Franciscan International Study Centre

Canterbury Studies in Franciscan History

General Editor

Philippe Yates, OFM

Volume One

*Acts of the Franciscan History Conference
held at the Franciscan International Study Centre
on 9th September 2006*

Editors

Michael Robson OFM Conv.

Jens Röhrkasten

Franciscan International Study Centre

Canterbury, England

2008

Cover Art: Greyfriars, Canterbury by Br. Bernard
Coleman OFM © OFM Immaculate Conception
Province of England

British Library Cataloguing in Publication Data

Canterbury studies in Franciscan history : acts of the 2006
  Franciscan History Conference
  1. Bacon, Roger, 1214?-1294 - Congresses 2. Franciscans -
  England - History - To 1500 - Congresses 3. Franciscan
  monasteries - England - History - Congresses 4. Theology,
  Doctrinal - History - Middle Ages, 600-1500 - Congresses
  I. Yates, Philippe, O.F.M. II. Robson, Michael, O.F.M.Conv
  III. Rohrkasten, Jens IV. Franciscan International Study
  Centre V. Franciscan History Conference (2006)
  271.3

ISBN-13: 9780954927219

Published by:
Franciscan International Study Centre
Giles Lane, Canterbury CT2 7NA
www.franciscnas.ac.uk

Printed in Sittingbourne, England by:
JEM Digital Print Services Ltd.
www.jem.co.uk
2008
ISSN 1757-9236
ISBN 978-0-9549272-1-9
© FISC and the authors 2008

Contents

Abbreviations 5

Preface 7

MICHAEL ROBSON, OFMConv. *The Greyfriars' Itinerant Ministry inside their limitatio: Evidence from the Custody of York, c.1230-1539.* 9

JENS RÖHRKASTEN. *The Creation and Early History of the Franciscan Custody of Cambridge.* 51

LUCA PARISOLI. *La Philosophie de l'argent dans l'école franciscaine. Un aperçu inspiré par l'anthropologie dogmatique de Pierre Legendre.* 83

AMANDA POWER. *'In the last days at the end of the world': Roger Bacon and the Reform of Christendom.* 135

EVA SCHLOTHEUBER. *Late Medieval Franciscan Statutes on Convent Libraries and Education.* 153

LUDOVIC VIALLET. *La Reforme en gestes et en textes. Autour de «l'Observance» Franciscaine.* 185

Index 217

Abbreviations

AF	Analecta Franciscana
AFH	*Archivum Franciscanum Historicum*
BF vols,	*Bullarium Franciscanum*, eds. J.H. Sbaraleae, C.Eubel et alii, 7 (Rome, 1759-1904), new series 1-4, i-ii (Rome, 1929-2003)
BL	British Library, London
BSC	Bibliotheca Seraphico-Capuccina
BSFS	British Society of Franciscan Studies
CCCM	Corpus Christianorum, Continuatio Mediaevalis
CCSL	Corpus Christianorum, series Latina
CF	*Collectanea Franciscana*
CPR	Calendar of Patent Rolls
CYS	Canterbury and York Society
FS	*Franciscan Studies, Franziskanische Studien*
MPG	J.-P. Migne (ed.), *Patrologiae cursus completus, series Graeca*, 161 vols. Paris, 1857ff.
Narbonne, 1260, Assisi, 1279, Paris, 1292 *AFH*	M. Bihl (ed.), 'Statuta generalia Ordinis edita in Capitulis generalibus Narbonae an. 1260, Assisii celebratis an.1279 atque Parisiis an.1292', 34 (1941) 13-94, 284-319.
OM	Roger Bacon, *Opus maius*, ed. J.H. Bridges, 3 vols., Oxford 1897

RS	Rerum Britannicarum et Hibernicarum Medii Aevi Scriptiores (Rolls Series)
TNA	The National Archives, London
VCH	Victoria County History

Preface

The Franciscans in Britain have long been engaged in the pursuit of wisdom. The friars' school at Oxford produced many of the leading lights of the Franciscan Intellectual Tradition. There is also a tradition of research into Franciscan history in this country which flourished in the work of the British Society of Franciscan Studies.

In the light of these traditions there was a desire for an ongoing British forum for sharing the fruits of research into Franciscan history and thought. Consequently, after consultation with Dr. Jens Röhrkasten of the University of Birmingham and Dr. Michael Robson OFM Conv. of St. Edmund's College, Cambridge, the *Franciscan History Conference* was established to be held at the Franciscan International Study Centre, Canterbury. The conference is held annually on the Saturday nearest the 10th September to offer an occasion to scholars of Franciscan Studies and allied subjects to come together and share the fruits of their research.

Jens and Michael have given invaluable advice and generously offered the fruits of their experience to ensure the continuing success and growth of the *Franciscan History Conference*. They have also participated in editing this volume which presents the papers from the first conference. Subsequent conference papers will form the basis of further volumes in this series. For this we owe them a debt of gratitude.

The Franciscan International Study Centre is dedicated through its courses, its publications and its open lectures, to promote Franciscan Studies in all their aspects. The publication of these papers and the inauguration of this series is an important contribution to this vocation.

Philippe Yates, OFM

Principal, Franciscan International Study Centre

The Greyfriars' Itinerant Ministry inside their *limitatio*: Evidence from the Custody of York, c.1230-1539

Michael Robson, OFMConv.

(St Edmund's College, Cambridge)

St Francis of Assisi knew instinctively that his vocation did not lie within the monastic enclosure with its attractive rhythm of the *opus Dei* in the choir and its meditation in the cloister. Although monasticism based itself on the life of the apostolic community in Jerusalem, Francis was convinced that God called him to another vocation. The itinerant and poor Jesus Christ was his model and inspiration. The result was a new expression of the religious life which stretched beyond the confines of monasticism. One of the first friars at Erfurt in 1225 responded to questions about the construction of a friary by declaring that he had never seen a cloister in the order.[1] The breadth of the friars' impact has long been recognised. Professor Barrie Dobson, the doyen of urban historians in England, observes that the ministry of friars was appreciated well beyond their immediate vicinity.[2] This raises the question of the organisation of the friars' ministry to the towns and villages away from their friaries. A convent's *limitatio* might be extensive, stretching for 30 or 40 miles into the countryside. This study assembles the strands of evidence

---

1 *Chronica Fratris Jordani*, ed. H. Boehmer (Collection d'études et de documents sur l'histoire religieuse et littéraire du Moyen âge, 6), Paris, 1908, 38-9.

2 R.B. Dobson, 'Yorkshire Towns in the Late Fourteenth Century', *Publications of the Thoresby Society* 59 (1983), 1-21, at 6.

drawn from the custody of York, despite the loss of the friars' own once rich archives.

I. The custody of York and the *limitationes* of its friaries

The constituent friaries of the custody of York were at Beverley, Boston, Doncaster, Grimsby, Lincoln, Scarborough and York. Each house was a *domus formata* or *conventus*; the custody had no *loca*,[3] which were probably the non conventual (*non conventualis*) houses of fewer than thirteen friars in continual residence envisaged by the general constitutions.[4] The friaries of York and Lincoln, cathedral cities and centres of political and commercial importance, probably drew alms from a larger area than the other friaries of that custody. Friaries, some of which might be described as a *parva domus*, were assessed in accordance with the services provided.[5] There are some indications that the friary at Grimsby was smaller than the other six.

The dimensions of the custody of York are reconstructed from a variety of sources. An early witness was the *Registrum Anglie*, which was compiled by the friars. This listed several religious houses in particular custodies, including that of Salisbury, which was dissolved in the middle of the thirteenth century. The register identifies the boundaries of the custody of York, which was one of the largest in the English province, stretching from Whitby in the north to Spalding in the south and from the east coast to the River Trent, with the exception of some parts of

---

3   P.M. Sevesi, 'Tavola capitolare della provincia dei minori conventuali di Milano, redatta nel 1498', *AFH* 24 (1931) 185-194, at 193-4, records that two of the six friaries (Desio and Oreno) in one custody were *loca* rather than *conventus*.

4   Narbonne 1260, Assisi 1279, Paris 1292, ed. Bihl, 295.

5   BF VII, no.172, p.55.

Nottinghamshire.[6] The custody was the friar's normal sphere of activity and he spent his life attached to friaries in that geographical unit. Friars were moved from one custodial house to another at the appointment of the custos, although some enjoyed a protracted residence in a single convent. Few friars were assigned to work outside the custody for specialised types of ministry.

Like any modern householder, religious houses were acutely aware of the extent of their property. *Limites* was a term employed by chroniclers commenting on the boundaries of monastic towns.[7] Similarly, the extent of a friary was known to its members. Each friary regarded the places nearest to it as its own territory, regardless of whether they crossed the borders of a diocese or county.[8] Its boundaries were set by the provincial chapters (*divisio custodiarum*).[9] These borders were carefully devised to prevent the activities of one friary impinging upon those of another. Alms were given to the friars within their *limitatio*.[10] Robert Scheffeld de Westbutterwick's will of 4 December 1419 mentioned the friars - *item lego quotuor [sic] ordinibus fratrum mendicantium limitantium*.[11]

The *limitatio* circumscribed the powers exercised by the guardians of the respective friaries; they were not permitted

---

6 *Registrum Anglie de libris doctorum et auctorum veterum*, eds. R.H. Rouse / M.A. Rouse (Corpus of British Medieval Library Catalogues 2), London 1991, 2-6.

7 *The Chronicle of Bury St Edmunds, 1212-1301*, ed. A. Gransden, Edinburgh 1964, 10, 44-5.

8 F. Delorme, 'Diffinitiones Capituli Generalis O.F.M.Narbonensis (1260)', *AFH* 3 (1910), 491-504, at 503.

9 Narbonne 1260, Assisi 1279, Paris 1292, ed. Bihl, c.10, no.17, p.303.

10 *Wills of the Archdeaconry of Sudbury 1439-1474: Wills from the Register 'Baldwyne', Part I: 1439-1461*, ed. P. Northeast (Suffolk Records Society, 44), Woodbridge 2001, no.18, pp.8-9.

11 *The Register of Richard Fleming bishop of Lincoln 1420-31*, vol.1, ed. N.H. Bennett (CYS, 73), 1984, no.5, pp.1-2.

to send friars beyond the limits of their friary (*extra terminum guardianiae suae*).[12] Neighbouring provinces entered into agreements about their boundaries.[13] There is evidence that details of the *limitationes* of the friaries were communicated to bishops and diocesan officials, who maintained up-to-date records of the friars licensed to preach and hear confessions. This information was important to bishops who authorised friars to minister in specified areas. For instance, John Dalderby, bishop of Lincoln, was petitioned by the custos of York and guardian of the Lincoln Greyfriars to license friars from Lincoln, Boston and Grimsby within the *limitacione de conventu Linc., (...) S.Botulphi,(...) de conventu et Grimesby*. These friars were authorised to hear confessions and to act in cases reserved for parish priests and curates.[14] John de Ebor', a friar of Boston, was licensed to hear confessions *infra limitacionem assignatam dictis fratribus* on 13 November 1347 for one year.[15] There are instances of friars who were licensed to serve as confessors in part of their *limitatio* which lay in another diocese.[16]

Testamentary dispositions are a barometer of the friars' itinerant ministry and they constitute a working guide to the extent of their *limitatio,* which might be reconstructed from

12 Narbonne 1260, Assisi 1279, Paris 1292, ed. Bihl, V, no.4, p. 63.

13 M. Bihl, 'Raymundus Gaufridi, Minister generalis, Parisiis 9 iunii 1292 confirmat conventionem initam inter Provincias Austriae et Alemaniae Superioris de terminis eleemosynarum conquirendarum in confiniis', *AFH* 36 (1943), 98-102.

14 A.G. Little, *Franciscan Papers, Lists, and Documents*, Manchester 1943, 237.

15 Lincolnshire Archives Office, Register 9C, f.40r.

16 On 21 February 1325 the rectors, vicars and parish priests of the diocese were informed that John de Witele, a friar of Winchelsea, had been licensed to preach and hear confessions in accordance with *Super cathedram*. The licence was confined *infra limitacionem fratrum minorum de Wynchelse. Registrum Hamonis Hethe diocesis Roffensis, A.D.1319-1352*, 2 vols., ed. C. Johnson (CYS, 48, 49), Oxford, 1948, I, 368.

these sources. Dr Rosemary Horrox, for instance, notes the level of support which the friars of Beverly received from the town 'and a wide area around it',[17] an observation buttressed by a wealth of evidence from the probate registers. Indeed, this extra-mural support for the friars' apostolate is rendered more intelligible by reflection on their work away from the cities and towns in which the friaries were located. It is also indicated by their gifts from monastic houses, such as Selby Abbey.[18] A small number of testators left legacies to the friaries without specifying them.[19] Although it was the practice of some to bestow alms upon friaries that were distant, such as friaries in a cathedral city, the vast majority supported the nearest friary[20] and expressly identified it in their will. These men and women were familiar with the friars' annual visits to their parishes and knew the friaries whence they came. In some instances they identified the nearest houses of the mendicants;[21] mistakes about friaries were comparatively rare and were probably caused by confusion on the part of the scribe

---

17 *VCH, Yorkshire*, VI, 76, note 72.

18 *Monastery and Society in the Late Middle Ages : Selected account rolls from Selby Abbey, Yorkshire, 1398-1537*, ed. J.H. Tillotson, Woodbridge 1988, 143.

19 *Halifax Wills : being abstracts and translations of the wills registered at York from the parish of Halifax*, ed. J.W. Clay, Halifax 1904, 30-1. For example, Oliver Witton of Skipton gave four shillings to the four orders of friars on 4 November 1502, leaving it to his executors to identify and pay the alms.

20 *Wills of the Archdeaconry of Sudbury 1439-1474*, ed. Northeast (cf. note 11), xlix, states that testators gave to the houses of each order geographically most convenient.

21 E.g. Thomas Wombwell, requested burial in All Saints de Derfield, on 4 February 1453, leaving 13s. 4d. to each of the mendicant houses, that is, the Austin Friars of Tickhill, the Greyfriars and Whitefriars of Doncaster and the Blackfriars of Pontefract. *Testamenta Eboracensia, or, Wills registered at York*, 6 vols., eds. J. Raine / J.W. Clay (Surtees Society, 4, 30, 45, 53, 79, 106), London

rather than the testator.[22] Some testators displayed a good knowledge of the nearest friaries of all four mendicant orders, even where these straddled diocesan and county boundaries. This is exemplified by Beatrice Haulay who requested burial in the Augustinian priory of the Blessed Virgin Mary at Thornton-on-Humber, Lincolnshire, on 28 November 1389. The sum of 13s. 4d. was left to each of the four nearest friaries, that is, the Austin Friars and the Greyfriars of Grimsby, the Whitefriars of Hull and the Blackfriars of York.[23] Testamentary evidence makes it clear that Halifax and Bradford belonged to the *limitatio* of Doncaster rather than York. On 28 May 1530 Walter Bradford of Houghton beside Pontefract left 6s.8d. to each friary of Doncaster. [24]

II. Friars and their necessary journeys

The friars' vocation differed markedly from the monastic *stabilitas loci* and presupposed a level of legitimate itinerancy. David of Augsburg, the celebrated novice master, talks of the travels that he had to make through different provinces (*vagando per diversas terras*).[25] The friars' movements and their involvement in matters away from their friaries emerge from a perusal of the correspondence of Adam Marsh, one of the most influential

---

1836-1902, II, 163-4.

22 *Lincoln Wills, 1532-1534*, ed. D. Hickman (Lincoln Record Society, 89), Woodbridge 2001, no.555, 370-1. William Hewton of Waltham, made bequests of 4d to the Franciscans and Carmelites of Grimsby on 12 October 1534. For Carmelites read Austin Friars, who with the Greyfriars were the only friars in the town.

23 Lincolnshire Archives Office, Register 12, f.363v.

24 Borthwick Institute of Historical Research in the University of York, Probate Register 10, f.17v.

25 *Fr. David ab Augusta De exterioris et interioris hominis compositione secundum triplicem statum incipientium, proficientium et perfectorum libri tres*, Quaracchi 1899, 64.

friars of his generation.[26] Friars were ubiquitous in English society. A ministry to the sick and dying took them to the bedside of Robert Grosseteste, bishop of Lincoln, at Buckden in October 1253[27] and some forty years later two friars of Bristol were called to the bedside of a canon of Wells.[28]

The upper echelons of English society drew upon the friars' services as preachers, confessors and counsellors. A notice of 30 July 1250 reveals that the friars had their own quarters (*camera fratrum minorum*) in the household of Queen Eleanor of Provence, wife of Henry III, at Clarendon.[29] In the same year Gregory de Bosellis joined the household of Simon de Montefort, earl of Leicester, in Gascony.[30] Edmund, earl of Cornwall, refers to John Russell, the twenty-second regent master of the Oxford Greyfriars as his *domesticus [frater Iohannes] familiarius* in a letter of 29 August 1293. Dr Rosalind Hill believes that the friar may have gone to Edmund's manor at Beckley, a few miles from Oxford, during the vacation.[31] On 30 December 1424 the dean and chapter of York authorised Robert Masuarii, a friar, dwelling with (*moranti cum*) Lord John Ashton, a soldier, to hear the confessions of his subjects in the deanery of Preston in Amounderness in the

---

26 *The Letters of Adam Marsh*, ed. C.H. Lawrence, I (Oxford Medieval Texts), Oxford 2006.

27 *Matthaei Parisiensis, monachi Sancti Albani, Chronica majora*, 7 vols., ed. H.R. Luard (RS, 57), London 1872-83, V, 408-9 and *Matthaei Parisiensis, monachi Sancti Albani, Historia Anglorum*, 3 vols., ed. F. Madden (RS, 44), London, 1866-69, III, 146-7, 330-1.

28 *Chronicon de Lanercost M.CC.I.- M.CCC.XLVI*, ed. J. Stevenson, Edinburgh, 1839, 153.

29 *Calendar Liberate Rolls* 1245-1251, 296-7.

30 *The Letters of Adam Marsh*, ed. Lawrence (cf. note 26), I. xl. Cf. Letters 141 and 142 in the second volume of Adam's letters.

31 R.M.T. Hill, *Ecclesiastical Letters-Books of the Thirteenth Century*, B.Litt. thesis, University of Oxford 1936, 8, 186, 187, 256-7.

archdeaconry of Richmond.[32] The plight of friars on the road entered the order's collections of *exempla*.[33] The friars' mobility led John Wyclif to complain that they *gon fro place to place and fro man to man to begge of pore men*.[34]

The Lanercost Chronicle, the work of a friar in the north of England, reports both local and international events with the ease of an author who combined an interest in events both at home and abroad.[35] When friars met for the profession of vows, ordinations and funerals and other celebrations, it was natural that they would exchange news about their friaries and their locality. On some occasions friars from different communities and custodies were ordained together, as happened when John Gynwell, bishop of Lincoln, conferred orders on friars from Grantham, Nottingham, Boston and Lincoln in Stowe prebendal church on 22 September 1352.[36] The friars' mobility is one of the reasons for their valuable contribution to the writing of history. Franciscan materials, for example, were incorporated into the Kirkstall[37] and the Anonimalle Chronicles.[38]

---

32 Borthwick Institute of Historical Research in the University of York, Register 5A, f.394v.

33 Cf. J.Th. Welter, 'Un nouveau recueil Franciscain d'exempla de la fin du XIIIe siècle', *Études Franciscaines* 42 (1930), 432-76, 595-629, at 627.

34 *The English Works of Wyclif*, ed. F.D. Matthew (Early English Texts Society, 74), London, 1880, 8.

35 *Chronicon de Lanercost* (cf. note 28), 98-9, 128-31, 187-8. His confrères supplied him with information on the experiences of friars in Italy and the Holy Land.

36 Lincolnshire Archives Office, Register 9D, ff.63v-64v.

37 *The Kirkstall Abbey Chronicles*, ed. J. Taylor (Thoresby Soc., 42), Leeds 1952, 25.

38 *The Anonimalle Chronicle 1307-1334 from Brotherton Collection MS.29*, eds. W.R. Childs / J.Taylor (The Yorkshire Archaeological Society, Record Series, 147), Leeds, 1991, 10, 12, 19, 20.

Although the friars' movements were regulated, their apostolate was itinerant in character. There were several legitimate reasons for which a friar might be absent from his mendicant precincts. The charge that such preachers were *girovagi* was firmly rejected by John Pecham, who refers to these friars as *rote Domini. ....euntes et redeuntes*.[39] John of Wales urged his confrères to avoid any potential distractions on their travels, to promote the values enunciated by Jesus Christ (*sic autem exeuntium debet esse tota intentio ad Deo lucrandas animas*) and to copy the example of St Cuthbert, who preached in out-of-the-way places.[40] The expectation of a friar's visit to villages is caught by Margery Kempe, who was travelling to Walsingham, when she heard that a friar would be preaching in a small village, where he attracted a good audience.[41] A later example is found in the will of Sir Humphrey Stafford of Hooke, Dorset and earl of Devon, from May 1469. He was killed after the battle of Edgecote during August of the same year. According to his will, two Franciscans of Exeter, Master Nicholas Goffe, Master Wattes, his confessor and the guardian of the friary, should

---

39 *Fratris Johannis Pecham quondam archiepiscopi Cantuariensis Tractatus tres de paupertate*, eds. C.L. Kingsford / A.G.Little / F.Tocco (BSFS, 2), Aberdeen, 1910, 24.

40 John of Wales, 'Ordinarium vitae religiosae', p.3, c.3, in *Summa Johannis Valensis de regimine vite humane seu Margarita doctorum ad omne propositum prout patet in tabula*, Lyons 1511, fol. 248rv, Cf. 'Vita Sancti Cuthberti auctore Beda', in, *Two Lives of Saint Cuthbert: A Life by an Anonymous monk of Lindisfarne and Bede's Prose Life*, ed. B. Colgrave, Cambridge 1940, c.9, 186-7, quoting this *vita*, John shows that Cuthbert went to villages that were far away and on steep and rugged mountains, which others dreaded to visit and whose poverty and ignorance prevented teachers from approaching them.

41 *The Book of Margery Kempe*, eds. S.B. Meech / H.E. Allen (Early English Text Society, 212), London 1940, lib.2, c.2, 227, she was travelling to Walsingham, when she heard that a friar was due to preach in a little village, where a great audience gathered.

visit every parish church in Dorset, Somerset, Wiltshire, Devon and Cornwall to deliver sermons in every church, town or other.[42] The friars' systematic visits to the cities and boroughs symbolise their strategy for the revitalisation of the rural Church. They soon developed the pattern of visiting their *limitatio* each year. There is evidence that they visited all the parish churches and dependent chapels in the course of a year. The planning of these visits was highly organised and it necessitated the absence of pairs of friars for some weeks, possibly a couple of months at a time. During this period friars lodged in nearby religious houses, with parish clergy[43] or with local families.[44]

Custodial officials were obliged to satisfy their administrative responsibilities, as were members of the communities, although it was ordained that they should travel in pairs, that is, in the company of a *socius*. The custos travelled long distances in the discharge of his duties and was responsible for the friars' dealings with the bishops in whose dioceses they ministered. He was required to visit the scattered manor houses of the bishops of Lincoln and the archbishops of York, regardless of whether they were located inside the custody. For instance, Thomas de Barneby (Barnby), probably the custos of York, was received by Bishop Dalderby on 12 October 1300 and

---

42 *Somerset Medieval Wills (1383-1500)*, ed. F.W. Weaver (Somerset Record Society, 16), London 1901, 196-201. Cf. C. Richmond, 'The English Gentry and Religion, c.1500', in: C. Harper-Bill (ed.), *Religious Belief and Ecclesiastical Careers in Late Medieval England*, Woodbridge 1991, 121-50, 128-9.

43 G.R. Owst, *Preaching in Medieval England: an introduction to the sermon manuscripts of the period c.1350-1450*, Cambridge 1926, 107, note 3, citing Pecham's constitutions of 1281, *de hospitalitate tenenda: et ut qui ibidem transeunt et praedicant verbum Dei necessaria recipiant corpori alimenta* (…).

44 *Ibid.*, 61, note3, Gray's Inn Library, London, MS.15, f.31r: *Item frater Radulphus de S[wyneland], cum socio suo semel veniens Londoniis, intravit villam quemdam.* The two friars entered the village at nightfall and were given lodging by a woman.

delivered a letter from the minister provincial. The bishop considered the number of Franciscans licensed in the diocese and proceeded to grant licences to friars from the custodial houses in Lincolnshire.[45]

A memorandum in the register of Bishop Dalderby on 15 March 1319 lifts the veil on the custos's travels and his sensitive negotiations with the ordinary of the diocese. The previous day, 14 March, John of Moreton of Gainsborough, the lector of Boston, made the journey to the episcopal manor at Buckden bearing two letters addressed to the bishop. The first was written by William of Nottingham, minister provincial, at Cambridge on 17 October 1318 and addressed to Robert, the custos of York, who was authorised to present friars selected by the provincial chapter for a licence to hear confessions, in accordance with the papal statute *Super cathedram*. The second was written by the custos of York at Boston on 12 March 1319, when he pleaded that the business of the order (*vice aliis negociis ordinis impeditus*) prevented him from travelling to Buckden. John de Moreton expanded on the terms of the custos's letter and explained that William of Barton and Roger of Deighton (Dighton), friars of Lincoln and Grimsby, already licensed by the bishop, had been transferred to the diocese of York. Henry of Beckingham, a friar of Boston similarly approved, was too infirm to exercise the office. Thomas of Toynton (Tynton), Thomas of Holbeach and John of Moreton of the Boston Greyfriars were licensed in their places until the next provincial chapter which was to be held on 15 August with special consideration of the last named on account of the affection which the bishop had felt for him for a long time. The former licences were accordingly revoked and the archdeacon of Lincoln's official was informed that the three friars had been licensed. The register contains a marginal

---

45 Lincolnshire Archives Office, Register 3, f.19v, Little, *Franciscan Papers* (cf. note 14), 238.

sketch of a friar's head and the caption *pro fratribus minoribus*.[46]

John de Thurgutthorp, custos of York, wrote to Adam de Ludeford, guardian of Lincoln, on 20 November 1321 and explained that pressing business prevented him (*certis negociis impeditus*) from visiting Henry Burghersh, bishop of Lincoln, to present eight friars, John Thurgutthorp, Geoffrey de Aynsham, John de Gaynesburgh, Richard de Multan, William de Ravenser, John de Barton, Richard de Haukerword and Robert de Quappelad senior, for licences to hear confessions. Ludeford was received by the bishop at his manor of Nettleham, north-east of Lincoln, on 7 December of that year, when he presented the custos's letter. Burghersh chose to license one friar, William de Ravenser, in place of John de Barton, who had died unexpectedly (*ab hac vita de medio sublati*).[47] Hugh de Staunton, custos of Oxford, acted for the custos of York and was received by Bishop Burghersh at Banbury on 17 November 1320. He explained that Hugh de Hothorp, Richard de Herice and Richard de Leyc', all licensed by Bishop Dalderby, had been transferred to undisclosed friaries in the diocese of York. On that occasion Burghersh licensed Richard de Shelton, John de Sisted and Robert Whatton.[48]

While the archbishop of York or his suffragans, some of whom were friars, held most of the ordinations in the county town and annually in the city's Greyfriars, the bishops of Lincoln selected a number of venues and frequently conferred orders in the churches adjacent to their manors, especially Liddington and Buckden. This emerges from an anecdote about an ordination conducted by Robert Grosseteste at Huntingdon during Lent. A friar, who was

---

46 Lincolnshire Archives Office, Register 3, ff.411v-12r.
47 *Ibid.*, Register 5, ff.299v-300r.
48 *Ibid.*, Register 5, f.265v.

ordained on that day, subsequently crossed the River Humber to Doncaster, where he recounted the anecdote half-a-century later as a *grandaevus*. At the time of his ordination he had probably been a member of a friary in Lincolnshire.[49] Some friars of Lincoln had to travel to Sleaford, Huntingdon, Buckden and Northampton for ordination. Four friars of Beverley travelled to Blyth, Nottinghamshire, where their suitability for ordination was examined on 20 September 1274, that is, two days before the ordination.[50] Three friars of York appear in the lists of ordinands in the diocese of Lincoln. Robert Greene and Godfrey de Saxonia, friars of York, were ordained at St Katherine's priory, Lincoln, on 6 June 1433,[51] even though two of his confrères from the same convent were ordained at Blackfriars, York, on that day by Nicholas Warter, the Franciscan bishop of Dromore.[52] John de Billam, another friar of York, made an even longer journey when he was ordained subdeacon on 19 December 1360 in Oakham parish church, that is, in the custody of Oxford.[53] On that day, too, John Thoresby, archbishop of York, ordained six friars at his manor chapel at Cawood.[54]

Although the friars found many of their penitents in the cities and boroughs in which they resided, they ministered to others who lived further afield. One such was John Harby (Harvy), formerly a friar at York. He was the guardian of the friary of Lincoln on 22 August 1493 when

---

49 *Chronicon de Lanercost* (cf. note 28), 187-8.

50 *The Register of Walter Giffard, lord archbishop of York, 1266-1279*, ed. W. Brown (Surtees Soc., 109), Durham 1904, no.697, pp. 197-8.

51 Lincolnshire Archives Office, Register 17, f.211r.

52 Borthwick Institute of Historical Research in the University of York, Register 19, f.244rv.

53 Lincolnshire Archives Office, Register 9D, f.97v.

54 Borthwick Institute of Historical Research in the University of York, Register 11, f.343r.

John Crokes, a parishioner of St John the Baptist at South Collingham, Nottinghamshire, left him six marks to celebrate Masses daily for his wife and all the faithful in the Greyfriars for a year. He was also Crokes's confessor and witnessed the will.[55] [Sir] Richard Hawe, a friar of Lincoln, was the confessor of William Bucknall of Canwick, east of the cathedral city. Bucknall left the Greyfriars of Lincoln half a quarter of malt and *a stryke of barly* in his will of 20 May 1531. The sum of 10s. was left to Hawe to celebrate a trental of Masses for him at Canwick parish church; he also witnessed the will. In this case it is not known whether the testator travelled to Lincoln for spiritual guidance or whether the friar made his way to Canwick.[56]

The names of streets, roads or estates frequently denote the site of a medieval friary. Fifteenth-century testators referred to *Francisgate* and the *Freris Mynors brigge* at Doncaster.[57] *Frere breyge* in the same town connoted the Greyfriars, whose house was at the north end of the bridge.[58] The term friar was used rather broadly in late medieval England, as the Robin Hood legends demonstrate. Some of these references are manifestly associated with the monastic rather than the mendicant cosmos.[59] In addition, it is conceivable that the surname Friar or a variant of it may lie behind some of these names, but it is doubtful if it

---

55 *Ibid.*, Probate Register 5, f.437rv.
56 *Lincoln Wills, III, A.D.1530 to 1532*, ed. C.W. Foster (Lincoln Record Society, 24), Lincoln, 1930, 137.
57 *Testamenta Eboracensia* (cf. note 21), V, 59.
58 A.H. Smith, *The Place-Names of the West Riding of Yorkshire*, 2 vols. (English Place-Name Society Publications, 30, 37), Cambridge 1961-63, I, 32.
59 E.g., V. Watts, *A Dictionary of County Durham Place-Names* (English Place-Name Society, Popular Series, 3), Nottingham 2002, 46, cites two examples. First, Friar House (*Freer House*) of Middleton in Teesdale was a vaccary of the lay brothers of Rievaulx Abbey established c.1165. Friarside in Chester (*Frerejohanside*) was a house for the lay brothers of Newminster Abbey.

accounts for every case. Vestiges of the friars' presence, nonetheless, are also to be found away from the cities and boroughs in which they settled and these may be echoes of their itinerant ministry. Friar Mere (*Frear Mer*) alluded to a Dominican house near Delph.[60] Friar's Ditch (*Freredik*), near Pickering, was mentioned in 1334.[61] There is a Friars' hill at Sinnington, near Pickering.[62] There is a Friars Ings in Barden.[63] Friar Head is two miles north of Gargrave, which is north-west of Skipton.[64]

III. Preaching

Friars were capable of presenting the Scriptures in an orthodox and attractive manner. They strove to bring the Gospel into the lives of merchants, tradesmen and artisans through their sermons delivered in the vernacular.[65] Their programme of preaching was not confined to their place of residence, as Federico Visconti, archbishop of Pisa (1253-77), attests. They did not cease from their preaching as much in cities as outside them (*tam in civitate quam extra*) on Sundays, feast days and celebrations of the deceased.[66] Piers the Plowman was a witness to the friars' sermons in diverse places : *that when the friars preach to*

---

60 Smith, *Place-Names of the West Riding of Yorkshire* (cf. note 58) II, 311. The Blackfriars are said to have had a house near Delph.

61 Idem, *The Place Names of the North Riding of Yorkshire* (English Place-Name Society Publications, 5) Cambridge 1928, 86.

62 *VCH, Yorkshire, North Riding*, II, 489.

63 *Ibid.*, I, 246.

64 *Ibid., Yorkshire*, II, 67.

65 *The Records of the Northern Convocation*, ed. G.W. Kitchin (Surtees Soc., 113), Durham 1907, 145-72, 150, 152.

66 *Les sermons et la visite pastorale de Federico Visconti archevêque de Pise (1253-1277)*, ed. N. Bériou (Sources et documents d'histoire du moyen âge publiés par le École française de Rome, 3) Rome, 2001, no.3, 658.

people in places all about. [67] An insight into the assistance provided by the friars emerges from reports of the visitation of a cell of Benedictine monks at Snaith, West Yorkshire, a dependent priory of Selby Abbey. On 7 October 1275 Alexander, the chaplain, testified that the parish had no vicar and that the Franciscans and Dominicans often visited it and preached there. The friars were well received by the monks;[68] they were probably from the Greyfriars at Doncaster. There are other northern references to friars being invited to serve a vacant chapel.[69] Friars were occasionally invited to preach at funerals or during the period of official mourning. In his will of 17 September 1537 John Woodward, vicar of All Saints at Darfield-upon-Dearne, left 6 shillings 8 pence to the unnamed doctor of divinity at the friary in Doncaster to preach to his parishioners either on the day of his burial or soon afterwards.[70]

Friars' sermons were not confined to churches, as the early biographies of Sts Francis of Assisi and Anthony of Padua confirm. Friars in England preached in chapter-houses, cloisters, churchyards, principal squares and market crosses. Their sermons in the open air are well

---

67 *The Vision of William concerning Piers the Plowman together with Vita de Dowel, Dobet and Dobest*, 5 vols. ed. W.W. Skeat (Early English Texts Society, 28, 38, 54, 67, 81), London 1867-84, V, 64, refers to the sermons which the friars preach to the people *in many place aboute.*

68 *Register of Walter Giffard, lord archbishop of York, 1266-1279*, ed. Brown (cf. note 50), no.918, pp.322-4.

69 On 2 August 1360 the Austin Friars of Penrith were licensed to provide a friar to serve the vacant chapel of Newton Reigny. *The Register of Gilbert Welton bishop of Carlise 1353-1362*, ed. R.L. Storey (CYS, 88), Woodbridge 1999, no.329, p.60.

70 Borthwick Institute of Historical Research in the University of York, Register 28, fol.177r-v.

documented.[71] The archbishop of York had friars assigned to various towns to preach the Crusade before stipulating that the friaries of Richmond and Preston should each send friars to preach wherever people gathered – *ubi major creditur esse congregatio populi in Coupland* and *in loco alio ubi creditur esse major concursus populi*.[72] Piers the Plowman refers to the friars' sermons at St Paul's Cross in London after the Black Death.[73] English historians talk somewhat tentatively about the friars' 'preaching tours',[74] although the documentation is limited. Sermon books used by itinerant friars are now attracting more scholarly attention.[75] One much quoted figure is Nicholas Philip whose travels between 1430 and 1436 are recorded in his booklet of sermons to be preached on diverse occasions in various parts of England. The friars embarked upon preaching tours, especially during the seasons of Advent and Lent.[76] On 23 October 1483 William Whelpedale, guardian of Beverley, was licensed to preach the word of God with Friar William Lator. On the same day Robert

---

71 *Chronicon de Lanercost*, (cf. note 28) 68, recounts the story of a loiterer at a sermon by a friar on Good Friday of 1259 in Haddington. The man went to the sermon more out of curiosity than for edification of soul and was leaning on a wall (*muro incumbens*).

72 *Historical Papers and Letters from the Northern Registers*, ed. J. Raine (RS, 61), London 1873, 95-6.

73 *The Vision of William concerning Piers the Plowman* (cf. note 67) V, 146. *The Register of Henry Chichele, archbishop of Canterbury, 1414-1443*, 4 vols. ed. E.F. Jacob (CYS, 42, 45, 46, 47), Oxford 1937-47, III, 139-57, at 141, William Russell, guardian of the London Greyfriars, preached there (*apud crucem in cimiterio ecclesie cathedralis Sancti Pauli*) on 28 January 1425.

74 E.g., Owst, *Preaching in Medieval England*, (cf. note 43), 61.

75 S. Gieben, 'Preaching in the Thirteenth Century: A Note on MS.Gonville and Caius 439', *CF* 32 (1962), 310-24.

76 Cf. A.J. Fletcher, *Preaching, Politics and Poetry in Late-Medieval England*, Dublin 1998, 41-57.

Bewchampe, *magister studentium* at York, was authorised to preach anywhere in that diocese.[77]

Shortly after they had settled at Oxford two friars went out to 'sow the saving seed of the Lord' in the approach to Christmas.[78] The mendicant chronicles and *exempla* collections offer an invaluable insight into the ministry and experience of the mendicant preachers. The author of the *Lanercost Chronicle* met two friars of Dumfries travelling to the region of Annandale, to the south of the friary, to preach during Advent of 1281.[79] While friars were accustomed to preach throughout the year, they were in particular demand during Advent and Lent, when people were preparing for the celebration of the major festivals. Humbert of Romans, master of the Dominicans, notes that Advent and Lent were the busy preaching seasons, when the friars were absent from their convents.[80] The friars' seasonal visits to parishes made their way into diocesan legislation. The synodal statutes of Bishop William Bitton I for the diocese of Bath and Wells in 1258 (?) urged that the friars' ministrations be received whenever they passed through parishes in Lent.[81]

There is some evidence that the friars visited parishes more than once a year (*in locis singulis per que semel aut bis transit per annum*),[82] although this may have referred more to the earlier period of their history in England.

---

77 Borthwick Institute of Historical Research in the University of York, Register 23, f.42v.

78 *Chronicon de Lanercost* (cf. note 28), 31.

79 *Ibid.*, 107.

80 B. *Humberti de Romanis, Opera de Vita Regulari*, 2 vols., ed. J.J. Berthier, 1956, II, 254.

81 *Councils and Synods with other documents relating to the English Church: A.D.1205-1313*, 2 vols., eds. F.M. Powicke / C.R. Cheney, Oxford, 1964, I, 586-626, at 595-96.

82 Little, *Franciscan Papers, Lists, and Documents* (cf. note 14), 119.

Richard FitzRalph, archbishop of Armagh (1346-60), contrasts the pastoral care provided by the parish priest and his curates with that of the friars who visit the parish once or twice a year.[83] The practice of making annual visits to towns and villages appears in contemporary literature. Giovanni Boccaccio devotes one of his stories to the disreputable Friar Onion (Fra Cippola) at Certaldo.[84] The friars' annual visits to parishes *ex consuetudine* were mentioned by Thomas Smyth of Ormesby on 5 November 1478[85] and Thomas Newhall of Stoxlay in Cleveland on 13 March 1479.[86] Their annual sermons in the parish church of All Saints, Batley, were noted by John Dale, vicar of that church, on 23 July 1435, leaving 3s. 4d. to each house of friars.[87] There are several examples of friars exercising their ministry in the *limitatio*. Friars of all four orders who preached in Leeds received a legacy from William Darlay,

---

83   L.L. Hammerich, *The Beginning of the Strife between Richard FitzRalph and the Mendicants, with an edition of his autobiographical prayer and his proposition Unusquisque* (Det. Kgl. Danske Videnskabernes Selskab. Historisk-filologiske Meddelelser, 26, iii) Copenhagen 1938, 65.

84   *Giovanni Boccaccio, Decameron, Filocolo, Ameto, Fiammetta*, eds. E. Bianchi / C. Salinari / N. Sapegno, (La Letteratura Italiana Storia e Testi, 8), Milan 1952, 451-64 (VI, 10). Cippola stands as symbol of the mendicants' excesses, although he is styled as a Friar of St Anthony.

85   Borthwick Institute of Historical Research in the University of York, Probate Register 5, f.132r. *Item lego iiii ordinibus fratrum mendicancium elemosinas in parochia de Ormesby predict' annuatim ex consuetudine collegen' xls.*

86   *Ibid.*, Probate Register 5, f.137r. He was buried in the church of Sts Peter and Paul at Stoxlay. *Item do et lego iiii ordinibus fratrum mendicancium elemosinas infra parochiam de Stoxelay predicte annuatim ex consuetudine colligen'[tibus] ac pro missarum trentali pro anima mea dicenda et per eosdem fide[liter] celebrand' xxs.*

87   R.B. Cook, 'Wills of Leeds and District', in: *Miscellanea VI* (Publications of the Thoresby Society, 22), Leeds 1915, 235-64, at

a member of the parish of St Peter in the market town, on 27 June 1448, leaving 20d. to each order of friars.[88]

A more negative note is struck by the protest of William Zouche, archbishop of York. On 24 October 1351 he informed his archdeacons, diocesan officials, rectors and chaplains of indiscipline and scandal caused by the friars whose order and communities remain unspecified. Friars arrived at churches and chapels between the Masses, when the laity were present in large numbers. They collected alms in contravention of the ancient practices (*moris solitus et antiquitatus observatus*). Their purpose was material gain and they appeared with their books open (*causa lucri cum libris apertis in manibus suis more per omnia questorum fidelium*). This conduct disturbed the ecclesiastical order. A marginal note provides this summary: *contra fratres mendicantes ne petant elemosinas in ecclesiis cum libris apertis*.[89] Three days later the archbishop wrote to the same officials and parochial clergy and reaffirmed that friars, duly licensed in accordance with the papal constitution, should be permitted to preach, hear confessions and collect alms in their churches and parishes.[90] Zouche's terminology was echoed a few years later, when similar complaints were voiced in the diocese of Carlisle.[91]

238-9.

88 W. Brigg, 'Testamenta Leodiensia', in: *Miscellanea I* (Publications of the Thoresby Society, 2), Leeds 1981, 98-110, 205-14, at 100-1.

89 Borthwick Institute of Historical Research in the University of York, Register 10, f.271r.

90 *Ibid.*, Register 10, f.263v.

91 *Register of Gilbert Welton bishop of Carlise 1353-1362*, ed. Storey (cf. note 69), no.201, pp.36-7. A mandate to the official of Carlisle was issued by the bishop on 8 January 1358. There had been reports of the mendicant friars interrupting services in churches and chapels. The friars did not preach. Instead, they offered indulgences with empty words, seeking money and not souls, with open books in their hands, as if they were questors, contrary to the canons, observances of their orders and ancient custom. The official was

IV. Confessors

The ministry of preaching was dovetailed with the sacrament of Confession, the last stage of preparation to receive the Eucharist. One of the benefits of sound and moving homilies was the examination of conscience and the act of penitence, formally seeking reconciliation with the Church for past failings. While many friars were licensed by the bishops of medieval England to preach, their number was greatly exceeded by the confessors. Friars were selected by the minister provincial for the office of confessor and presented to the bishop for a licence. Many were authorised to hear confessions inside their *limitatio*. For instance, on 30 May 1267 Walter Giffard, archbishop of York, wrote to the custos and the guardians of the friaries in the diocese asking the friars to hear confessions.[92] Similarly, John le Romeyn, archbishop of York, authorised friars to hear confessions in the archdeaconry of York on 26 June 1287.[93] Controls were placed on the friars' activities and this is exemplified in the directive that the friars should not hear the confessions of parishioners of Sts Mary and Martin at Beverley.[94] Friars licensed by the ordinary were required to present their letters of appointment for inspection by the local clergy.

After sixty years of sometimes vexed relations between the local hierarchy and the order, the promulgation of Boniface VIII's bull *Super cathedram* on 18 February 1300

---

instructed to inform all the deans and parochial clergy, under pain of excommunication, not to admit any friar or questor, particularly during services, unless they displayed the episcopal licence.

92 *Register of Walter Giffard, lord archbishop of York, 1266-1279*, ed. Brown (cf. note 50), no.709, p. 209; *Historical Papers and Letters from the Northern Registers*, ed. Raine (cf. note 71), 9-10.

93 *The Register of John le Romeyn, lord archbishop of York, 1286-1296*, 2 vols., ed. W. Brown (Surtees Soc., 123, 128), Durham 1913-17, I, no.160, pp.67-8.

94 *Register of Walter Giffard, lord archbishop of York, 1266-1279*, ed. Brown (cf. note 50), no.726, pp. 226-7.

introduced new and durable regulations. Thereafter the nominated friars were presented by the minister provincial, custos or the guardian of the community closest to the manor where the bishop was in residence. The bishop was not obliged to approve all the names which were placed before him, a factor demonstrated in Bishop Dalderby's rejection of John Duns Scotus on 26 July 1300.[95] Episcopal licences were generally issued to friars active in a particular locality, such as a group of parishes, a deanery, an archdeaconry or, in some cases, an entire diocese. As mentioned earlier, friars from the Lincolnshire houses in the custody were authorised to work within their *limitatio*. Some licences were granted for a specific term, such as one or two years.

The range of licences granted to the friars and the territory for which they were valid indicates the amount of travelling that a friar might face in the discharge of his office. William de Carlisle was at York when he was licensed to hear confessions in the city and diocese on 27 October 1326 and again on 8 April 1327.[96] Thomas Burton, *sacre theologie doctor*, Thomas Boynton and William Awne were licensed for the diocese on 5 January 1444,[97] as was William Selby on 4 November 1446.[98] Thomas Kyrkham, *sacre theologie professor*, William Symys, Richard Todde and George Humlocke and John Stott were licensed to preach to the clergy and people *in ecclesiis et capellis* in the city of York and the diocese on 24 July 1534.[99]

Nicholas Banestre, a bachelor of theology resident at Oxford, was appointed as a confessor and penitentiary of

---

95 Little, *Franciscan Papers, Lists, and Documents* (cf. note 14), 235.

96 Borthwick Institute of Historical Research in the University of York, Register 9, ff.204v, 207r.

97 *Ibid.*, Register 19, f.86v.

98 *Ibid.*, Register 19, f.107v.

99 *Ibid.*, Register 28, f.85v.

the archbishop's subjects in the county of Lancaster on 4 November 1408.[100] John de Hoveden, *sacre pagine professor*, another friar of York, was licensed as a confessor and penitentiary for one year on 19 February 1348, especially in the archdeaconry of Richmond; his authority in matrimonial cases was mentioned.[101] Oliver Standich, Edward Bradekirk, Ralph Knoll and Richard Leylond, *scolares in sacra theologia*, were commissioned on 10 September 1444 to hear confessions, presumably in the archdeaconry.[102] William Booth, archbishop of York, wrote to William Awne, a friar of Beverley, on 8 April 1457, appointing him as his penitentiary in that town and deputing him to hear confessions in the archdeaconry of the East Riding.[103] Thomas Richmond, a friar of York, was appointed as the archbishop's penitentiary in the county town and as a confessor in the city and archdeaconry of York on 16 August 1458.[104]

Friars were sometimes appointed to areas some distance from their friaries. For instance, on 8 April 1339 the bishop of Lincoln licensed William de Tykhill, probably a friar at Boston, to hear confessions in the parish church of St Peter at Ingoldmells for one year.[105] Thomas de Barneby was commissioned in the diocese of Lincoln for the Isle of Axholme on 23 September 1338 for one year.[106] The friars' itinerant ministry is reflected in the policies of Robert Grosseteste, the patron and friend of the order. He informed Innocent IV on 13 May 1250 that, from the time of his consecration, he made a systematic visitation of the archdeaconries and rural deaneries of his far-flung diocese.

---

100 *Ibid.*, Register 17, f.14v.
101 *Ibid.*, Register 10, f.278r.
102 *Ibid*, Register 19, f.214v.
103 *Ibid.*, Register 20, f.130r.
104 *Ibid.*, Register 20, f.199r.
105 Lincolnshire Archives Office, Register 5, f.150v.
106 *Ibid.*, Register 5, f.151v.

Clergy and people were summoned to meet him to hear a sermon and to confess their sins. While the bishop preached to the clergy, a friar, Franciscan or Dominican, preached to the laity in the vernacular. The friar would be assisted by four others who heard confessions and assigned penances.[107]

In an age when people were increasingly authorised to seek their own confessors, friars ministered to individuals and noble households. John de Couton' was mentioned as the confessor of Richard Oysel, who was described as infirm, on 8 January 1307.[108] Martin de Alnwick, *sacre pagine professor*, was licensed to hear the confessions of Sir Henry Fitzhugh and Sir Robert de Hastang, knights, Garnius de Weston, Nicholas de Ask, Lady de Charmues and Sara her servant, in the parts of Richmond and Hexham, from 1 October 1318.[109]

The sacramental ministrations of friars were deemed suitable for female religious communities, especially the Poor Clares.[110] This aspect of their work appears in paintings and drawings from the fourteenth and fifteenth centuries. The psalter commissioned by Sir Geoffrey Luttrell (1276-1345), a wealthy landowner in Lincolnshire who had family associations in south Yorkshire, exemplifies this with a miniature of a corded friar kneeling

---

107 S. Gieben, 'Robert Grosseteste at the Papal Curia, Lyons 1250. Edition of the Documents', *CF* 41 (1971), 340-93, at 376.

108 *The Register of William Greenfield, lord archbishop of York 1306-1315*, 5 vols., eds. W. Brown / A.H. Thompson, (Surtees Society, 145, 149, 151, 152, 153), Durham 1931-40, IV, no.2083, p.202.

109 Borthwick Institute of Historical Research in the University of York, Register 9, f.159r.

110 C. Richmond, *John Hopton: a fifteenth century Suffolk Gentleman*, Cambridge 1981, 223, note 252. Sir William Willoughby left 6s. 8d. to each friar (presumably those ministering to the Franciscan nuns) at the monastery of Bruisyard in 1498.

to hear the confessions of a nun.[111] The registers of the archbishops of York and the bishops of Lincoln contain numerous licences to hear the confessions of Benedictine or Cistercian nuns, many of which were some distance from the nearest friary.

Archbishop Giffard appointed Franciscans as confessors to the Cistercian nuns of Sinningthwaite at Bilton in Ainsty on 17 February 1276. On the same day he instructed the prioresses of the same order at Hampole, Nun Appleton and other prioresses in the diocese to turn to the Dominicans and Franciscans for confessors.[112] Robert de Wyntringham had been licenced to hear the confessions of the nuns of Nun Appleton on 17 October 1300;[113] he was still described as a friar of York on 12 April 1318 when the licence was renewed.[114] The officials of William Greenfield, archbishop of York, visited the Benedictine monastery of Arden and the Cistercian priory of Rosedale during October 1306 and identified certain scandals and irregularities. On 14 October the archbishop instructed the prioress of Arden to select two friars, Blackfriars and Greyfriars, as confessors.[115] The prioress of Rosedale was castigated for choosing unauthorised confessors for the sisters and on 19 October of that year Greenfield instructed them to nominate two suitable friars, Dominican or Franciscan, for an episcopal

---

111 Cf. M.P. Brown, *The World of the Luttrell Psalter*, London 2006. BL, MS. Add. 42130, f.74r.

112 *The Register of Walter Giffard, lord archbishop of York, 1266-1279*, ed. Brown (cf. note 50), no.892, p.295.

113 *The Register of Thomas of Corbridge, lord archbishop of York, 1300-1304*, 2 vols., eds. W. Brown / A.H. Thompson (Surtees Soc., 138, 141), Durham 1925-28, I no.94, p.34.

114 Borthwick Institute of Historical Research in the University of York, Register 9, f.155r.

115 *Register of William Greenfield, lord archbishop of York 1306-1315*, eds. Brown / Thompson (cf. note 107), III, no.1153, pp.5-9.

licence.[116] Benedict of Malton and Thomas de Husthwayt' were appointed as confessors to the Augustinian nunnery of Moxby on 12 August 1314.[117] Adam de Brantingham was licensed as confessor to the Benedictine nuns of Wilberfoss on 26 June 1322.[118] John Francis, a friar of Scarborough, was the confessor of the Benedictine priory of Yedingham in 1532.[119]

Laurence Wetewang', a friar of Beverley, was commissioned to hear the confessions of the prioress and convent of the Cistercian nunnery at Swine in the East Riding on 4 April 1318.[120] Philip de Toumby, probably a friar of York, was licensed as a confessor for the same nunnery on 4 December 1335.[121] At least three friars and confessors to the Cistercian nuns of Hampole, West Yorkshire, are known to us: William de Calverley, on 19 March 1315[122] and 31 January 1318,[123] Adam de Acastr on 9 April 1375 for one year[124] and John Wotton on 10 September 1426.[125] It is probable that they were all friars assigned to Doncaster.

---

116 *Ibid.*, no.1154, pp.9-11.

117 *Ibid.*, no.1326, p.85.

118 Borthwick Institute of Historical Research in the University of York, Register 9, f.348v.

119 Borthwick Institute of Historical Research in the University of York, CP, G216.

120 Borthwick Institute of Historical Research in the University of York, Register 9, f.323v.

121 *Ibid.*, f.251r.

122 *Register of William Greenfield, lord archbishop of York 1306-1315*, eds. Brown / Thompson (cf. note 107), II, no.1110, p.210.

123 Borthwick Institute of Historical Research in the University of York.Register 9, f.481r.

124 *Ibid.*, Register 12, f.18r.

125 *Ibid.*, Register 19, f.28r.

The episcopal registers of Lincoln contain numerous references to friars appointed as confessors to the monasteries of female religious, [126] although many were to the south of the diocese and thus outside the custody of York.[127] Robert de Wynthorp, a Dominican, and Adam de Ludeford, a former guardian of the Lincoln Greyfriars, were authorised to hear the confessions of the Benedictine nuns of Stainfield on 26 March 1322.[128] Adam de Patrington and Thomas de Gressebey were licensed to hear the confessions of the nuns of Stainfield on 29 September 1325 for two years.[129] John de Morton, a friar, and Alan, perpetual vicar of Calthorp were licensed to hear the confessions of the nuns of Cistercian nuns of Legbourne on 9 December 1339 for one year.[130] John de Barton was re-licensed to hear the confessions of the nuns on 4 December 1338.[131]

V. Limiters

The term limiter carries some ambiguity, although it has latterly acquired a pejorative dimension. In its literal sense it denoted a friar appointed to pursue his ministry of preaching, hearing confessions and collecting alms inside a prescribed territory, the *limitatio*. One application is the straight-forward allusion to a friar working as a confessor

---

126 L.J. Wilkinson, *Women in Thirteenth-Century Lincolnshire*, (Royal Historical Society, Studies in History, new series), Woodbridge 2006, 165-95.
127 Lincolnshire Archives Office, Register 5, f.152r.
128 *Ibid.*, f.306v.
129 *Ibid.*, f.383v.
130 *Ibid.*, f.154v.
131 *Ibid.*, f.152r.

inside the friary's territory.[132] The term is equally applicable to preachers.

The limiter became a satirical figure in the vernacular literature of the fourteenth century. Boccaccio's portrait of Frate Cippola, already mentioned, evokes the image of a corrupt limiter and his *socius* and accomplice. The friar's open-air sermon was an occasion for peddling fables and superstitions; its purpose was to swell the order's coffers. The limiters mentioned by Piers the Plowman were scarcely more impressive. They, too, were associated with mendacity and lechery.[133] Geoffrey Chaucer's 'Summoner's Tale' paints a cynical portrait of a pair of disreputable and dishonest friars in Holderness. The sermon of one of the friars encouraged the laity to invest in trentals for the liberation of souls from purgatory and to support the order's building programmes; the two projects were often united. When the limiter had finished his sermon, pennies were put on his plate. After writing the donors' names on a tablet with a promise to pray for them, he went around the houses to beg for meal, cheese or corn. Meanwhile his companion, *socius*, carried a staff and two ivory tablets to record the names of those who provided food. Out of sight, he surreptitiously erased the names.[134] William Woodford confirms that the limiters were accustomed to write the benefactors' names on tablets and in the books ordained for

---

132 Cambridge University Library, Ely Diocesan Registers, G/1/1, f.121r, Montacute: *Item ix die decembr' anno domini m ccc xlii apud Downham dominus [episcopus Eliensis] concessit fratri Iohanni de Wetynge de conventu fratrum minorum Cantebrig limitatori insule Elien.quod posset audire confessiones xii personarum elien. dioc. sed confiteri volencium.*

133 *The Vision of William concerning Piers the Plowman* (cf. note 67) V, 64, 383.

134 *The Riverside Chaucer*, ed. L.D. Benson, 3rd ed. Oxford 1988, 128-36.

this purpose.[135] While satire is situated inside a credible framework for the sake of plausibility and credence, it is prone to caricature. Despite the literary image of the decadent friar, the order's work in visiting the territories assigned to the convents endured until the religious revolution of the sixteenth century. Furthermore, friars were the beneficiaries of a large number of wills until the Dissolution of the friaries in 1538-39.

The friars of Doncaster were authorised by William Melton, archbishop of York, to beg for alms on 3 June 1335.[136] The practice of the friars seeking alms (*for ther lyffyng*) within their territory was occasionally mentioned by testators such as William Eyre of Saleby on 11 July 1531. Saleby, a village north of Alford, was on the boundary of the limitation of the friaries of Lincoln, Boston and Grimsby.[137] Limiters were mentioned by John Sothill of Dewsbury on 28 September 1498,[138] and Richard Peke of Wakefield on 4 June 1516.[139] Some of them were named by testators in the decade before the suppression of the friaries. The evidence suggests that each friary sent a regular limiter to preach, hear confessions and collect alms. Both examples concern priests. Edward Morton of Little Wassand in Holderness, who asked for burial in the parish of Sigglesthorne, left the friars of Beverley a motte wheate and gave 12d. to [Sir] William White, limiter, on 8 March

---

135 E. Doyle, 'William Woodford, O.F.M.: His Life and Works together with a Study and Edition of his *Responsiones contra Wiclevum et Lollardos*', *FS* 43 (1983), 17-187, at 150.

136 *The Register of William Melton, Archbishop of York, 1317-1340*, 5 vols., eds. R.M.T. Hill / R. Brocklesby / T.C.B. Timmins (CYS, 70, 71, 76, 85, 93), York / Woodbridge 1977-2002, III, no.242, p.140.

137 *Lincoln Wills* (cf. note 22), 146-7.

138 *Testamenta Eboracensia* (cf. note 21), IV, 168-71. His offering distinguishes between the itinerant friars and yem yt kepes ye qwers at home at y' plays.

139 *Ibid.*, V, 73-6.

1527.[140] Thomas Cottis was asked to celebrate a trental of masses for John Serlle, a parishioner of St Cuthbert's at Sessay, whose will of 26 November 1532 refers to this friar as *our lemyto.*' Sessay is a village approximately 16 miles north of York. By this stage Cottis had been ordained for some twenty years.[141]

The limiter symbolised the itinerant work of the friars, who *ab initio*, displayed a strong interest in the evangelisation of the rural areas. This aspect of the friars' work has received less attention than their urban contribution, but it was nonetheless, a central feature of their itinerant ministry, as some recent studies have shown.[142] The model was provided by Sts Francis and Anthony. The former went through the villages and churches in the vicinity (*per illas villas et ecclesias in circuitu civitatis*) to preach[143] and the latter preached in cities (*civitates*), castles (*castra*), villages (*vici*) and the countryside (*campestria*).[144] Perhaps smarting from the allegation that they preferred large urban centres to the countryside, friars were exhorted not to avoid sparsely populated places.[145] David of Augsburg instructs young

---

140 Borthwick Institute of Historical Research in the University of York, Probate Register 9, f.375r.

141 *Ibid.*, Probate Register 11, f.34r.

142 Cf. M. Robson, 'Benefactors of the Greyfriars in York: Alms From Testators, 1530-1538', *Northern History* 38 (2001), 221-39.

143 *The Writings of Leo, Rufino and Angelo Companions of St.Francis*, ed. R.B. Brooke, Oxford 1970, cc.18-19, pp.118-19.

144 *Vita prima o Assidua*, ed. V. Gamboso (Fonti agiografiche antoniane, 1), Padua 1981, c.9, no.3, pp.318-9.

145 *Determinationes quaestionum circa regulam fratrum minorum*, in S Bonaventura, *Opera Omnia*, 10 vols., Quaracchi, Florence, 1898-1902, VIII, 337-74, at 370. *Non quod omnino debeamus alios in locis desertis deserere, sed prout se opportunitas obtulerit, debemus etiam eis doctrinam salutis offere. Illos tamen praedicatores et confessores non excuso a peccato negligentiae, qui magis pro commodo corporis frequentant loca illa, ubi sunt bona*

religious that the friars' work outside the convent should be conducted under obedience and for a good and useful purpose; friars should not seek every opportunity to absent themselves from the Divine Office and to roam away from the cloister. The golden age of monasticism in Egypt had seen no wandering around, begging or fawning upon people.[146]

A further fruit of this mobile ministry was the enrolment of men and women in the third order of St Francis. Sir John de Meux de Beswick, a soldier in Holderness who asked for burial in the church of St Bartholomew in Aldbrough, informed his executors on 1 June 1377 that at his funeral he wished to be clothed in the Franciscan habit, *quia frater sum in eodem ordine*, perhaps in association with the friary at Beverley, one of the eight mendicant houses in the locality to which he made a bequest.[147] The degrees of spiritual kinship to which the friars admitted laymen and women represent another manifestation of their outreach beyond their cities and boroughs. This is exemplified by the wills of Anne, Lady Scrope of Harling, widow of John Lord Scrope of Bolton, on 28 August 1498[148] and Robert Abbott of Austhorpe, in the parish of Whitkirk, south-east of Leeds, on 7 April 1502. The former gave 26s.8d. to the Greyfriars of Babwell, where she was a sister; she was also a sister at the Austin Friars of Norwich. The latter bequeathed 12d. to the Franciscans of York 12d. for prayers as *a broder of yr house*. He also had a letter of brotherhood

---

  hospitia, et nolunt pro salute fraterna divertere ad villas pauperculas et ibi pro Christo paupertatem, quam illi homines ibidem semper sustinent, apud illos aliquamdiu tolerare... paupertatem.

146 Fr. David ab Augusta *De exterioris et interioris hominis compositione* (cf. note 25), 28-31, 133, 156.
147 *Testamenta Eboracensia* (cf. note 21), I, 100-1.
148 *Ibid.*, IV, 149-54, 151.

from St Robert at Knaresborough and described himself as a brother of that house also.[149]

VI. The proclamation of the Crusades and the Scottish wars

The reverses experienced in the Holy Land during the 1220s led Gregory IX to enlist friars in the proclamation of the Crusade from the 1230s onwards. On 26 May 1252 Henry III wrote to Walter de Gray, archbishop of York, asking him to arrange that suitable Dominicans and Franciscans be selected to preach the cross, in accordance with the apostolic mandate.[150] On 14 July 1275 Archbishop Giffard wrote to the archdeacons of his diocese, instructing them to give every assistance to the Greyfriars and their custos who were preaching the Crusade.[151] Both the popes and local prelates relied heavily on the friars to stimulate local interest in this international cause. John Le Romeyn, archbishop of York, issued a mandate to the friars of the diocese on 4 September 1291. At least two or three friars were to preach the Crusade in the following places in the diocese: the Greyfriars of Doncaster were instructed to have one in Doncaster, another at Blyth, Nottinghamshire, and a third at Retford. The friary at York was to have one at Howden, another at Selby and a third in Pocklington. The Beverley Greyfriars were to have one at Driffield, another at Malton and a third at South Cave. The Greyfriars of Scarborough one at Bridlington and another at Whitby. A similar summons was dispatched to the Dominican friaries in the diocese.[152]

---

149 Cook, 'Wills of Leeds and District' (cf. note 87), 85-102, at 102.
150 *Calendar of Close Rolls, Henry III, A.D.1251-1253*, 219.
151 *Register of Walter Giffard, lord archbishop of York, 1266-1279*, ed. Brown (cf. note 50), no.818, p.264. *Historical Papers and Letters from the Northern Registers*, ed. Raine (cf. note 71), 46.
152 *Ibid.*, 93-6.

The Scottish wars disturbed the rhythm of life in the northern province in the early fourteenth century, leading to incursions and demands for money to buy off attacks or for ransom. The mobile friars were deemed to be useful instruments of national and diocesan policies. Archbishop Greenfield wrote to the heads of the four mendicant houses of York on 14 January 1315. Rehearsing the horrendous crimes perpetrated by Sir Robert Bruce and the Scots against churches and manors, the archbishop asked the priors and the guardian to appoint friars to preach in the vernacular [*denuncient in vulgari*] against Bruce in their convents and in the various parish churches in the diocese [*tam in ecclesiis vestrae religionis quam in aliis conventualibus et parochialibus ecclesiis ac ceteris locis insignibus*]. He particularly desired that the warden of the convent at Richmond should be one of the preachers. An indulgence of forty days was to be granted to those who helped to resist the enemy.[153]

Friars were ubiquitous in medieval society and it should come as no surprise to find them on the battlefield. On 19 June 1300 Thomas Corbridge, archbishop of York, granted the petition of Henry de Lacy, earl of Lincoln (1249-1311), and one of the major benefactors of the friary in York, that two friars, Michael de Merton and Reginald de Kingston, should hear the confessions of those who were accompanying the earl to fight in Scotland.[154] The same earl was successful in securing a papal indult on 15 January 1305 for him to be accompanied by his confessor, Michael

---

153 *Register of William Greenfield, lord archbishop of York 1306-1315*, eds. Brown / Thompson (cf. note 107), II, no.1097, pp.201-2, *Historical Papers and Letters from the Northern Registers*, ed. Raine (cf. note 71), 238-9, n.239.

154 *The Register of Thomas of Corbridge, lord archbishop of York, 1300-1304* (cf. note 112), I, no.61, pp.23-4, *Historical Papers and Letters from the Northern Registers*, ed. Raine (cf. note 71), 143.

de Merton, a friar who had full faculties except in reserved cases.[155]

The Scottish gains in the north of England were recorded by the *Lanercost Chronicle*. About 8 September 1318 two cardinals, papal delegates, were still in England, when they wrote to the English bishops to arrange that at every solemn mass the excommunication of Robert Bruce and his supporters might be announced. The presence of marauding Scottish armies as far south as Boroughbridge in the summer of 1319 galvanised the citizens of York to attack the Scots near the town of Myton-on-Swale, in the North Riding, twelve miles north of the city. Their forces were led by Archbishop Melton and Bishop John Hotham of Ely, chancellor of the realm, and included a large number of priests and clerics, among whom were sundry religious, including mendicants (*diversi religiosi, possessionati et mendicantes*). The disordered English lines were easily outmanoeuvred by the Scottish army which pursued the English, killing clergy and laymen; about four thousand people perished; some of them drowned in the River Swale. Thereafter the battle was known as the chapter of Myton on account of the number of clergy engaged. It ended in defeat for the English forces with a huge loss of life.[156]

The friars' ministry towards the captured is reflected in the fate of John of Brittany, earl of Richmond, who had a strong affection for the order.[157] The earl was captured by the Scottish forces on Blackhowe Moor near Byland Abbey

---

155 *Calendar of Entries in the Papal Registers relating to Great Britain and Ireland, Papal Letters, II, A.D.1305-1342*, ed. W.H. Bliss, London 1895, 7.

156 *Chronicon de Lanercost* (cf. note 28), 237-9.

157 E.g. Lincolnshire Archives Office, Register 3, f.257r: on 13 July 1312 Bishop Dalderby wrote to Geoffrey Brusshyn, a friar, at the request of Sir John of Brittany, count of Richmond, and authorised him to absolve Sir John of the same family from excommunication incurred for an assault on a cleric, monk or canon of the diocese of Lincoln.

on 14 October 1322 and held as a prisoner in Scotland. Robert de Stayndorp, the guardian of the Greyfriars in York, and another friar, his English *socius*, were given a safe conduct on 27 October 1322 by Edward II to remain with the earl for his recreation and solace until Whitsuntide.[158] Following his death on 17 January 1334, the earl was buried in the church of the Cordeliers at Nantes, bequeathing various relics to that church.

Friars were sometimes engaged as messengers. The account rolls of Bolton Abbey, a house of Austin Canons, contain records of the payment of debts to Lord Roger *per manum* of the Greyfriars of York and Preston in 1311-12.[159] The crown made good use of the friars as mediators and envoys from the 1230s. The friars' presence on the battlefield at Lewes is well documented. They worked closely with Stephen Bersted, bishop of Chichester.[160] Two friars, John Beckingham and Geoffrey de Fugeriis, members of another custody, travelled through the northern part of the custody of York in the early summer of 1290 as royal envoys in negotiations for a marriage between Edward of Caernarfon, son of Edward I, and Margaret of Scotland, the daughter of Eric II, king of Norway. Expenses were paid for eleven days for their journey from London to Hartlepool.[161] The accounts of Edward I record a payment made on 12 October 1301 to the friars who served as messengers and envoys of the crown.

---

158 *Calendar of Patent Rolls, Edward II, iv, A.D.1321-1324*, 210; *Calendar of Documents relating to Scotland preserved in her majesty's Public Record Office, London, III, A.D.1307-1357*, 4 vols., ed. J. Bain Edinburgh 1881-88, III, no.793, p. 147.

159 *The Bolton Priory Compotus 1286-1325 Together with a Priory Account Roll for 1377-78*, eds. I. Kershaw / D.M. Smith (The Yorkshire Archaeological Society, Record Series, 154), Woodbridge 2000, 312.

160 *The Song of Lewes*, ed. C.L. Kingsford, Oxford 1890, xix-xx.

161 *Documents illustrative of the History of Scotland, 1286-1306*, 2 vols., ed. J. Stevenson, Edinburgh 1870, I, 138-9.

Among the recipients were Henry de Barton and his *socius*, friars of York, who received 40s. for travelling from York to London *pro negocio regis pro expensis suis, eundo, morando et redeundo in denar. eisdem liberatur per scutum XII dierum.*[162]

IX. Friars in residence

Fluctuations in the size of the friars' communities have puzzled historians. One tentative answer is that friaries maintained a base community of friars who rarely left their conventual complex as well as those who were sent out to work in the *limitatio*. The friary and its church required the constant presence of a significant number of men to sustain the conventual life. A certain number of friars was required to celebrate the masses at particular hours. It is unlikely that a particular group of friars, for example, the sacristan, cook or librarian, went far from their cloister. The granting of licences to preach and hear confessions probably created distinctions among the ordained members of the community; not every priest was selected for these ministries. For instance, testamentary dispositions hint at some distinctions in the clerical ranks. Some friars, styled as *capellani*, were required to satisfy the demand for suffrages in the form of masses to be celebrated for the benefit of the living and the deceased in the various chapels of the friary church.[163]

There is ample information regarding the friars' movements around their *limitatio* in various English sources. It is indisputable that a group of friars remained legitimately absent from the friary for periods of some weeks as they worked in parishes distant from the friaries.

---

162 British Library, MS Add. 7966, f.26v.

163 Cf. *Item lego fratribus Minoribus de Notyngham v marcas. Ita quod inveniant unum capellanum ad celebrandum pro anima mea pro anno post obitum meum. Testamenta Eboracensia*, I, 211.

The assumption that some friars might be absent from the community was enshrined in the prayers *pro fratribus absentibus* during the Divine Office. Friars were assigned to specified communities after the chapters and they lived under obedience to the local guardian, who was appointed by the annual provincial chapter. However, from the outset friars were invited to undertake tasks which took them away from their own communities for varying periods of time.

Evidence that the mendicant communities in a neighbourhood did enter in agreements with each other comes from the series of documents concerning the Carmelites and the Austin Friars, who had recently established themselves at Hull. The agreement was confirmed by the two priors in the chapter house of the Carmelites on 24 October 1320 and it was copied into the register of Archbishop Melton on 30 October of that year at Bishopthorpe. This was followed by declarations from the Austin Friars on 21 October and a second one on 3 November 1321 regarding the building of an oratory in the priory. There was also a document issued by the Carmelites on 25 October 1321.[164] Such agreements between neighbouring mendicant communities bolster the hypothesis that the friars were far from being a group of casual religious who responded to the circumstances in which they found themselves. There is a formidable body of material to indicate that the friars were well organised and highly efficient in their administration. Note the speed with which the custos of York was dispatched across the River Humber to explain to the bishop of Lincoln that some of the friars whom he had licensed as confessors had been transferred to friaries in Yorkshire, had become incapacitated or had died. Urged by the minister provincial, the custos tendered new names to the bishop. An episcopal

---

164 Borthwick Institute of Historical Research in the University of York, Register 9, ff.345v, 46r.

response comes from Bishop Burghersh on 18 November 1320, when he informed his officials about the movement of licensed friars to houses in Yorkshire.[165]

The northern sources do not reveal any unseemly clashes between friars from different convents preaching, hearing confessions or seeking alms. Neither are there reports of disputes between the different mendicant orders active in the same parish simultaneously. One clue may lie in the terminology employed by Roger Marcand, rector of St Michael's in Laxton, Nottinghamshire, who left alms to the mendicants in the following terms in his will of 20 October 1427:

> *item lego cuilibet ordini Fratrum Minorum, Praedicatorum et Augustiniorum qui sunt limitatores venient ad Laxton ad praedicandum diversis temporibus annuatim.*

This implies a level of agreement between the four mendicant orders to avoid any ugly encounters with members of one or more orders arriving in a parish at the same time. Special mention of the Carmelites occurs just after this statement.[166] In other parts of the country there was co-operation between the mendicant orders, which is exemplified in a licence granted by John Sandale, bishop of Winchester, on 12 March 1317, permitting the Carmelites to preach in the cathedral every third turn after the Dominicans and Franciscans, unless one of the monks

---

165 The custos of York explained that William de Calverley, licensed in the diocese of Lincoln, had been transferred to the diocese of York, where he died. Simon de Castre was licensed in his place. Lincolnshire Archives Office, Episcopal Register 3, f.427r.

166 Borthwick Institute of Historical Research in the University of York, Probate Register 2, ff.547r, 650r. The Carmelites are mentioned a little later.

wished to preach.[167] It is probable that the custos of York was in discussion with his opposite number among the other three mendicant orders to negotiate and regulate the dates at which friars of one order would visit a particular deanery or parish in order to avoid any overlapping activities.

The assumption that friars would be absent from their convents during particular seasons of the year informs the picture of the Dominican lector painted by Humbert de Romans in 1265. His counsel was that the lector should take his vacation only when the greater part of the community was absent, that is, during the summer or the busy preaching seasons of Advent and Lent.[168] The inference that the followers of St Francis, too, may have had similar arrangements finds a textual basis in a contract for masses signed on 26 March 1458, when John Kyry, guardian of the London Greyfriars, entered into an agreement with William Cantelowe, a citizen, merchant and alderman of London, for masses for himself and others. He acknowledged that the community had received £200 in alms from Cantelowe for the repair of their church and for various other necessities. The friars placed on record their debt of gratitude. The chapter of that community, with the express consent and wish of the minister provincial, Thomas Radnor, ordained that there should be a daily Mass in the friary in perpetuity for the soul of Thomas Gloucestre, soldier, and Anne, his wife, and for the souls of

---

167 *The Registers of John Sandale and Rigaud de Asserio, bishops of Winchester (A.D.1316-1323), with an appendix of contemporaneous and other illustrative documents*, ed. F.J. Baigent (Hampshire Record Society, 8), London 1897, 32-3, 422-3. The licence was renewed on 8 August 1321.

168 L.Boyle, 'Notes on the Education of the *Fratres communes* in the Dominican order in the Thirteenth Century', in: *Xenia Medii Aevi Historiam Illustrantia oblata Thomae Kaeppeli O.P.* eds. R. Creytens / P. Künzle (Storia e Letteratura raccolta di Studi e Testi, 141), Rome 1978, 249-67, at 256-7.

the said William [Cantelowe] and for Margaret and Elizabeth, his deceased wives, family and his benefactors; an exception was to be made for the sacred *triduum*. Moreover, this mass should generally be celebrated in the chapel of St Mary, where these benefactors were interred. In addition, the friars undertook to enter the names of the above among their major benefactors to be recommended each week during the domestic chapter. On the day of their anniversaries mass should be celebrated annually around the feast of St Agatha, the virgin, 5 February. And for more recent memory the anniversary should be observed around the feast of All Saints, when the greater number of the friars would be in residence:

> *quando maior multitudo fratrum fuerit in dicto conventu.*[169]

This would represent the lull between the end of cycle of visits to the parishes in the *limitatio* and the beginning of Advent about four weeks later, when preaching missions were resumed.

X. Conclusion

St Francis's vocation opened new vistas and brought novel dimensions to the lexicon of religious life. Despite their different outlook, the friars were no more tolerant of purposeless travel than were the monks, who abhorred the *gyrovage*. One legitimate reason for the friars to be absent from the community was the exercise of their itinerant apostolate, which brought them to every parish inside the community's *limitatio*. which might be as far as thirty miles from their convent. These services were appreciated by people in the parishes of the custody of York, many of whom made offerings and left legacies to the order. In addition, a smaller band of friars served as messengers,

---

169 C.L. Kingsford, *The Grey Friars of London* (BSFS, 6), Aberdeen 1915, 208-11.

envoys, diplomats, chaplains and penitentiaries. This sample of the evidence from the custody of York illuminates a central aspect of the friars' apostolate away from the shadow of their own cloisters.

The Creation and Early History of the Franciscan Custody of Cambridge

Jens Röhrkasten

(University of Birmingham)

The expansion of the Franciscan order in the thirteenth century was a complex process. The development of a new type of religious life by Francis of Assisi and his immediate followers led to an enthusiastic response in the area of his Umbrian hometown which soon attracted people of all walks of life from different areas of the Christian world. Communities modelled on those of the Portiuncula soon emerged in other parts of Italy and a religious order began to emerge, not least because Francis himself also acted as an itinerant preacher who travelled widely in the Mediterranean. Despite the emphasis on humility and simplicity, the order's growth was not left to chance but was instead guided by processes of planning which ensured that the new spirituality was represented in all parts of the continent within a generation. While much attention has been given to Franciscan spiritual innovation, there was another aspect which still needs to be fully understood: a new attitude to space. Within a few decades the Franciscans - like the Dominicans - were represented in all parts of Christian Europe and the organisations they formed in provinces, vicariates and custodies covered the whole of the available area. In parallel to the Dominicans[1] the Franciscans did not just expand into all areas of Europe by establishing provisional residences in the towns, they

---

1 G.G. Merlo, *Nel nome di san Francesco. Storia dei frati Minori e del francescanesimo sino agli inizi del XVI secolo*, Padua 2003, 73-97.

approached the task in an organised and carefully planned manner.[2] Their intention to achieve universal representation emerges already from the fact that they gave priority to the major towns - Italy during the life of St Francis is an exception here - in order to set up networks from there, identifying and exploiting existing urban hierarchies.

This creation of a comprehensive network of convents in European towns in the first half of the thirteenth century occurred with great speed.[3] The development in England, where the friars arrived in the summer of 1224, conforms to the general pattern: by 1256 forty-nine houses had been established in English towns.[4] The English kingdom was defined as one of the order's provinces which was subdivided into four, later seven, custodies. This pure statistical data only becomes meaningful if it is set in a wider context. How were the custodies defined geographically and how were they organised? What is the meaning of 'establishment of a friary'? In London the small group of friars spent their first year in a possibly derelict

---

2   H.-J. Schmidt, *Kirche, Staat, Nation. Raumgliederung der Kirche im mittelalterlichen Europa*, Weimar 1999, 375-6.

3   H. Hefele, *Die Bettelorden und das religiöse Volksleben Ober- und Mittelitaliens im 13. Jahrhundert* (Beiträge zur Kulturgeschichte des Mittelalters und der Renaissance, 9), Leipzig 1910, 76; B. Gratien, *Histoire de la Fondation et de l'Évolution de l'Ordre des Frères Mineurs au XIIIe siècle*, Paris 1928, 77, 225, 513ff; M. Heimbucher, *Orden und Kongregationen der katholischen Kirche*, 2 vols., Paderborn 1933-34, I, 691-3; J.B. Freed, *The Friars and German Society in the Thirteenth Century* (The Mediaeval Academy of America, 86), Cambridge (Mass.) 1977, 21-2. W. Emery, *The Friars in Medieval France. A catalogue of French mendicant convents, 1200-1550*, New York 1962, 3, 7, 16-7.

4   A.G. Little (ed.), *Fratris Thomae vulgo dicti de Eccleston Tractatus de Adventu Fratrum Minorum in Angliam*, Manchester 1951, xxx, 11; Idem, *Franciscan Papers, Lists and Documents*, Manchester 1943, 217-21.

house in Cornhill[5], in Cambridge they were assigned the old synagogue which shared an entrance with the town gaol[6] and the first residences in other English towns were similar. From these beginnings it was a long way to extensive monastic precincts with cloisters and large churches, a process sometimes completed only as late as the middle of the fourteenth century. These changes were part of a general transformation of the order as a whole which affected its attitude to economic management, study and its architectural representation in the localities. There were other changes. The Franciscans began to influence their environment by offering the example of a religious life in the communities, through their sermons and through their availability as religious advisors. In many instances the effects of this influence on religious practices and beliefs of the laity remain to be studied. However, it is clear that this was not a one-sided process but an exchange which affected the order itself. The attitudes of the faithful, perhaps most strongly expressed in the wishes of lay patrons, had an impact on local Franciscan communities. The composition of these communities also changed with members of local families being represented, reflecting their social environment. Local and regional studies can help to illustrate and perhaps explain these larger historical processes and it is with a view to contribute towards this end that a few preliminary observations on the custody of Cambridge shall be presented.

---

5   Little (ed.), *Tractatus de Adventu Fratrum Minorum in Angliam* (cf. note 4), 10; C.L. Kingsford, *The Grey Friars of London* (BSFS, 6), Aberdeen 1915, 15-6; J. Röhrkasten, *The Mendicant Houses of Medieval London* (Vita Regularis, 21), Münster 2004, 43-4.

6   Little (ed.), *Tractatus de Adventu Fratrum Minorum in Angliam* (cf. note 4), 22; J.R.H. Moorman, *The Grey Friars in Cambridge*, Cambridge 1952, 8-9.

Local studies can fall back on checklists of questions developed by Jacques Le Goff and André Vauchez which help to structure the contextual aspects of mendicant life.[7] The identification of founders and supporters, the sometimes ambivalent attitudes of the local secular and regular clergy as well as the relationship between the members of different mendicant orders were factors to which Le Goff drew attention, adding the further dimension of the urban topography, the location and possible relocation of mendicant houses and their impact on urban development. Vauchez was able to refine this list of criteria significantly, focusing on aspects related to the foundation, the location, the convent plan and architecture, recruitment, mendicant influence on the religious life of the laity and the friars' involvement in local politics. The first items on this questionnaire are relevant for the early phases of foundation and consolidation: who took the initiative for a foundation? Who provided land and material assistance? What were the reasons for a possible later relocation? What is known about the plan of the friary? Where was it located and how did it influence urban development?

The survival of sources poses a problem. The archives of the friaries in question share the fate of other mendicant document repositories in the British Isles in that they have been almost completely lost. The only exception is the fragment of an account book from Cambridge, discovered and published by Moorman in his monograph on the Cambridge Grey Friars and possibly a deed from Lynn, allowing the friars to lead the pipes of their aqueduct over

---

[7] J. Le Goff, 'Apostolat mendiant et fait urbain dans la France médiévale: l'implantation des ordres mendiants', *Annales ESC* 22 (1968) 335-52; M. de Fontette, 'Villes médiévales et ordres mendiants', *Revue Historique de Droit Français et Étranger* 48 (1970), 390-407. A. Vauchez, Introduction, in: 'Les ordres mendiants et la ville en Italie centrale (v.1220-v.1350)', *Mélanges de l'École Française de Rome* 89 (1977), 561ff.

private land.[8] Archaeological remains are scarce and not very informative about the custody's early history. Even though much of the house in Walsingham remains, this was a mid-fourteenth century foundation which is unlikely to have formed part of the original plan for the new custody.[9] Contemporary information is difficult to obtain. Relatively little use has yet been made of the urban archives of Lynn, Norwich, Yarmouth, Colchester and Ipswich which offer excellent and sometimes complete collections of deeds, wills, accounts and court minutes.[10] Records from the dioceses of Ely, London and Norwich and the much better preserved archives of other religious institutions in the region also need to be tapped[11] while further information can be found among the records of the royal administration. Taken together these collections may allow at least a partial reconstruction of the lost mendicant archives but this is work for the future.

---

8   Moorman, *Grey Friars in Cambridge* (cf. note 6), plate facing p.70; Norfolk Record Office, KL/C50/524.

9   A.R. Martin, 'The Greyfriars of Walsingham', *Norfolk Archaeology* 25 (1935) 227-71; *Idem, Franciscan Architecture in England* (BSFS, 18), Manchester 1937, 124-5.

10 B. Brodt, *Städte ohne Mauern. Stadtentwicklung in East Anglia im 14. Jahrhundert* (Veröffentlichungen des Deutschen Historischen Instituts London, 44), Paderborn 1997, 198-202; H. Harrod, *Report on the Deeds and Records of the Borough of King's Lynn*, King's Lynn 1874, 69, 130; *Idem, Repertory of the Records and Evidences of the Borough of Colchester, 1865*, Colchester 1865, 7; *Idem, Report on the Records of the Borough of Colchester*, Colchester 1865; W. Hudson / J.C. Tingey (eds.), *The Records of the City of Norwich*, 2 vols. Norwich 1906-10, I, 364-8, 369; II, 49. D. Owen (ed.), *The Making of King's Lynn. A Documentary Survey* (Records of Social and Economic History, n.s. 9), Gloucester 1984, 317-8, 324. H. Ingleby / R.F. Isaacson (eds.), *The Red Register of King's Lynn*, 2 vols., King's Lynn 1919-21, I, 2-3, 76-9; W.M. Palmer (ed.), *Cambridge Borough Documents*, Cambridge 1931, xxx-xxxii, 1.

11 D.M. Owen, 'Ely Diocesan Records', in: C.W. Dugmore / C. Duggan (eds.), *Studies in Church History I*, London 1964, 176-83.

The custody of Cambridge was one of initially four, later seven, regional subdivisions of the English Franciscan province. By the time the province was structured into custodies, probably in 1228[12], Minorites could already be found in at least two towns in the area: Cambridge itself and Norwich, where the first friars arrived in 1226.[13] Precise dates at this stage are unknown, partly because there were only a handful of friars in the English province whose places of residence were improvised and temporary. With the foundation of the house at Walsingham in 1347, the creation of the custody in one of the kingdom's most densely populated areas, was completed.

Thomas of Eccleston provided a detailed account of the poor and improvised lodgings of the first Franciscans in the kingdom. Their precarious and sometimes marginal existence conveys the impression that the friars' lives were determined by coincidence and chance. However, it is highly likely that Franciscan settlement was planned and the Cambridge custody may serve as an example. The choice of Norwich as the greatest centre of population and commerce seems natural. The case of Cambridge is more difficult. The town was an emerging regional capital of education and learning but the university was still in its infancy. The Franciscan arrival in Cambridge was also before the order showed an interest in systematic intellectual training in the universities.[14] For these reasons it

---

12 Little (ed.), *Tractatus de Adventu Fratrum Minorum in Angliam*, (cf. note 4), 34.

13 *Et praedicatores et minores coeperunt habitare in Norwyco*. H.R. Luard (ed.), *Bartholomaei de Cotton monachi Norwicensis Historia Anglicana* (RS, 16), London 1859, 113.

14 The Franciscans came to Oxford already in 1224 but it took about five years before they opened a school of their own, M.W. Sheehan, 'The Religious Orders 1220-1370', in: J.I. Catto, R. Evans et al. (eds.), *The History of the University of Oxford*, 8 vols., Oxford 1984-94, I, 193-223, at 194. A.G. Little, 'The Franciscan School at

is unlikely that the emerging university attracted the friars even though their role in the faculty of theology of the medieval university of Cambridge was to be very important.[15] There was a different appeal. Cambridge, like Norwich, was a county town and by this time it had probably also become a centre of administration for the diocese of Ely.[16] Apart from its own population the town attracted visitors and merchants. It is likely to have been a deliberate decision by the order to have a presence in Cambridge rather than in the cathedral town nearby, even though the first group of friars was small. Another factor may have been the welcome they were given by at least a section of the population: it is said that they were called by the citizens who also provided them with a place of residence for them.[17] Only a few years later, probably by 1230, Franciscans were resident in Lynn and they had arrived in Ipswich and Colchester, the administrative

Oxford', in: *Idem, Franciscan Papers* (cf. note 4) 55-71; *Idem, The Grey Friars in Oxford* (Oxford Historical Society, 20), Oxford 1892, 30.

15 A.G. Little, 'The Friars and the Foundation of the Faculty of Theology in the University of Cambridge', in: *Idem, Franciscan Papers* (cf. note 4), 230 note 6. Moorman, *Grey Friars in Cambridge* (cf. note 6), 7, assumes that there were important schools in the town while the university "was only in its infancy."

16 Moorman, *Grey Friars in Cambridge* (cf. note 6), 7-8; E.O. Blake, 'Ely', in: *Lexikon des Mittelalters*, 9 vols., Munich 1977-98, III, col. 1865-68; J.A. Brundage, 'The Cambridge Faculty of Canon Law and the Ecclesiastical Courts of Ely', in: P. Zutshi (ed.), *Medieval Cambridge. Essays on the Pre-Reformation University* (History of the University of Cambridge, Texts and Studies, 2), Woodbridge 1994, 21-45, at 21, 41, suggests the link but admits that it cannot be proved, cf. D.R. Leader et al., *A History of the University of Cambridge*, 4 vols., Cambridge 1988-93, I, 192-3. It has been doubted whether Cambridge had this role already in the twelfth century, N. Karn (ed.), *Ely 1109-1197* (English Episcopal Acta, 31), Oxford 2005, lvi.

17 Little (ed.), *Tractatus de Adventu Fratrum Minorum in Angliam* (cf. note 4), 22.

centres of Suffolk and Essex before 1237. An effort to establish a presence in the monastic town of Bury St Edmunds in 1233 failed due to the resistance of the Benedictine monks and it appears to have been repeated with equal lack of success five years later,[18] but unlike the Dominicans who were equally frustrated in their attempt to settle, the Franciscans returned in 1257 only to find the monks' resistance undiminished. The struggle between the order and the prestigious Benedictine house became a classic example of confrontation between monks and friars. The eventual compromise saw the friary outside the banleuca of the town, just on the northern approach at Babwell. Further moves to the port towns of Yarmouth (before 1271) and Dunwich (before 1277) completed the creation of the custody. At this stage Walsingham, still a small settlement with a priory of Augustinian canons, was not deemed to be of sufficient importance to attract the attention of the Franciscans. However, King Henry III's regular visits to the priory gradually changed its status and by the early fourteenth century the shrine at Walsingham had become a major centre of pilgrimage. The foundation of a Franciscan convent here was only possible with the help of a major figure and such a patron emerged in the person of Elizabeth de Burgh, a relative of the Plantagenets and co-heiress of the Clare estates.[19] She provided land for the friars and her protection may have helped to overcome the canons' vociferous resistance to the new friary. Of all the Franciscan host towns in the priory, Walsingham is the most likely to have lacked an urban character, making it an

---

18 Annales de Dunstaplia, in: H.R. Luard (ed.), *Annales Monastici*, 5 vols. (RS, 36), London 1864-69, III, 134; A.G. Little, *Studies in English Franciscan History* (Publications of the University of Manchester, Historical Series, 29), Manchester 1917, 96.

19 J.C. Ward, 'Elizabeth de Burgh, Lady of Clare (d. 1360)', in: C.M. Barron / A.F. Sutton (eds.), *Medieval London Widows 1300-1500*, London 1994, 29-45.

untypical choice for a Franciscan house.[20] Untypical was also the foundress's social background.

Even though the origins of the friary at Colchester are unknown, it is fairly certain that the other houses were not founded by members of the aristocracy. Thomas of Eccleston's account of the Cambridge foundation with its reference to the *burgenses* is corroborated by independent evidence. The initial residence, part of the town's old synagogue, was deemed insufficient by 1230 and an alternative was offered, again *ex parte burgensium* of Cambridge.[21] The evidence concerning the other houses is not contemporary but is based on the early modern antiquarians. For Ipswich there is a reference to Sir Robert Tibtot and his wife Una, probably local landholders[22], the house in Yarmouth is said to have been founded by Sir William Gerbrigge, very likely the member of a family from whose ranks a bailiff of the town came in the late thirteenth century.[23] The men traditionally regarded as founders of Norwich, John de Hastingford, and Lynn, Thomas Feltham, can also safely be located in the urban elite,[24] as can Richard Fitz John and Alice his wife, who are said to have created the necessary preconditions for the

---

20 Even in the sixteenth century Walsingham only had a low place in the ranking of English towns according to taxpaying (1524-25) and taxable wealth, A. Dyer, 'Ranking lists of English medieval towns', in: D.M. Palliser / P. Clark / M. Daunton (eds.), *The Cambridge Urban History of Britain*, 3 vols., Cambridge 2000, I, 747-70, at 762, 766.

21 Moorman, *Grey Friars in Cambridge* (cf. note 6), ch.1.

22 *VCH Suffolk*, II, 126.

23 *VCH Norfolk*, II, 436.

24 J. Kirkpatrick, History of the Religious Orders and Communities, and of the Hospitals and Castle, of Norwich [written about the year 1725], Yarmouth 1845, 108, quoting Weever; F. Blomefield, An Essay Towards a Topographical History of the County of Norfolk,

friary at Dunwich. Only when the house had to be relocated, did the king step in as second founder.[25]

While the civic elites welcomed and supported the representatives of the new order, two powerful religious houses objected to the friars' presence: the Benedictines of Bury St Edmunds and the canons of Walsingham. Such resistance was not restricted to England. Dossat has pointed out that old established abbeys did not refrain from using their privileges and seigneurial rights to keep the mendicants at bay. The examples from Figeac, Rabastens, Mézin, Castre and Toulouse point to a pattern, especially since emerging civic elites were sometimes keen to have access to venues of worship independent of those provided by the dominant local religious house.[26] Despite obvious parallels in antagonism between the friars and older religious institutions, background conditions varied and the cases of Bury St Edmunds and Walsingham show that local factors played an important role.

The Franciscan attempt to establish a permament presence in Bury St Edmunds in 1233 coincided with the effort to obtain a foothold in Reading in the same year. The Annals of Dunstable provide some detail on the friars' preparations in Reading, where they are alleged to have appeared armed with papal and royal letters which were essential for their success. It is not known whether similar protection had been obtained for the prospective convent at Bury St Edmunds but it is unlikely since the planned settlement failed.[27] The presence of the papal legate Otho encouraged the Dominicans in 1238 to request permission

---

11 vols., 2nd edn. London, 1805-10, IV, 107.

25 *VCH Suffolk*, II, 125; *VCH Norfolk*, II, 427, 430.

26 Y. Dossat, 'Opposition des anciens ordres à l'installation des mendiants', in: *Les mendiants en pays d'Oc* (Cahiers de Fanjeaux, 8), Toulouse 1973, 263-306. English cases are discussed by Little, *Studies* (cf. note 18), 92-100.

27 Luard (ed.), *Annales Monastici* (cf. note 18) III, 134.

for the construction of a convent in the monastic town in a place which had been offered to them by the countess of Oxford. Having travelled to the town and inspected the monks' privileges, the legate refused and this refusal also referred to a Franciscan petition apparently made at the same time.[28] While these appear to have been rather half-hearted efforts by the English Minorites, the situation was very different when they returned to Bury St Edmunds twenty years later. This time the Franciscans were determined to succeed and the level of support they mobilised and the nature of their preparation indicates that the attempt to establish a convent in the Benedictine liberty was co-ordinated by the province rather than at a more local level. Henry III and other members of the royal family and the earl of Gloucester and other members of the aristocracy became involved and Matthew Paris as hostile Benedictine observer noted that *introducti sunt et instituti violenter per laicorum manum*.[29] The arrival of the Franciscans resulted in five years of conflict with the monks. On occasion the dispute led to instances of physical violence but more common were appeals to the king and to the Curia. The litigation ended with a humiliating defeat for the Franciscans who were ordered by pope Urban IV in late May 1263 to dismantle their convent and to leave the town.[30] By the end of the year the friars had had to make a public submission to the monks. Despite royal and aristocratic support, the Franciscans technically never had a convent in Bury St Edmunds. Instead they were given a site at Babwell, outside the privileged area, officially as a sign of grace by the monks but probably as part of a negotiated

---

28 A. Gransden (ed.), *The Chronicle of Bury St Edmunds 1212-1301*, London 1964, 9.

29 H.R. Luard (ed.), *Matthaei Parisiensis, monachi sancti Albani, Chronica Majora*, 7 vols. (RS, 57), London 1872-83, V, 688.

30 T. Arnold (ed.), *Memorials of St Edmund's Abbey*, 3 vols. (RS, 96), London 1890-96, II, 281-5. L. Dorez / J. Guiraud (eds.), *Les Registres d'Urbain IV (1261-64)*, 4 vols., Paris 1899-1929, I, 308.

settlement. This site was the third Franciscan precinct in Bury St Edmunds and its suburbs since their arrival in 1258. The initial structures on the first plot of land, granted by a local knight, had been dismantled by servants of the abbey shortly after the friars' arrival. A different strategy was pursued in the second attempt when an alternative plot was donated to Henry III for the use of the Franciscans by another Suffolk landowner. Since this settlement also had the support of pope Alexander IV the position of the friars seemed unassailable. However, the balance of power in England shifted significantly in the following years and Alexander IV, who had been the Franciscans' cardinal protector[31], was replaced by a pontiff less attached to the order.[32]

While the canons of Walsingham were equally opposed to a Franciscan friary in their town, the situation was different. The Augustinians never enjoyed privileges similar to those of the monks of Bury St Edmunds. The status of their community was not based on the charisma of a royal saint but their convent had originated as a much more humble private foundation which had remained unremarkable in prestige and wealth until Henry III began to make regular visits.[33] When the priory became a centre of pilgrimage in the second half of the thirteenth century, its property began to increase significantly, eventually making

31   L. Pellegrini, *Alessandro IV e i Francescani (1254-1261)*, (Studi e testi francescani, 34), Rome 1966, 21.

32   R. Yates, *History and Antiquities of the Abbey of St. Edmund's Bury*, London 1843, 117-20; H.R. Barker, *History of and Guide to Bury St. Edmund's*, Bury St. Edmund's 1885, 18; J.R. Thompson, *Records of Saint Edmund of East Anglia. King and Martyr*, 2 vols., London 1890-91, II, 153-4; A. Goodwin, *The Abbey of St. Edmundsbury*. The Gladstone Memorial Prize Essay, 1926, Oxford 1931, 38-9; M.D. Lobel, *The Borough of Bury St. Edmunds. A Study in the Government of a Monastic Town*, Oxford 1935, 125-6; J.R.H. Moorman, *Medieval Franciscan Houses*, New York 1983, 47.

33   J.C. Dickinson, *The Shrine of Our Lady at Walsingham*, Cambridge 1956, 4-19.

it one of the most wealthy religious houses of East Anglia. The priory was not only a pilgrimage site of national importance, it was also at the centre of a local network of parish churches and religious houses who had to share available resources. This balance was threatened when Elizabeth de Burgh proposed to found a Franciscan convent in the town in the 1340s. The canons drafted a carefully worded petition to the lady Clare listing a number of arguments against such a foundation. The foundation of a Franciscan convent - it was claimed - would reduce the tithe income of local parish churches because the new religious precinct took up land of the parish or parishes affected. In addition it was said to be likely that the friars would attract parishioners away from their local churches so that all the revenues derived from the *cura animarum* would go to the new convent rather than to the parish clergy. The canons reminded lady Clare of the fact that the friars were dependent on such income since they had no property of their own. However, the canons' own economy was also portrayed as being under threat. Offerings from pilgrims were more likely to go to the Franciscans than to the priory because public access to the chapel had to be closed after dark in order to protect the many valuables there from thieves. The canons were concerned that pilgrims would turn to the friars rather than wait until access to the priory would be granted again in the morning; potentially this was a serious problem because such offerings were an important part of their economy. A Franciscan foundation in Walsingham would add yet another mendicant house to the area which already had to provide resources to two Carmelite communities in the close vicinity, at Burnham Norton and *apud Sniterle* (Blakeney). These were valid arguments even though the canons probably overstated the effects of a Franciscan presence in their town. They implored Elizabeth de Burgh not to endanger a religious community which owed so much to her ancestors and to desist from her plans. The fact that lady Clare established a Franciscan community at Walsingham in 1347 does not necessarily mean that the canons' petition was ineffective. There may well have been compensation arrangements in order to minimize the impact on the local Church.[34]

The Franciscan expansion in the area was largely complete by the late thirteenth century, but the development of the custody continued. With the exception of the Walsingham friary, this was now an internal development of churches and friary buildings, including the acquisition of additional plots of land, the construction of aqueducts and the setting up of schools. The replacement of initial primitive structures by more conventional monastic buildings which centred around a church with a large preaching nave, the acquisition of more land and the creation of an infrastructure which often included walls, gates, water supplies, schools and libraries marked a new phase in the order's history. This transition in which the spiritual ideals had to be adapted to local realities appears to have affected the order as a whole. The general statutes of 1260 prescribe restrictions on the roof architecture and prohibit the construction of elaborately decorated church windows and steeples.[35] The structural changes could take decades, even a century or more, depending on the friars' aims and the level of outside support.[36]

---

34 J. Lee-Warner, 'Petition of the Prior and Canons of Walsingham, Norfolk, to Elizabeth, Lady of Clare, circa A.D. 1345', *Archaeological Journal* 26 (1869) 166-73; the Latin text of the petition, preserved in the cartulary of Walsingham Priory, has also been printed by Martin, 'Greyfriars of Walsingham' (cf. note 9), 269-71. Dickinson, *Shrine of Our Lady at Walsingham* (cf. note 33), 26. On lady Clare's household cf. Ward, 'Elizabeth de Burgh' (cf. note 19), 29-45.

35 Narbonne, 1260, Assisi, 1279, Paris 1292, p.48 nos. 17, 18.

36 This transition has been noted in a number of local studies, e.g. A. Cazenave, 'Les Ordres mendiants dans l'Aude et l'Ariège', in: *Les mendiants en pays d'Oc au XIIIe siècle* (Cahiers de Fanjeaux, 8),

Since the situation in Cambridge, where the Franciscans shared an entrance with the town gaol, was soon inadequate, 5 marks sterling were offered by the citizens of the town to the king in October 1230 to obtain a plot of land for the friars. This can only have been the beginning of a lengthy process because apparently there were no buildings on this land.[37] In 1238 the bailiffs of the town were ordered by Henry III to give the seisin of the house formerly

---

Toulouse 1973, 143-74, at 146-7; C. Cotton, *The Grey Friars of Canterbury 1224 to 1538* (BSFS, extra series, 2), Manchester 1926, 8-24; Freed, *The Friars and German Society* (cf. note 3), 36, 50; Gratien, *Histoire* (cf. note 3), 164-5; Little, *Grey Friars in* Oxford (cf. note 14), 12-22; H. Martin, *Les ordres mendiants en Bretagne (1230-1530). Pauvreté volontaire et prédication à la fin du moyen âge*, Rennes 1975, 14, 179, 196, 277-301; P. Müller, *Bettelorden und Stadtgemeinde in Hildesheim im Mittelalter* (Quellen und Studien zur Geschichte des Bistums Hildesheim, 2), Hanover 1994, 32-4; M. Robson, *The Franciscans in the Middle Ages*, Woodbridge 2006, 95-6; Röhrkasten, *Mendicant Houses of Medieval London* (cf. note 5), 43-51; A. Rüther, *Bettelorden in Stadt und Land. Die Straßburger Mendikantenkonvente und das Elsaß im Spätmittelalter* (Berliner Historische Studien, 26. Ordensstudien XI), Berlin 1997; H.-J. Schmidt, *Bettelorden in Trier. Wirksamkeit und Umfeld im hohen und späten Mittelalter* (Trierer Historische Forschungen, 10), Trier 1986, 32-3; M. Sehi, *Die Bettelorden in der Seelsorgsgeschichte der Stadt und des Bistums Würzburg bis zum Konzil von Trient*, Würzburg 1981, 36-7, 114-5; W. Simons, *Stad en apostolaat. De vestiging van de bedelorden in het graafscahp Vlaanderen (c.1225 - c. 1350)* (Verhandelingen van de Koninklijke Academie voor Wetenschappen, Letteren en Schone Kunsten van België, Klasse der Letteren, 121), Brussels 1987, 118; L. Viallet, *Bourgeois, prêtres et cordeliers à Romans. Une société en équilibre* (C.E.R.C.O.R. Travaux et Recherches XV), Saint-Étienne 2001, 61; M. Wehrli-Johns, 'Stellung undWirksamkeit der Bettelorden in Zürich', in: K. Elm (ed.), *Stellung und Wirksamkeit der Bettelorden in der städtischen Gesellschaft* (Berliner Historische Studien, 3, Ordensstudien, II), Berlin 1981, 77-84, at 79.

37 *De quodam pladam placea vacua que est in Cantebrig' pro qua habenda ad opus fratrum minorum Nicholaus Pilate, offert ex parte urgensium de Cantebrig' V m.*, C. Robinson (ed.), *The Memoranda Roll of the King's Remembrancer for Michaelmas 1230 - Trinity*

belonging to Benjamin the Jew to the friars *ad clausum domorum predictorum fratrum dilatandum*. This referred to the house which up to then had been used as the town gaol, next to the friars' lodgings. The entrance which they had had to share with gaolers and prisoners for more than ten years was now reserved solely for them. The annual rent of this property, amounting to 1 mark, formed part of the farm of the town and the king was aware that the friars would find it difficult to make the regular payments. For this reason the bailiffs were authorised at the same time to spend 10 marks for the purchase of the rent so that the overall burden of those obliged to contribute to the farm remained the same.[38] The original little chapel, the timber framing of which had been put up by one carpenter in a day must have been replaced in the intervening years. According to Moorman, the friars remained on their original site for about forty years until they moved to a new location. In 1269 a payment to the Franciscans was made by the royal administration in return for timber taken from their convent, perhaps from their old site.[39] The new precinct extended over six acres and was made up of a number of smaller plots. Although there is no direct evidence for building activity, a gradual process of construction must have taken place since the new Franciscan church was consecrated only in 1348.[40] By this time the area of the friary had been significantly expanded. In 1328 they obtained licence to enclose a lane to the east

---

1231 (Pipe Roll Society, 49, n.s. 11), Princeton 1933, 8.

38 Close Rolls 1237-42, 61; Calendar of Liberate Rolls, 1226-40, 338; Moorman, *Grey Friars in Cambridge* (cf. note 6) 15.

39 Calendar of Liberate Rolls, 1267-72, no. 580; Moorman, *Grey Friars in Cambridge* (cf. note 6), 9.

40 Little, 'The Friars and the Foundation of the Faculty of Theology in the University of Cambridge' (cf. note 15), 139; *Rotuli Hundredorum*, 2 vols. (Record Commission, 13), London 1812, II, 360; Moorman, *Grey Friars in Cambridge* (cf. note 6) 17.

of their precinct and further land was acquired in 1331.[41] The enlargement of the precinct came only to a conclusion after a further land acquisition in 1353.[42] The process of consolidation was not restricted to the Cambridge Grey Friars but happened in all other houses but one: Babwell outside Bury St Edmunds. The nature of the evidence does not allow a conclusive chronological analysis but it needs to be pointed out that activities related to the enlargement and improvement of the friaries occurred at different times in different places which could suggest that local conditions, were an important factor. However, it remains to be seen whether there is not a common pattern despite the differences in local conditions.

In Colchester the Franciscan church was under construction in 1269 when the friars received a royal gift of seven oak trees as building material.[43] By 1278 a fountain had been obtained outside the Roman walls and the convent was negotiating the construction of its own water supply. The royal command to hold an inquest *ad quod damnum*, dated 27 October 1278, only led to a reaction on 19 January 1279 when a jury of the town reported that losses in rent income to the king would amount to 2 shillings 2 pence but that the city wall would not be affected as long as the friars would cover the water conduit. Within a week of the inquest the friars obtained the royal licence to carry out the necessary construction work.[44] Only a few years later, in March 1285, a similar jury dealt with another Franciscan petition, this time concerning the acquisition of land. The area of the friary, located in the north-eastern corner of the Roman fortification, near the town's East Gate, was to be expanded towards the royal castle. This time the assessment

---

41 TNA, C143/202/20; CPR 1327-30, 260. TNA C143/218/14; CPR 1330-34, 261.
42 CPR 1350-54, 436.
43 Close Rolls 1268-72, 49.
44 TNA C143/4/20; CPR 1272-81, 299.

by the jury was negative. The land in question – an area of more than three acres – was close to the castle defences and would hinder the provisioning of the castle in time of war.[45] There does not appear to be a royal licence for the acquisition of this land which had an annual rent value of 9 shillings, however, it is likely that the friars actually obtained the property because their convent eventually occupied most of the land between the castle, the walls and the street leading to the gate. There was a clear determination on the part of the Franciscans to lay the foundations for a substantial residence. The next inquest, dealing with another parcel of land, was held already in November 1289[46] and a further half acre was added in 1293, the royal licence being enrolled in the Patent Rolls.[47] Although this intense activity over eight years is well documented, the evidence is not conclusive. In 1285 concern was expressed about the impact on the defence of town and castle and there is no confirmation of a land transfer. In 1289 no objection was raised but again there is no licence while the friars' request of 1293 clearly did lead to an enlargement of their precinct. This process of land acquisition was not completed until the middle of the fourteenth century. A very substantial extension of four and a half acres was granted in 1309, when no objection was

---

45 TNA C143/9/8: *qui dicunt per sacramentum suum quod si dominus rex concedit fratribus minoribus Colecestr placiam quam petunt possit esse ad dampnum et nocumentum domini regis pro eo quod illa placia adiacet ex una parte castello domini regis Colecestr distans a fossato eiusdem castri per novemdecim particatas que partica continet in se sexdecim pedes et dimidia. Et ex alia parte est contigua muro ville. Et pro eo quod si guerra moveretur in regno Anglie periculum possit evenire predicto castri et villate Colecestr si predicta placia esset inclusa eo quod placia illa iacet prope castrum et infra muros ville. Et pro eo quod predicta placia multum valeret ad sustentationem warnesture predicti castri tempore guerre unde quod dampnum domino regi possit evenire nesciunt estimare.*

46 TNA C143/12/22.

47 TNA C143/19/9; CPR 1292-1301, 14.

raised from the jurors.[48] Soon afterwards, in the summer of 1310, the precinct of the Franciscans in Colchester was further extended, this time by half an acre.[49] In 1338 the convent obtained land from Colchester's old Benedictine abbey of St John and this was followed by a further grant in April 1348.[50] There is no other evidence on building activity but the surviving sources show that the phase of consolidation of the Colchester friary extended over eighty years.

The development of the Norwich friary which occupied a central site between castle and cathedral priory was of a similar nature but the process was much faster and apparently better organised. It was completed before the end of the thirteenth century. The creation of a religious precinct had a substantial impact on the town's topography. The enclosure of a lane with a length of about sixty metres in 1285, when the friars had already acquired several tenements which were liable to taxation,[51] was followed by a substantial grant of land from eighteen parties in 1292.[52] Five years later, in 1297, another lane of ca. thirty metres' length was enclosed.[53] In a complicated sequence of transactions the expansion of the priory was completed in 1299 when a messuage was granted to the canons of Walsingham in return for a grant of similar property to the Franciscans who at the same time obtained the right to enclose yet a third lane. Two further messuages were given

---

48 TNA C143/71/1; CPR 1307-13, 157; CCR 1307-13, 110, 152.

49 TNA C143/77/5; CCR 1307-13, 335-6.

50 CPR 1338-40, 110; CPR 1348-50, 85; TNA C143/291/2.

51 W. Hudson (ed.), *Leet Jurisdiction in the City of Norwich During the XIIIth and XIVth Centuries*, (Selden Society, 5), London 1892, 21: *Jurati presentant per sacramentum suum quod ... fratres minores appropriaverunt sibi plura tenementa que solebant dare domino Regi langabulum. Presentant quod fratres Sancti Augustini appropriaverunt eis similiter.*

52 TNA C143/9/14; CPR 1281-92, 155, 493.

53 TNA C143/26/3; CPR 1292-1301, 256.

at the same time.[54] The friars made use of built-up areas and the legal transactions within a period of fourteen years show a high degree of co-ordination between the order, its supporters and the secular authorities at various levels. In order to assess the effect of this process it is important to note that there is a suspicion that not only the town's topography but also the arrangement of the districts of its court leet was affected. The number of presentment districts in the area was reduced from eleven to ten after 1313, presumably because the number of residents had declined since not only the Franciscans but also the Austin Friars had built up substantial precincts here.[55]

Additions of land to the Yarmouth friary are documented in the same period, beginning in 1271 when king Henry III requested the town to enlarge the precinct by granting a lane to the community.[56] Apparently the initiative had been taken by his eldest son, on crusade at the time, but the insufficiencies may well have been pointed out to him by the friars themselves. In any case they appear as petitioners in 1285, when a citizen of the town granted property adjacent to the friary to the king with the intention of letting the Franciscans have the use of it.[57] The addition of another parcel of land in 1290 appears to have completed the transformation of the friary into a modern religious convent.[58] The friary at Lynn was extended in 1287 and the fragment of a deed dated October 1295 and referring to properties *ex quibus augmentatur area fratrum minorum* proves that the process of site enlargement was also taking

---

54 TNA C143/30/3, CPR 1292-1301, 412-3.

55 Hudson (ed.), *Leet Jurisdiction in the City of Norwich* (cf. note 51), xix.

56 CPR 1266-72, 530.

57 TNA C143/9/4; CPR 1281-92, 161.

58 *Ibid.*, 358.

place in the west Norfolk port town.[59] In Lynn the development of the friary included the construction of an aqueduct. This important project began with the acquisition of a fountain before 1314, when they were given a retrospective licence in accordance with the mortmain legislation.[60] Four years later they made an agreement with a neighbouring landowner who gave permission to have their aqueduct on his property.[61] This facility must have been very valuable because legislation from the later fourteenth century indicates that the supply with drinking water in Lynn was a problem.[62] Large additions to the friary are not recorded with the exception of a grant in 1340 when two citizens of the town gave a house to queen Isabella for the use of the Franciscans.[63]

The picture is similar for Ipswich where there is evidence for three additions to the friary. The sources in question are dated 22 July 1331 when two inquisitions *ad quod damnum* were ordered to be held. In one of them the jurors were to concern themselves with a projected donation of a house with land adjacent to the conventual precinct. The other inquiry was retroactive. A house and a piece of land had already been given to the community by two lay donors and the purpose of the inquest was to justify a royal licence. The licences were granted shortly afterwards.[64] The situation in Dunwich was more complicated because here the friars had occupied a site close to the seashore which soon turned out to be unsuitable. The town provided a new

---

59 Norfolk Record Office, KL/C50/525; Blomefield, *Topographical History of the County of Norfolk* (cf. note 24), VIII, 526; Martin, *Franciscan Architecture* (cf. note 9), 102.
60 TNA C143/101/9; CPR 1313-17, 128.
61 Norfolk Record Office, KL/C50/524.
62 Ingleby / Isaacson (eds.), *Red Register of King's Lynn* (cf. note 10), II, 50.
63 Norfolk Record Office, KL/C50/526.
64 TNA C143/218/9; C143/218/13; CPR 1330-34, 247-8.

apparently empty site covering an area of more than four and a half acres which was enclosed in 1290.[65] There is no information about building activity but it is likely that material was removed from the old site. The old cemetery remained and the order was permitted to hold on to it in 1328.[66] Walsingham, finally, was yet another different case. Elizabeth de Burgh's original foundation was extended shortly after the Black Death, in 1351. Two other grants of land followed in the fifteenth century.[67]

These sources are not complete but they do allow some conclusions. 1.) There is a contrast between the development of the friaries in Colchester, Cambridge and Norwich on the one hand and the coastal towns of Lynn, Dunwich, Yarmouth and Ipswich on the other. The houses of Cambridge and Norwich saw significant expansions, which in the case of the latter was clearly carefully planned, while there was a move to another site in the case of the former. In Colchester the order wanted to extend into a corner of the Roman wall and it eventually succeeded in doing so. In all three towns the precincts were carefully built up of small plots, potentially lengthy processes which required careful coordination. Development in the coastal towns was on a more modest scale and it may well be that the local topography played a role here. There were other factors apart from geography and topography. The house at Babwell outside Bury St Edmunds seems to have seen little development and it is not clear whether an extension was planned for Walsingham or whether the friars merely accepted additional land when it was offered, eventually ending up with a friary extending over thirteen acres which relied on pilgrims to the shrine and never had a stable urban constituency. Local political conditions may have been an obstacle to the further development of the Babwell friary although, as we are going to see, the number of friars here

---

65 TNA C143/13/24; CPR 1281-92, 383.
66 CPR 1327-30, 324.
67 Martin, 'Greyfriars of Walsingham' (cf. note 9), 231-3.

could be quite high. 2.) The sources reflect the specific situation of each friary, providing important information on relations with local supporters who provided land and very likely also other material assistance. These supporters consisted of members of the urban elites acting collectively or of high-ranking individuals who passed on some of their family property. In the case of the Colchester friary rent obligations linked to the land given to the Franciscans were taken over by some local landholders in the early fourteenth century, a different social group whose members had already shown their appreciation of the order after the friars' first arrival. 3.) The evidence also gives insight into the physical transformation of the custody, with beginnings in derelict and provisional accommodation, a situation the order's founder would have recognised and approved and a result where modern convents had a firmly established place in the urban topography of the region's major towns. Most of the activity occurred in the years between 1250 and 1350.

The topographical development of the friaries into large and modern precincts, some with their own water supplies, was only a symptom of a more general transformation. In the Cambridge custody other aspects of this change can also be tracked, so that it is possible to study the process more closely. By the middle of the fourteenth century the custody could boast two outstanding centres of learning, the theology faculty at Cambridge, largely created by the Franciscans and the order's study at Norwich, where Adam Wodeham was lecturing in 1329.[68] Lay support and lay wills are indirect evidence that the pastoral care given by

---

68 V. Doucet, 'Le studium franciscain de Norwich en 1337 d'après le MS Chigi B.V. de la Bibliothèque Vaticane', *AFH* 46 (1953) 85-98, W.J. Courtenay, *Adam Wodeham. An Introduction to his Life and Writing* (Studies in Medieval and Reformation Thought, 21), Leiden 1978, 31.

the friars was appreciated and this is also borne out by the high number of novices who joined the order in the first decades. The number of friars rose sharply to level out in the second half of the thirteenth century. From Thomas of Eccleston's account it is known that in Cambridge there were only three Franciscan clerics shortly after the friars' arrival in the town. By 1285 the number had increased to forty-two friars and in 1290 seventy were resident.[69] Figures remained at these levels: fifty-five friars in 1297[70], thirty-six friars in 1302[71] and again seventy in 1325. According to Little, the Cambridge convent was the third largest in the English province. Figures available for Babwell outside Bury St Edmunds for 1278 and 1285 point to the presence of thirty Franciscans; between 1296 and 1297 it may have fluctuated between sixty and forty, a rapid increase from the nine friars suspended by the abbot of St Augustine's Canterbury in 1263, when the earlier convent was suppressed.[72] Between 1300 and 1302 the number of friars in Babwell stood at twenty, forty-four and forty-six.[73] Colchester may have had twenty-nine friars in 1296[74], in Ipswich there were probably forty-six in December of the same year and fifty-one in the following month.[75] In Norwich the number of Minorites may have been as high as sixty in 1285[76] and the Franciscan community of Lynn

---

69 TNA C47/4/2 fol. 26r, Little, 'The Friars and the Foundation of the Faculty of Theology in the University of Cambridge' (cf. note 15), 138.
70 TNA C47/4/6 fol. 1r.
71 TNA E101/361/15 m 5d, 6d.
72 TNA C47/4/1 fol. 51v; C47/4/2 fol. 25v; BL MS Add. 7965 fol. 6r, v. Arnold (ed.), *Memorials of St Edmund's Abbey* (cf. note 30), II, 274.
73 BL MS Add. 35291 fol. 26v, 28r; TNA E101/361/13 m 2d.
74 BL MS Add. 7965 fol. 6r.
75 *Ibid.* fol. 6v.
76 TNA C47/4/2 fol. 25v.

numbered forty friars in 1300.[77] Transfers of friars from one house of the custody to another and their constant involvement in preaching and administrative tasks will explain the fluctuations in the figures which overall indicate a stable number. Little could also show that about a third of the Franciscan masters at the university were men from East Anglia.[78] If this were true for the ordinary friars in the custody's other convents, the order would have acquired strong links to the local population. Although this can only be shown to be true for the Dominicans at Lynn in the fourteenth century and not for the Franciscans and although relations between friars and their host towns were not always without tension[79], the Cambridge evidence supports the hypothesis.

The form of the Franciscans' presence in the towns meant that they had no choice but to become involved in the local land market and the local economy, a process recently analysed in detail by Paul Bertrand in his study of Liège.[80] Urban property had to contribute a share of a town's annual farm at the Exchequer and sales of land often added further financial burdens. In late thirteenth-century Norwich the Franciscans sold a plot of land to a citizen in return for the man to take over an annual rent of 16 pence

---

77 Society of Antiquaries, London, MS 119 fol. 18v; BL MS Add. 35291 fol. 25v.

78 Little, 'The Friars and the Foundation of the Faculty of Theology in the University of Cambridge' (cf. note 15), 138, 139.

79 The jurors who dealt with the Inquisition *ad quod damnum* in Colchester did not always give a favourable assessment and in Yarmouth the Franciscans were involved in litigation, later also complaining about damage done to their precinct by townsmen, TNA C47/4/4 fol. 42v; CPR 1301-7, 85, cf. A.R. Saul, Great Yarmouth in the Fourteenth Century. A Study in Trade, Politics and Society, unpublished PhD. thesis, Oxford 1975, 243-4.

80 P. Bertrand, *Commerce avec dame Pauvreté. Structures et fonctions des couvents mendiants à Liège (xiiie - xive s.)* (Bibliothèque de la Faculté de Philosophie et Lettres de l'Université de Liège, Fascicule CCLXXXV), Geneva 2004.

which they had to pay for one of the parcels which made up their precinct.[81] The problem for the friars was the accumulation of small sums which were demanded in perpetuity. The tax due to the king for a property granted in Ipswich in 1331 was 2 pence but a further 12 pence of rent were due to other people who had a right in it.[82] Land earmarked for the Yarmouth friary in 1285 had an annual rent value of 5 marks sterling and jurors in Norwich reported in the same year that the Franciscans had appropriated several tenements which used to pay a tax to the king.[83] An area coveted by the Colchester friars in 1289 had an annual tax value of 11 pence to which a further 12 pence were added when the area was further enlarged in 1293.[84] The cemetery of the Dunwich friary had an annual rent value of 2 shillings and a lane enclosed by the Cambridge friars in 1328 was worth 6 pence a year.[85] Since the friaries – probably with the exception of Bury St Edmunds – were made up of several plots of land, the regular annual financial demands could be significant. Strategies were developed to avoid or reduce the burden. Examples from Norwich (1299) and Colchester (1348) show that the rent obligation could simply be taken on by the donor of the property.[86] The alternative was for the friars to find supporters who were willing to burden their own property with the rent.[87] In Bury St Edmunds a donor

---

81 Norfolk Record Office DCN 45/34/4.
82 TNA C143/218/9.
83 TNA C143/9/4; Hudson (ed.), *Leet Jurisdiction in the City of Norwich* (cf. note 51), 21.
84 TNA C143/12/22; C143/19/9.
85 CPR 1327-30, 324; TNA C143/202/20.
86 *Et dicunt etiam quod predicta terra et tenementa sic predicto Johanni ultra donationem et assignationem predictas emanentia sufficiant ad consuetudines et servicia tam pro predicta terra sic data quam pro aliis terris et tenementis predicto Johanni retentis debita facienda* (…), TNA C143/291/2. C143/30/3; CPR 1292-1301, 412-3.
87 TNA C132/19/9.

even gave his land to the king, reducing the payment requirement.[88] Coping with the financial demands required careful planning by those friars who were involved in the administration of the custody. They had to make their choice between different models and negotiate with supporters, neighbours, civic authorities and even the royal administration. These tasks were an addition to their constant concern to ensure the communities' material welfare, their supply with food, clothing and fuel and to continue the construction programmes that went on largely unrecorded in the background.

It is important to draw attention to the fact that the Franciscans were not the only regular religious in the towns of the custody. They had to compete with other equally attractive mendicant orders in the region who were faced with identical tasks at the same time. The creation of the Franciscan custody of Cambridge was part of a much more extensive development, coinciding with the overall mendicant settlement in the area. Only two of the towns on which the custody centred, Bury St Edmunds and Walsingham, where powerful religious houses had offered resistance to the Minorites, had no other mendicant convent. In all the others the Franciscans had to coexist with at least one, in Cambridge and Norwich there were even five other mendicant groups until the disappearance of the Friars of the Sack and the Friars of St Mary (Fratres de Areno). In Cambridge the Franciscans appear to have had a head start, the Dominicans being first recorded only in 1238. The two were joined by the Carmelites perhaps as early as 1251; the White Friars' church was certainly nearing completion in 1267. In 1258 the Friars of the Sack established a residence in the university town and the Friars of St Mary de Areno were present in 1279, five years after the decision taken by the second Council of Lyons to suppress the order by prohibiting new recruitment. The last

---

88 CPR 1247-58, 623.

to arrive, perhaps in 1290, were the Austin Friars. The pattern in Norwich was very similar: an early arrival of the Dominicans (1226) and the Franciscans, the two then being joined by the Carmelites and the Friars of the Sack in the mid-thirteenth century. The Austin Friars were slightly earlier here, perhaps in the first years of Edward I's reign and the Friars of St Mary were also able to extend their presence beyond the fatal date of 1274, when the decision against the smaller mendicant orders was taken. In Colchester the Franciscans remained the only mendicants until the arrival of the Flemish Friars of the Cross after 1250 and Dunwich had two mendicant houses, the Dominicans probably preceding the Franciscans. In Lynn, where a mendicant presence seems to have been established fairly late, around the middle of the thirteenth century at the earliest, the Carmelites had arrived by 1261. The Austin Friars, who were present by 1295, arrived at a time when the Friars of the Sack, who can be traced in 1277, must already have been on the decline. In Ipswich the Franciscans seem to have been the sole mendicant group for a long time since Henry III's foundation of a Dominican house dates only from 1263. By 1278 the two had been joined by the Carmelites. In Yarmouth the Minorites had been preceded by the Dominicans by about a decade. Franciscans and Carmelites arrived at about the same time and the creation of permanent residences does not appear to have gone smoothly. There was a legal dispute about land in the late 1280s and soon afterwards the Franciscans complained about damage done to their property.[89] In all towns except Bury St Edmunds the arrival of the mendicants and the creation of their religious houses contributed to the general urban development, shaping the local topography and imposing material burdens on the population although the decision to bear them was

---

89 TNA C47/4/4 fol. 42v.

voluntary.[90] The mendicant presence changed in the course of the fourteenth century, the four houses of the Friars of the Sack and the Friars of St Mary de Areno disappearing. However there were other mendicant priories in the area, Dominicans in Sudbury, Chelmsford and eventually also in Thetford, communities of the Austin Friars in Clare and Thetford and Carmelites in Blakeney and Burnham. Although some of these houses, e.g. those of the Austin Friars at Clare and Thetford, were founded by aristocrats who defrayed much of the building cost, the majority of mendicant houses was built by successful merchants and local landowners. Even though the sources are lacking it is safe to assume that significant contributions were also made by members of other social groups who also ensured the mendicants' long-term survival. For the lay supporters of the mendicants, these costs were an addition to the tithes and other material contributions they made to the local parishes. For the mendicants it meant that they had to compete for resources, a competition which required them to define their identities clearly by developing distinctive forms of spirituality.

The example of the Cambridge custody shows the effects of external pressures, e.g. the land market, the legal framework within which the communities' material requirements had to be met and probably also the expectations of founders and supporters. At a time when there were debates about the interpretation of the Rule within the order, in October 1240, the Franciscans of Cambridge were given royal alms of 10 marks sterling in cash.[91] The friars of Colchester were assigned 10 marks from the profits of judicial proceedings in 1247 and the first

---

90 *VCH Cambridge*, II, 269, 282, 286-7, 290; *VCH Essex*, II, 179, 181; *VCH Norfolk*, II, 426-9, 431-3, 435, 437; *VCH Suffolk*, 122, 130; H.F. Chettle, 'The Friars of the Sack in England', *Downside Review* 63 (1945) 239-51, at 246.

91 *Calendar of Liberate Rolls* 1226-40, 501.

royal cash payment to the Franciscans of Bury St Edmunds was recorded in 1278.[92] Surely there were spiritual friends in the background who would deal with the coins and when a friend of the order assigned an annual rent of a penny to the convent at Lynn in c. 1282 he gave it to the town.[93] This evidence has to be assessed in the wider context of the practices pursued in the English Franciscan province. There is clear proof that determined efforts were made to adhere to the principles laid down in the Rule in other custodies. The Franciscans in Worcester were content with the sum of £4 out of £10 offered as a royal subsidy in 1243-44 and even someone as ambivalent towards the mendicants as the Benedictine chronicler Matthew Paris judged it a *factum laudabile* when the Franciscans refused to accept goods confiscated from merchants as royal alms in 1252.[94] There is even undisputable proof of adherence to the spiritual ideal from the very end of the thirteenth century. When the friars assembled for the 1297 provincial chapter in London were offered the customary food for three days from Edward I they refused: *quia per alios magnates pascebantur per duobus de eisdem tribus diebus noluerunt pecuniam recipere.*[95] However, this decision by the provincial chapter was not representative of current economic practice. By this time the Franciscans of Cambridge (and those of Oxford) were already in receipt of an annual pension from the royal Exchequer.[96]

---

92 *Calendar of Liberate Rolls* 1245-51, 113; C47/4/1 fol. 51v.

93 Norfolk Record Office, KL/C50/339.

94 J. Röhrkasten, 'Mendikantische Armut in der Praxis - das Beispiel London', in: G. Melville / A. Kehnel (eds.), *In proposito paupertatis. Studien zum Armutsverständnis bei den mittelalterlichen Bettelorden* (Vita regularis, 13), Münster 2001, 135-67, at 140; Luard (ed.), *Chronica Majora* (cf. note 18), V, 275-6. Little, *Studies* (cf. note 94) 39.

95 BL MS Add. 7965 fol. 9v.

96 A grant during royal pleasure was made by Edward I in 1304, CPR 1301-7, 239 but the practice went back at least to 1285, TNA

It is well known that the Franciscan order underwent painful changes in the decades following its founder's death, if not already in the years preceding it. It is also accepted that these changes cannot be reduced to problems relating to the observance of the poverty ideal, there were many other factors involved and some of them depended on local or regional conditions. These conditions need to be further analysed, perhaps with the sets of questions outlined by Le Goff and Vauchez. This approach will show up parallels between custodies and provinces but it will also highlight differences. The friars were not only operating in different legal frameworks, under different economic conditions and in situations where orthodoxy was challenged or not, they had themselves been shaped by these conditions. Perhaps here is an opportunity to obtain a more differentiated picture of the order as a whole.

E403/51 m 1. Even though payments were not always made in full, the grant remained at 50 marks each per annum for the convents of the two orders in Oxford and 25 marks each per annum for the two convents in Cambridge until the reign of Henry VIII with the last recorded payment on 13 October 1537, TNA E404/101.

La Philosophie de l'argent dans l'école franciscaine. Un aperçu inspiré par l'anthropologie dogmatique de Pierre Legendre.

Luca Parisoli

(University of Calabria)

I. L'obéissance et la pauvreté

Dans ses *Admonitions* saint François donne une place capitale à l'obéissance au supérieur hiérarchique. Plus tard les querelles autour de la soi-disant 'question franciscaine' concernent tout d'abord la pauvreté. Il s'agit d'un débat historiographique que le protestant Sabatier a initié à la fin du dix-neuvième siècle et qui ne pouvait qu'attirer l'attention des modernistes jusqu'aux partisans de l'interprétation la plus sécularisée du Concile Vatican II.[1] En effet, la visée finale est celle d'établir que certains franciscains ont bien fait de se rebeller contre la méchante Curie, ou bien que la même Curie a domestiqué (voire étouffé) la pureté de l'esprit des origines. La confiance de saint François dans l'obéissance n'a pas grand intérêt dans cette perspective, par ailleurs dominante à la fin du vingtième siècle. Le chapitre III des *Admonitions*, consacré à 'l'obéissance parfaite', utilise le langage du 'rien avoir', mais sans références de la sorte aux biens extérieurs. Il s'agit en revanche des biens intérieurs, le corps et la volonté, dont il faut perdre la possession pour s'abandonner à Dieu. Mais le franciscain ayant perdu sa volonté ne peut même pas désobéir: «l'assujetti (*subditus*), voyant qu'il y a des possibilités meilleures et plus utiles pour son âme que

---

[1] Cf. L'introduction de Claudio Leonardi à *La letteratura francescana*, II, Milano 2005.

celles que le prélat (supérieur) lui impose, est censé se sacrifier pour Dieu» – il s'agit de l'obéissance dans la charité, en référence à la première lettre de Pierre, 1, 22, où la vérité découle de l'obéissance. Mais si le prélat lui ordonne une action étant un péché mortel (*contra animam suam*), l'assujetti doit s'abstenir d'agir contre son salut, mais il ne peut nullement contester son supérieur (*tamen ipsum non dimittat*), jusqu'à accepter d'être sanctionné et persécuté, aimant son persécuteur en Dieu (*magis eo diligat propter Deum*). L'assujetti et le supérieur sont nettement distingués, et l'assujetti ne peut rêver de prendre la place du supérieur invoquant des ordres injustes. Le refus de la révolte s'appuie sur l'évangile de Jean 15, 13 («il ne peut pas y avoir de plus grand amour que de donner sa vie pour ses amis»), et la délégitimation du supérieur est une opération de ceux revenant aux vomissements de leur volonté (Proverbes, 26, 11 – «le chien revient à son vomissement, et l'insensé retourne à sa folie»; deuxième lettre de Pierre, 2, 22, concernant les faux enseignants comparés aux chiens dont parle le passage des Proverbes) et étant des assassins (*homicidae*) par leur mauvais exemple capable de tuer les âmes d'autrui. Il s'agit d'une obéissance reliée à une très-haute pauvreté intégralement intérieure, précédant la très-haute pauvreté concernant les biens extérieurs matériaux. On ne peut contester l'autorité hiérarchique au nom de la violation de la pauvreté, car l'obéissance précède la pauvreté, et celui qui conteste l'autorité est un assassin. Les franciscains plaçant en revanche la valeur de la pauvreté matérielle avant cette obéissance, peuvent refuser l'obéissance en appelant à la défense de cette pauvreté absolue. Or, par ce renversement de la priorité de l'obéissance sur la pauvreté, ils ont dénaturé le message normativiste de saint François, ouvrant une lecture intimiste et gnostique de son héritage. Ce qui nous concerne ici est la donnée d'un phantasme de confusion: le respect de la pauvreté érigé en critère conditionnel pour l'obéissance conduit les franciscains

Spirituels à un questionnement permanent sur la légitimité de la hiérarchie catholique n'approuvant pas leur propre interprétation de la Règle. Le phantasme de confusion consiste dans le passage à l'acte dans le souhait de remplacer un évêque, un cardinal ou un pape 'malheureusement' pas assez parfaits: il s'agit d'une attitude qui a toujours été minoritaire à l'intérieur de l'Ordre franciscain, comme le montre la très grande majorité des franciscains demeurant fidèles au Pape à l'occasion des mouvances schismatiques. Pourtant cette attitude a connu l'honneur de l'historiographie au moment de la sécularisation de la pensée européenne. En effet, la bourgeoisie européenne a aussi connu son phantasme dans la confusion entre la pauvreté volontaire et involontaire au vingtième siècle: l'histoire des idées collectives en témoigne largement par ce qui le philosophe italien Armando Plebe[2] appelle «l'hystérie révolutionnaire» de la deuxième moitié du vingtième siècle.

Les conflits et les différends avec le Siège apostolique naissent par l'interaction entre une spiritualité voulant devenir une forme de vie, et non pas une simple expression mystique, et les exigences normatives régissant toute forme de vie collective, dans le cas d'espèce la communauté franciscaine à l'intérieur de la société de l'Église catholique. L'injonction de saint François de 'rien avoir' (devenant *nihil sibi approprient* dans la Règle) parcourt la Règle. Dans un recueil de *Determinationes* (fin XIIIe) concernant la Règle (I, 24) on oppose le verbe «avoir» (*habere*) – trop générique – au verbe «s'approprier» (*appropriandi*) – plus précis. La Règle utilise le verbe «s'approprier», mais saint François n'avait pas dans son langage ces soucis de précision normative et il employait le verbe bien plus courant avoir ou bien le verbe recevoir. Par exemple, il écrit dans ses *Admonitiones*, 18, 2: «heureux le serviteur qui rend tous les biens au Seigneur Dieu, car celui

---

2   A. Plebe, *Filosofia della reazione*, Milan 1969.

qui garde quelque chose pour lui cache en lui-même l'argent (*pecuniam*) du Seigneur son Dieu et ce qu'il pensait *avoir* lui sera enlevé». Le passage revient dans l'hagiographie, par exemple la *Legenda maior* de saint Bonaventure, au chapitre VI, et la phrase est reprise aussi dans l'*Imitation du Christ* de Thomas de Kempis, III, 50. On peut voir enfin la description de l'attitude des premiers franciscains par Thomas de Celano dans sa légende, *Vita prima*, § 39, une description plongée dans l'absence de soucis pour le devenir en dépit de toute précision juridique.

Cette injonction de saint François résonne aussi dans son *Testament*: «ceux qui venaient pour recevoir la vie franciscaine, tout ce qu'ils pouvaient avoir, ils le donnaient aux pauvres; et ils se contentaient d'une seule tunique, rapiécée au dedans et au dehors, avec une ceinture et des braies.» (16) «Et nous ne voulions pas avoir plus» (17). Cette injonction, en latin *et nolebamus plus habere*, pouvait rester dans une dimension mystique, et des centaines de mystiques de tout âge ont répété l'idée du dépouillement mondain pour mieux approcher la sphère divine; en ce cas, l'originalité de l'injonction de 'rien avoir' serait bien mince, car chaque Père de l'Église, latine ou grecque, a fait à sa manière l'apologie de la pauvreté du chrétien. Mais dans cette tradition on a souligné que la détermination du superflu est subjective: au début du treizième siècle, Guillaume d'Auxerre affirme que la complaisance dans la boisson n'est pas un péché mortel, car il est difficile de déterminer le superflu par nature et les jugements ne sont pas uniformes (*difficile enim est scire quod sit superfluum naturae: quoniam aliquid dicitur superfluum quod non est superfluum: et a converso; et aliquid superfluum uni non est superfluum alii*).[3] Dans cette lignée, 'rien avoir' n'est

---

3 *Summa aurea*, III, 7, q. 3. Gratien avait quand même souligné que les biens de l'Église appartiennent aux pauvres, d. 42, c. 1, et C. 16, q. 1, c. 68 – qu'il vaut mieux éviter le superflu en général, d. 35, c. 4; d. 41, c. 1; d. 47, c. 8; C. 12, q. 2, c. 70 – la nature de certains biens superflus dans la nourriture, d. 44, c. 1; dans l'habillage, d. 41,

pas une règle effective dans sa brutale littéralité, mais est une norme symbolique à harmoniser avec la réalité sociale. Au contraire, la même injonction aurait pu devenir un message de rébellion sociale, par l'argumentation selon laquelle étant obligatoire de ne rien avoir, ceux qui se refusent à abandonner leur richesse doivent y être obligés: avant et pendant l'essor du mouvement franciscain l'Europe occidentale a connu plusieurs mouvances hérétiques de rébellion sociale, contestataires de l'enseignement et de la pratique de l'Église catholique en vue d'implanter avec force l'Évangile (à leur guise) dans la société, à tout prix. Le millénarisme sociale de Joachim de Flore (1202†) a connu bien des partisans jusqu'à la théorisation athée de Karl Marx. Joachim était un pauvre mystique inconscient (peut-être) des issues sociales de sa pensée, notamment par une dénaturation plaçant l'humanité à la place de Dieu. En revanche Marx, avec son compagnon Engels, ont toujours su 'que cet idéal d'une humanité devenant consciente d'elle-même dût nécessairement finir dans une liberté anarchique'.[4]

Mais comme le dit Jacques Leclercq dans son ouvrage *Les Chrétiens devant l'argent*[5], la mise en commun des biens de la première communauté chrétienne, en dépit de sa valeur morale, «aboutit à une faillite complète». C'est la faillite du soi-disant 'communisme chrétien'. Mais saint François a affiché ouvertement sa volonté de bloquer la naissance de ces pistes de développement ordonnant de ne pas juger ceux qui ne vivent pas la radicalité évangélique, soulignant avec force que la forme de vie du 'rien avoir' n'engage qu'à titre individuel, sans aucune implication ni de vie collective (les hérétiques sont toujours des groupes),

---

c. 5; dans les bâtiments, C. 12, q. 2, c. 71.

[4] C. Schmitt, *Théologie politique*, Paris 1988, (éd. orig. *Politische Theologie. Vier Kapitel zur Lehre von der Souveränität*, Munich 1922).

[5] J. Leclercq, *Les Chrétiens devant l'argent*, Paris 1954.

ni de perfection (les hérétiques se prétendent souvent ou 'parfaits', ou vrais-amis des 'parfaits'). Le franciscain, dans l'intention de saint François, n'est pas pauvre en tant que moins riche que quelqu'un d'autre, jusqu'à devenir le premier des moins riches: cette pauvreté évangélique ne vit pas de comparaison aux autres, elle est une condition d'absence de matière comparable, à savoir absence de droits humains sur les choses. Dans cette condition, par ailleurs idéale et surhumaine, le franciscain ne peut pas envier la chose possédée par l'autre, ni parce qu'elle lui fait défaut, ni parce qu'il voudrait être le seul à la posséder. Comme le dit le psaume 34, 11 «les riches n'ont plus rien et ils ont faim, mais ceux qui espèrent en le Seigneur, les bonnes choses ne leur font pas défaut».[6] N'ayant rien, le franciscain est pauvre dans un sens tout à fait différent du pauvre de la sociologie contemporaine, déjà dessiné par Georg Simmel qui affirme: «est pauvre celui dont les moyens ne suffisent pas à atteindre ses fins».[7] Mais tandis que les franciscains se donnent des fins surnaturelles, indépendantes d'une liaison avec les autres hommes (le salut est essentiellement individuel), dans une société principalement humaine et immanente les fins sont décidées par les hommes eux-mêmes. Simmel peut affirmer qu' «en fait, chaque milieu, chaque classe sociale a ses besoins typiques; l'impossibilité de les satisfaire signifie pauvreté». Les pauvres du vingtième siècle sont ceux acceptant les finalités que la structure sociale (la classe politique

---

6   *La Bible des peuples*, Paris 1998. La traduction de la *Bible de Jérusalem* préfère conserver un langage métaphorique, et au lieu de 'riches' utilise l'expression 'jeunes fauves' (cf. la liturgie des heures, samedi 3ᵉ semaine, *hora sexta*, psaume 33). Le texte latin de la *Vulgata*, la version latine de saint Jérôme utilisée évidemment au Moyen Âge, évite de conserver les métaphores idiomatiques de la langue juive, en raison de sa finalité éminemment pastorale et non purement érudite.

7   G. Simmel, *Les pauvres*, Paris 1998, 91, (éd. orig. *Der Arme*, in: Idem, *Soziologie. Untersuchungen über die Formen der Vergesellschaftung*, Berlin 1908).

dominante, l'*intelligentsia* dominante, les organisations internationales, etc.) considère devoir être celles de chaque individu. Les pauvres sont le résultat d'une conception mathématique et technocrate des besoins et des exigences de la nature humaine. A défaut de cette domination d'une 'misère des valeurs' dans les régimes se proclamant 'démocraties occidentales', il serait toujours possible «que la pauvreté individuelle – l'insuffisance de moyens pour les fins d'une personne – n'existe pas pour quelqu'un, alors qu'il y a pauvreté sociale» et aussi «qu'un homme soit individuellement pauvre bien que socialement aisé».[8] L'empire de la pensée unique, berceau du relativisme moral et de l'universalisme de la technocratie du Management[9], prétend apprendre à chacun sa sensation subjective de pauvreté, bien plus qu'une mensuration objective (pouvant en soi être ignoré par l'individu). Et la légitimité de cette prétention s'appuie sur un soi-disant coût de la démocratie: celui qui n'accepte pas la technocratie des valeurs est quelqu'un qui n'accepte pas la démocratie. D'une part, il s'agit d'une erreur, car le peuple peut gouverner tout en ayant au centre de ses soucis des valeurs morales et non pas la mathématique des statisticiens, des économistes, des démographes; d'autre part, il s'agit de la meilleure façon de nous faire douter du fonctionnement réel des démocraties occidentales, pouvant être, comme l'avaient prévu il y a un siècle les penseurs Gaetano Mosca et Wilfredo Pareto, une nouvelle forme historique de gouvernement d'une élite technocratique. En revanche, la pauvreté franciscaine est tout d'abord refus des finalités dictées par une société exclusivement humaine, renfermée dans une téléologie mondaine. Cette pauvreté ne peut qu'être pensée en relation à un état de nature précédant la Chute, la perte de l'innocence originaire: cette pauvreté ne peut qu'être pensée en relation à la sphère divine non-humaine. Les

---

8   *Ibid.*, 92.

9   P. Goodrich / L. Barshack / L. Schütz (éds.), *Law, Text, Terror: Essays for Pierre Legendre*, London 2006.

franciscains, par cette pauvreté, essayent de goûter la béatitude éternelle avant leur mort corporelle. Rien à voir avec les besoins et les exigences liées à la dignité sociale, définissant la pauvreté selon Simmel. Il en découle que l'acception du mot 'pauvreté' est complètement différent dans les deux contextes de discours.

II. L'argent et la Règle

Finalement, saint François n'avait pas directement mesuré la portée de son injonction de 'rien avoir' et de 'rien accepter' pour la très-haute pauvreté, voulant être bien plus qu'une idée mystique à l'instar d'une tradition chrétienne ancienne. En consignant à la Règle de son ordre religieux l'interdiction de manipuler l'argent, il répétait une interdiction déjà énoncée par les dominicains, de la source commune des Évangiles, notamment Luc 9, 3 («Ne prenez rien pour la route: ni sac qu'on accroche à son bâton, ni pain, ni argent: n'ayez pas une seconde tunique») et Mathieu 10, 9-10 (texte similaire). Il s'agit d'un interdit crucial, longuement répété dans la Règle *non bullata* (parfois appelée 'première' selon une indication simplement chronologique), réaffirmé plus brièvement dans le chapitre IV de la Règle définitive (et promulguée, donc véritable règle de droit). Or, le long chapitre (VIII) de la Règle provisoire consacré à l'interdit de toucher à l'argent s'appuie sur deux passages de l'Évangile de Luc, 12, 15 («Soyez bien en garde contre tout désir de posséder, car même quand on a tout, ce n'est pas cela qui donne la vie») et 21, 34 («Veillez sur vous-même: il ne faudrait pas que la bonne chère, les excès de vin ou les soucis matériels vous endorment, et que ce jour tombe sur vous à l'improviste» – il s'agit du jour de l'arrivée du Royaume de Dieu). L'argent semble ainsi stigmatisé en tant que symbole du désir de posséder, car la vie (ou la Vie comme l'écrirait un phénoménologue) est étrangère au désir de posséder: en effet, en songeant à l'anthropologie franciscaine, nous savons qu'Adam et Eve avant le péché originel n'avaient aucune envie de possession, tandis qu'en perdant la Vie (par le péché originel) ils ont justement connu l'envie de posséder. Et comme le dit Alexandre de Hales, dans l'état d'innocence le superflu n'existe pas (*si enim essemus in statu innocentiae, nullus haberet superfluum*)[10] et il s'oppose au droit naturel de l'état d'innocence.[11] Ce qui n'existe pas dans le Paradis est l'anxiété pour l'avenir, une évacuation largement soulignée comme indispensable dans la vie du franciscain par les récits de la vie de saint François: saint Bonaventure, commentant la méfiance de la communauté franciscaine à l'égard de l'accumulation des provisions dans les caves des couvents, souligne que les Évangiles sollicitent l'homme à s'abandonner à la volonté de Dieu (Math. 6, 34) et à ne pas se soucier de l'avenir comme les oiseaux et les lys des champs, mais ils n'interdisent pas la pratique commune des provisions alimentaires[12]. L'évangile de saint Mathieu condamne l'attitude de se *soucier* constamment de l'avenir, donc il condamne un état d'esprit qui détourne du présent et de la confiance de l'aide de Dieu pour demain: en revanche, il ne condamne pas la constitution de *provisions*. En effet, se soucier du devenir (*sollicitudo*) indique la volonté de constituer des provisions du superflu, marquée par une avarice ignorant la puissance de Dieu (l'avare accumulant les provisions de grains meurt en laissant ces immenses provisions à autrui sans les avoir même pas touchés, de plus ayant ignoré le salut de son âme). En revanche, constituer des provisions de biens nécessaires est tout à fait licite, notamment pendant une période déterminée et spécifique,

---

10 *De superfluo*, q. 17, 13.
11 *Ibid.*, q. 17, 26.
12 *Determinationes questionum circa Regulam*, I, q. 7, in: *Bonaventurae Opera Omnia*, 11 vols., Quaracchi 1882-1902, VIII, 342a. La critique philologique a avancé l'hypothèse que le vrai auteur de cet ouvrage est un franciscain allemand de la fin du XIIIe siècle. Il s'agit d'une possibilité qui ne change en rien notre argumentation.

de manière à ce que le franciscain ne puisse les obtenir par la quête en dehors de cette période déterminée. Saint Bonaventure ne donne pas des précisions spécifiques, mais il songe à des biens indisponibles à la quête car rares pour la population, ne pouvant s'en priver pour les offrir à autrui, tandis que dans une autre période il y a surabondance et la population peut les offrir à la quête. C'est la phrase finale de son analyse qui montre à elle seule toute une mentalité: il se réfère à la constitution de provisions de ces biens à grande disponibilité périodique et poursuit «nous aidons ceux auxquels nous demandons la quête bien plus que nous-mêmes, car en leur demandant au moment de l'abondance nous leur donnons la possibilité de nous la faire plus aisément». Donc, ceux qui donnent par la quête ont une plus grande chance de faire le bien.

Saint Bonaventure rédigea les Constitutions Générales des franciscains, connues comme Constitutions de Narbonne (1260): à propos du chapitre IV de la Règle définitive, il reprend la thèse du premier commentaire de la Règle, intitulé *Expositio* des Quatre Maîtres[13] (parmi lesquels les auteurs du traité philosophique et théologique *Summa fratris Alexandri*). Etant donné que le texte du chapitre IV inclut l'expression *denarios vel pecuniam*, le mot latin *pecunia*, objet interdit pour les franciscains, est compris pour indiquer l'argent (au sens strict de l'objet indiqué en tant que pièces et monnaies, *denarios*) et tout autre bien utilisé en tant que moyen d'échange[14]. On interdit la présence de l'argent dans le couvent (III, 1), car il s'agirait de la preuve explicite d'une intention d'utiliser la monnaie en tant qu'outil d'achats. Pourtant il est prévu que les franciscains ne disposent de l'argent leur étant destiné que de façon indirecte et par le biais d'un intermédiaire

---

13 L'édition critique est parue dans L. Oliger, *Expositio Quatuor Magistrorum super Regulam fratrum minorum*, Rome 1950, 141-8.

14 *Constitutiones generales*, III, 2, Narbonne 1260, Assisi 1279, Paris 1292.

agréé explicitement par la hiérarchie, interne à l'Ordre ou bien externe, à savoir les évêques et les cardinaux (III, 4). Ce qui transforme un objet en équivalent de l'argent est l'intention de l'utiliser pour une vente: la monnaie est objectivement destinée à l'achat et à la vente, mais tout autre bien peut devenir un équivalent de la monnaie une fois associé à cette volonté de ne pas utiliser directement ce bien, et en revanche s'en servir comme remplacement de l'argent. Il s'agit, pour paraphraser une expression de David Hume, d'un 'bundle of rights and claims'. Or, tandis que Hume utilisait cette notion de faisceau pour dénier toute réalité ontologique à la personne humaine, les franciscains l'utilisent pour souligner la vacuité ontologique de l'argent quand notre discours se place au niveau de la réalité ontologique la plus 'dure', celle notamment de la personne humaine. La nature volontariste de l'école franciscaine s'affiche ouvertement: c'est l'intention de celui qui reçoit pouvant qualifier un usage licite (le bien est utilisé en tant que ce-bien-là) ou bien un usage illicite (le bien est échangé ou vendu). Finalement, le droit est forgé par la volonté (ne pouvant émaner que d'une personne – agent moral par définition), la monnaie aussi: dans cette ontologie sociale, l'argent vaut autant que droit à échanger. Le franciscain ne peut toucher à l'argent, car il ne doit pas être titulaire d'un droit quelconque: ayant de l'argent, il possède un droit qui un tiers pourra lui acheter en échange d'un bien, ce qui viole la Règle.

Il convient de souligner que saint Bonaventure consacre 24 normes aux modalités de la pauvreté franciscaine dans une rubrique explicitement consacrée à la question, détaillant ce qu'il faut éviter, et *a contrario* ce qu'on peut envisager. Beaucoup d'autres normes dans d'autres parties des Constitutions poursuivent ce travail de précisions juridiques (par exemple, la qualité du vêtement – la bure –, les règles alimentaires, etc.), jusqu'aux détails les plus concrets. Les Spirituels condamnés par Jean XXII par la

Quorundam exigit (1317) n'accepteront jamais le bon sens bonaventurien et son pragmatisme, lui préférant le perfectisme radical, totalitaire et sans nuance. Il convient de préciser l'enjeu de ce différend: cet acte pontifical, la *Quorundam exigit*, va devenir le premier chapitre d'une section du recueil de droit canonique composé par les actes pontificaux de Jean XXII, appelé *Extravagantes*. Or, cette section est celle *De verborum significatione* (numérotée comme XIVème): Jean XXII est conscient d'avoir à définir l'espace de la normativité contre les débordements d'une pratique reniant une correcte normativité, notamment de ceux qui «prétendent une croyance infondée et aveugle».[15] Il s'agit de repousser l'idée que la constitution de provisions alimentaires est un péché mortel pour les franciscains, selon les dires des frères mineurs de la mouvance la plus anarchiste, par ailleurs contestataires farouches des autres franciscains reproduisant les pratiques d'une vie communautaire visant à assurer la continuité des repas. Il s'agit finalement pour Jean XXII d'imposer le bon sens de la vie quotidienne sur cette terre.

Dans ce sens d'élimination de tout souci pour l'avenir, la stérilité de l'argent n'est pas une notion économique ou matérielle, car cette stérilité est tout à fait intérieure à l'homme. L'argent est le moyen universel de l'envie de posséder, et il est donc étranger à la vie: les franciscains ont élaboré une conception des dangers de l'argent en soi indépendantes des circonstances économiques et sociales, car ils sont en train de stigmatiser une propriété structurelle de la monnaie produisant des dégâts par l'interaction avec la nature déchue de l'homme après le péché originel. Comme l'a affirmé il y a quelques années le philosophe américain John Searle, l'argent est un fait institutionnel, à savoir notamment la croyance sociale partagée est capable de déterminer la nature de l'argent, celui-ci n'étant pas une

---

15 Cf. la glose au mot *scrupolositatis* dans les éditions du *Corpus iuris canonici*.

espèce naturelle. Evidemment, les franciscains n'utilisent pas cette terminologie sophistiquée de la contemporaine philosophie analytique du langage, mais ils expriment très clairement l'idée que c'est justement la nature humaine, qui est tachée par le péché, à constituer l'argent comme moyen du désir de possession (car la possession et la confusion sont les éléments du péché originel). Notamment, la volonté pouvant mener à la béatitude ou bien aux maux du monde, cette même volonté peut constituer et construire un objet social, comme c'est le cas de l'argent.

Il convient quand même de souligner que le treizième siècle offrait aux yeux des frères mineurs un développement impressionnant de l'utilisation de la monnaie. La prospérité des villes communales amène à frapper des monnaies tout d'abord en argent, ensuite en or.[16] Venise et Gênes frappent une monnaie appelée *grosso* en argent, dans les premières années du treizième siècle; par la même appellation, d'autres villes italiennes suivent de près, Verona, Siena et Pisa dès 1220, Florence dès 1230. Le nom de la devise est repris par saint Louis en France frappant le *gros tournois* dès 1266. En ce qui concerne la monnaie en or, il y a l'*augustale* de Frédéric II à Messina et Brindisi, mais il ne s'agit que d'une frappe reliée aux rêves de l'Empire: en revanche, la prospérité commerciale amène Florence à frapper le *fiorino* en or dès 1252, et à la même date Gênes frappe le *genovino* – le nom de la ville est associé à l'appellation de la devise, manifestant un orgueil tout à fait compréhensible. Venise suit dès 1252 avec le *ducato*, tandis que saint Louis frappe l'*écu* à la même date du *gros tournois*. Cette histoire monétaire, associée aux manipulations de la valeur légale de la monnaie pratiquée par les gouvernants ou aux fraudes consistant à manipuler le poids (par limage) de la pièce de monnaie, amène Nicole Oresme vers 1340, dans sont *Traité de la monnaie* écrit en

---

16 P. Spufford, *Money and its use in medieval Europe*, Cambridge 1988.

langue française, à proclamer que l'argent est propriété de la collectivité, et le prince en changeant la valeur devient un tyran. Oresme s'avance dans une perspective aristotélicienne et son jugement appliqué aux démocraties européennes conduit à qualifier de tyrannique le gouvernement des pays de l'Europe occidentale après la deuxième guerre mondiale, jouant largement avec l'inflation et le cours des devises. Il se montre ainsi moderne et réactionnaire en même temps, moderne dans sa conception immatérielle de la monnaie, dont la valeur est un patrimoine collectif fixé par le fondement de la politique économique, réactionnaire car il ne pourrait que mépriser la conception contemporaine faisant de la politique monétaire un moyen pour l'État de pomper les ressources des citoyens à sa guise pour des finalités supérieures à la volonté du peuple. Ce n'est pas là l'approche franciscaine notamment des origines du mouvement, beaucoup plus centrée sur la personnalité des acteurs sociaux et marquée par une allure éminemment spirituelle et anthropologique. De la sorte, la mise en garde de saint François contre les dangers de l'argent, tout en étant enracinée dans une réflexion spirituelle et morale – clairement dépourvue de toute nuance de rébellion sociale, devient quand même un message très parlant pour les frères et les gens vivant en société, une société marquée par la monétarisation des échanges.

Finalement, le Royaume de Dieu est le retour de la Vie, et pour ce jour là il faudra ne pas être enveloppé par la mortification de l'argent, nous menant à dénier la vie. Les frères mineurs sont censés se tourner vers le Royaume de Dieu, donc ne doivent même pas toucher à l'argent à l'exception d'une maladie mettant en danger le salut d'un confrère: l'argent aux yeux des franciscains, récite la Règle provisoire, doit posséder la valeur d'une pierre. Comme pour le péché d'Adam et Eve, l'illusion de la valeur de l'argent n'est rien d'autre que l'œuvre du diable.

L'interdiction est fortement symbolique, mais sa violation est aussi fortement sanctionnée: le franciscain voulant avoir de l'argent est tout simplement un faux frère, et à moins d'une sincère repentance et l'acceptation de la punition il ne peut qu'être expulsé de l'Ordre. Même la demande d'aumônes impose le refus d'une offre en argent: les franciscains doivent demander l'aumône, mais ils ne peuvent accepter l'argent, car il s'agit de l'outil du diable pour solliciter le désir de possession des hommes. Encore une fois, ils peuvent accepter une aumône en argent seulement pour aider les lépreux, mais la Règle provisoire y ajoute tout de suite une admonition très forte contre les dangers du simple et bref contact avec l'argent.

Ce n'est pas surprenant de constater que cette mise en garde vigoureuse contre l'argent devient beaucoup plus synthétique dans la Règle définitive, promulguée par le Pape et rédigée sous le contrôle des canonistes de la Curie romaine. Il est de la tâche des commentateurs de la Règle de rappeler la spécificité de l'argent vis-à-vis des autre biens: les *Quatre Maîtres* rappellent que recevoir de l'argent signifie disposer de son utilisation, et son usage est permis aux franciscains, à défaut de tout titre de propriété. Mais l'argent possède des propriétés spécifiques, comme le dit le droit romain (*Digeste*, 50, 16, 178-222), à savoir qu'il est l'outil principal de la vente. Il ne s'agit pas du troc, car les biens s'échangent, et non l'argent. L'usage de l'argent est la vente ou tout autre opération monétaire: il s'agit de moyens par excellence afin de s'approprier des choses, donc l'usage même de l'argent est interdit aux franciscains. En effet, il n'y a pas un usage en soi de l'argent, au même titre que lire un livre ou manger une poire sont des usages en soi du livre et de la poire: l'argent est un bien dont l'usage renvoie toujours à la tension vers un autre bien (le plaisir du collectionneur de monnaies concerne les pièces, non pas l'argent). L'argent est un droit très général, il est la possibilité d'user licitement des biens convoités dans le cadre du marché.

Hugues de Digne, dont le commentaire à la Règle est disponible dans une excellent édition critique par Damien Ruiz, montre la même conscience juridique des *Quatre Maîtres*. Les *denarios* sont une espèce concrète d'argent, à savoir que les monnaies sont de la *pecunia*, mais l'argent ne se réduit pas aux monnaies courantes. L'argent est toute chose reçue en vue de la vente: c'est là la raison de l'interdiction pour les franciscains de toucher à l'argent. Hugues emploie la formule *pecunie ut pecunie* pour expliquer qu'il n'y a pas d'*usage en soi de l'argent* ouvert aux franciscains. Ce n'est pas l'or en tant que bien naturel ou artificiel qui est interdit aux franciscains, car ils peuvent l'utiliser en maniant les calices pendant la messe, ou bien pour soigner une maladie par ce minéral précieux. En revanche, quand l'or devient l'équivalent de l'argent, à savoir *pecunie ut pecunie*, il doit disparaître de l'univers vital des franciscains. Dans un autre ouvrage, *Libellus de finibus paupertatis*, cet ouvrage aussi édité par Damien Ruiz qui a été capable de montrer son importance encore récemment complètement méconnue, il utilise un néologisme éclaircissant: *proprietarietas*, qu'il convient de traduire par «propriétairité», à savoir l'essence du fait normatif d'être propriétaire. En particulier, pour Hugues le pauvre et le propriétaire s'opposent car au pauvre fait défaut la «propriétairité», la qualité mentale de vouloir devenir propriétaire selon la réglementation en vigueur. Mais alors Hugues ne parle pas du même pauvre dont parlait Marx dans le contexte de la lutte de classe. Le pauvre dont parle Hugues n'est que le pauvre volontaire ayant renoncé à la «propriétairité», tandis que le pauvre involontaire peut être rongé par l'avarice (tout comme le prolétariat se destinant à sa propre dictature). Et pour renoncer radicalement à la «propriétairité» il faut renoncer à manipuler l'argent, l'outil majeur des aspirants propriétaires.

Jean Pecham, dans son commentaire à la Règle attribué autrefois fautivement à saint Bonaventure[17], argumente que la *pecunia* est un mot plus apte à soulever un reproche d'avarice qu'un indicateur de richesse, à l'instar du chapitre XII de la *Cité de Dieu* de saint Augustin. Et pour justifier la notion de l'argent comme mesure de la vente il ne renvoie pas au droit romain, mais aux Écritures saintes (Actes, 5, 20; Proverbes, 7, 20) et au IVe livre de l'*Éthique à Nicomaque* d'Aristote (chapitre 1). Comme nous l'a indiqué Joel Kaye dans sa démarche d'histoire des idées[18], la monétarisation de la société européenne occidentale s'accompagne de la redécouverte d'Aristote par les biais de sa traduction en latin, faisant ainsi de la réflexion d'Aristote sur la monnaie et l'échange (notamment, le Ve livre de l'*Éthique à Nicomaque*) le fondement des analyses de l'économie chez des penseurs scolastiques comme Jean Buridan, Nicole Oresme, Walter Burley, et beaucoup d'autres. Mais ce qui caractérise l'approche des penseurs franciscains contemporains comme Pierre de Jean Olivi, Jean Duns Scot ou Gérald Odon c'est l'attention spécifique vers la dimension concrète de l'échange économique en comparaison avec la bien plus abstraite attention portée sur le même phénomène par l'école intellectualiste de tradition thomiste. Il convient de souligner que la monétarisation de la société est un phénomène de taille, tout d'abord circonscrit aux villes communales commerçantes du douzième siècle, ensuite élargi à la dimension des nations européennes[19]. Et le marchand devient un sujet social

---

17 Il est pour le moment exclusivement disponible dans l'*Opera Omnia* de saint Bonaventure (comme note 11), (VIII, 391).

18 J. Kaye, *Economy and Nature in the Fourteenth Century*, Cambridge 1998.

19 Par exemple, P. Spufford, *Le rôle de la monnaie dans la révolution commerciale du XIIIe siècle*, in: J. Day (éd.), *Études d'histoire*

capable d'attirer le désir d'imiter ses vertus et ses capacités, comme le montre efficacement Raymond Cazelles.[20] C'est là que les franciscains établissent leur originalité de pensée: tandis que Walter Burley peut établir que l'argent est la mesure de toute chose en laissant planer l'idée qu'il est en train de s'opposer à la littérature patristique moralisante, les franciscains peuvent délimiter cette notion de «mesure de toute chose» dans les confins de la vie mondaine, et grâce à leur anthropologie dualiste empêcher tout affaiblissement de l'approche moralisante vers les dangers de l'argent pour l'âme humaine. L'intellectualiste Burley, à l'instar de saint Thomas et révisant son attitude éminemment naturaliste, peut affirmer que «l'argent mesure la qualité commune des besoins humains (*indigentia*) associée aux biens échangés, par l'institutionnalisation et non pas en soi» (commentaire à Aristote, V^e livre, 84ra). Les volontaristes franciscains réduisent encore plus l'espace des lois naturelles, pour laisser libre cours à l'argent comme fait institutionnel complètement déterminé par les actes de volonté des acteurs du marché. Mais il convient aussi de souligner que l'image d'une patristique blâmant lourdement le commerce en tant qu'activité usuraire, et assimilant tout intérêt commercial à une activité usuraire – donc illicite – , est une image répandue dans la pensée chrétienne du Haut Moyen Âge et dans les siècles suivant, mais il est possible qu'il s'agisse en partie d'une déformation de l'intention des Pères de l'Église. En effet, comme l'a fait remarquer l'historien de la Rome antique Andrea Giardina, la civilisation grecque et latine avait confié aux Pères de l'Église un véritable mépris du petit commerçant, de la petite activité commerciale, dépourvue de toute vertu et chargée des vices les plus effrayants, tandis que le grand commerce trouvait de la considération en raison des

---

monétaire, Lille 1984.

20 R. Cazelles. *Nouvelle Histoire de Paris. De la fin du règne de Philippe Auguste à la mort de Charles V, 1223-1380* (Paris 1972),

capacités nécessaires pour l'entreprendre[21]. Cicéron dans son *De officiis* oppose la *magna mercatura*, où le gain est justifié par les dangers du déplacement des biens sur la longue distance, à la *tenuis mercatura*, où le gain n'est déterminé que par la tromperie. Le petit commerçant, qui revend rapidement ce qu'il achète, est un voleur de temps, car rien ne justifie son gain: il est un profiteur, un maître de la ruse, une plaie sociale. Il ne s'agit là que de la position abstraite d'un philosophe et d'un homme politique: le poète Martial dans ses *Satires* (10, 3) méprise l'un de ses collègues le comparant à un *proxeneta* de verres brisés. A la lettre il s'agit d'un médiateur, mais pour Martial c'est un petit commerçant et donc un menteur et un trompeur, en somme un trafiquant (ce n'est pas un hasard si les mots dans la langue italienne et française calqués sur *proxeneta* indiquent celui qui gagne sa vie en faisant prostituer des femmes). La patristique reçoit cet héritage sans faire trop de différence entre grand commerce et petit commerce, mais bouleverse le jugement méprisant que la civilisation classique portait sur l'activité manuelle, indigne de l'homme honorable: saint Basile le Grand fait l'apologie de l'artisan, en particulier en usant l'image de la forge, établissant un parallèle entre le couple matière-artisan et le couple fidèle-Dieu (*Regulae fusius tractatae*[22]). De plus, l'artisan est opposé au *negotiator*, le commerçant, car le premier transforme la matière, tandis que le deuxième achète et vend la même chose.[23] On revient au jugement de Cicéron, mais dans un cadre de valeurs tout autre: pour la pensée chrétienne il n'y a pas de défaut d'honneur dans l'activité manuelle, mais elle aussi – comme la pensée classique – n'arrive pas à saisir un véritable travail dans

---

85-118.

21 A. Giardina / A. Gurevic, *Il mercante dall'Antichità al Medioevo*, Roma-Bari 1994.

22 MPG, XXXI, 921.

23 MPG, LVI, 840.

l'activité commerciale, donc la méprise comme le faisait la pensée classique. Or, la pensée chrétienne patristique ne s'interroge pas sur la différence entre grand commerce et petit commerce, et sans une conscience spécifique du problème, le jugement négatif se porte sur le commerçant tout court, de manière à ce que la sévérité de la pensé classique contre le seul petit commerçant, celui qui vit de la tromperie à la différence des autres commerçants, glisse jusqu'à viser un commerçant indéterminé. Mieux, les Pères de l'Église ne se posent pas la question d'une analyse des typologies de commerçants, et sous l'étiquette de *negotiator* visent notamment le petit commerçant. Mais leurs lecteurs chrétiens du Haut Moyen Âge comprennent dans les passages de Grégoire de Nisse contre les usuriers[24] la condamnation de tout commerçant, peut-être parce que la société féodale ne connaissait pas de grand commerçant. Or, il n'est pas exclu que dans ses pages de feu contre les usuriers Grégoire de Nisse ne songeait point aux banquiers et aux financiers; elles ne visaient que les profiteurs de la détresse et des besoins des pauvres gens.

Dans le nouveau climat du dialogue serré entre la redécouverte de la philosophie païenne et de la philosophie chrétienne traditionnelle, à peu près quarante ans après les commentaires des *Quatre Maîtres*, la philosophie vole au secours de la normativité de la Règle davantage que par l'évocation du droit romain, mais l'esprit de la norme ne change pas. En effet, le droit romain n'offrait pas les outils pour alimenter la méfiance envers l'argent. Le droit canonique ne pouvait également fournir une position proche de celle des franciscains, méfiants envers l'argent mais en même temps prêts à différencier l'usure licite de l'usure illicite. Il n'y a pas de romaniste au treizième siècle qui ne souligne les dangers de l'argent pour l'âme; les canonistes oscillent entre la condamnation générale de tout prêt à intérêt et la justification prudente de cette activité

---

24 MPG, XLVI, 436-452.

commerciale prévoyant un intérêt, créant un discours embrouillé et ambigu typique d'un auteur comme le cardinal Hostiensis, Henry de Suse, ou Sinibaldo Fieschi, devenant ensuite Pape Innocent IV. Et à la fin du treizième siècle, le grand canoniste Jean d'Andrée, par ailleurs très sensible aux acquis de la pensée franciscaine en ce qui concerne le droit subjectif, pour sortir de l'embarras de positions dialectiques jusqu'à l'extrême, évite tout simplement de s'engager sur le terrain de l'intérêt au-delà des formules stéréotypées. Il y a peu de juristes qui pouvaient adopter la position radicale de Jacobus Butrigarius (1348†), le maître de Bartolus et de Baldus: commentant la loi romaine *Improbum foenus* (*Code de Justinien*, 2, 11, 20) il compare l'usure, à savoir l'intérêt sur le prêt, au crime de stellionat, à savoir la tromperie exercée par une partie au contrat contre l'autre partie. Il en tire la conséquence que le prêt à intérêt doit être sanctionné dans les mêmes conditions du stellionat, à savoir (*Digeste* 47, 20, 3, 1 et 2) par les juges à défaut de loi écrite selon une peine déterminée de façon arbitraire. Il s'agit d'une position entraînant potentiellement une répression féroce de l'usure, mais elle n'a pas était suivi ni par Bartolus, ni par Baldus. Les lois laïques depuis longtemps permettaient l'usure, au moins quand l'intérêt sur le prêt ne dépassait pas des limites censés être raisonnable (pouvant aller jusqu'au 20% en France et à Gênes et Venise au treizième siècle). Les romanistes ont davantage essayé de cantonner, et non pas de justifier une répression de l'usure, par ailleurs censée être nécessaire dans sa forme de grand prêt par les banquiers aux souverains des nations européennes. Les canonistes ont justifié l'immoralité de l'usure, mais il n'ont pas pu ignorer sa dimension pratique fonctionnelle à la nouvelle société urbaine s'imposant au treizième siècle. Tous les efforts de la papauté contre l'usure ne se plaçaient que sur le terrain doctrinal, et non pratique, tout en produisant le résultat de rendre plus rigide la législation laïque après le concile de Vienne (1312), quand il fût décidé que les juges préférant l'application d'une loi laïque tolérante à l'égard de l'usure davantage qu'une loi ecclésiastique étaient censurés. Il s'agissait de l'abandon définitif de la soi-disant exception de saint Ambroise, ayant interprété le passage du Deutéronome interdisant le prêt à intérêt (23, 21) comme concernant le seul frère dans la foi (la même lecture rigide – mais inversée – a été reproché aux Juifs par Sombart, à savoir que l'usure est licite vers le Chrétien et non vers le frère juif). Il est licite de nuire à l'ennemi en le chargeant du prêt usuraire – *ubi jus belli, ibi etiam jus usurae*[25], affirme saint Ambroise, mais sa position est vite oubliée car elle affaiblie l'unité doctrinale de la position catholique, qui se veut universelle et non pas communautaire. Léon Poliakov souligne que la thèse même selon laquelle les juifs, à cause de leur *pravitas*, auraient été autorisés par le Seigneur à emprunter chargeant d'intérêts les étrangers, encore soutenue par saint Thomas, devient toujours plus faible se réduisant plutôt à un simple préjugé anti-juif supposant une moralité partielle[26]. En effet, la décision prise d'excommunier les usuriers au Concile de Latran III sous la pression du feu Alexandre III (1187, *Extra*, 5, 19, 3), la poursuite de la lutte contre les usuriers chrétiens au IVe concile de Latran (1215) tout en prenant acte de la diffusion de la pratique chez les juifs par un effet de remplacement, les décisions de frapper de nullité les testaments des usuriers et de leur empêcher de louer des maisons prises au concile de Lyon (1274, *Sexte*, 5, 5, 1-2), celle de considérer hérétique la personne affirmant que l'usure n'est pas un péché prise au concile de Vienne (1312, *Clémentines*, 5, 5, *Ex gravi*) ont sûrement troublé la conscience des usuriers chrétiens, comme nous le témoignent les chroniques – notamment à la fin de leur vie, mais ils n'ont aboutit qu'à pousser la législation laïque à sanctionner l'usure grave, à savoir l'intérêt exorbitant, et

---

25 F. Raphaël, *Judaïsme et capitalisme*, Paris 1982, 132.
26 L. Poliakov, *Les Banchieri juifs et le Saint Siège*, Paris 1965.

point l'intérêt raisonnable, désormais outil inévitable de la société urbaine au début du quatorzième siècle. En dehors de toute sorte de pragmatisme ménageant les réalités du monde, pour les franciscains l'argent est l'outil par excellence de l'avarice, du désir de posséder le superflu. La licité de certaines activités commerciales prévoyant l'intérêt ne concerne pas la vie des franciscains, car ils ont formulé le vœu de vie évangélique, et l'activité commerciale n'existe que dans la vie mondaine.

La Règle définitive exprime la même méfiance symbolique vis-à-vis de l'argent exprimée dans la première Règle provisoire et dans les légendes franciscaines, mais sans en détailler les raisons: le chapitre IV pose la règle d'aucune possession, directe ou indirecte, de l'argent pour les franciscains. L'exception à cette règle concerne la possibilité pour les responsables d'une communauté franciscaine de solliciter des «amis spirituels» afin de recevoir de l'argent pour aider des frères malades en raison des conditions géographiques et climatiques. Mais le chapitre IV répète que les franciscains ne doivent pas «recevoir» de l'argent, ce stimulateur de l'envie d'acquisition de propriété comme le répètent les *Quatre Maîtres* en soulignant que le salaire d'un franciscain pour son travail ne peut être payé par de la laine ou des peaux, biens ayant la même fonction de l'argent (commentaire au chapitre VI de la Règle). En effet, la réception de ces matières premières «stimule la propriété» (*proprietatem inducit et importat*): les franciscains, finalement, comme le dit le chapitre VI de la Règle, «comme des pèlerins et des étrangers en ce monde ... ils iront quêter leur nourriture avec confiance, sans rougir». Afin de faire retentir l'écho du psaume 39, 13 (*peregrinus sicut omnes patres mei*) et de la première lettre de Pierre, 2, 11, l'argent est une entrave à débarrasser du chemin du frère mineur. Comme le dit Pecham, le franciscain est le serviteur utilisant les biens possédés par son maître (chapitre VI).

Je crois que le législateur a fait preuve ici de prudence: au lieu de donner l'impression que toute exception à la règle d'interdiction ne peut qu'être énoncée dans la Règle et que la violation de l'interdiction est un péché mortel (chapitre VIII de la Règle provisoire), les juristes professionnels rédigeant la Règle définitive préfèrent énoncer une interdiction ferme tout en laissant une clause ouverte d'exception, dont les responsables de la communauté franciscaine doivent fournir l'interprétation et les modalités d'application. Si les frères touchant à l'argent violent une norme fondée sur les Évangiles, ils sont fortement coupables – c'est le cas de la Règle provisoire; si les frères touchant à l'argent violent une norme voulue par le chef de l'Ordre, ils sont également coupables, mais leur péché n'est pas contre la Parole Sacrée des Évangiles – c'est le cas de la Règle définitive. Ce n'est pas un hasard si les modernistes anti-normativistes de l'époque et d'aujourd'hui ont levé des lamentations pour la perte de la pureté originaire de la Règle provisoire, tandis que les normativistes chrétiens de l'époque et d'aujourd'hui ont avancé les dangers d'une utopie totalitaire de la perfection sur terre comme seul condition humaine souhaitable.

Carl Schmitt a observé dans *Le Nomos de la terre*[27] qu'il y avait à l'origine une différence entre le *nomos* et la loi, mise en ombre depuis les sophistes: le *nomos* est relié à l'occupation de l'espace physique (à savoir, le territoire où le *nomos* s'exerce), tandis que la loi n'est qu'une simple règle. Le *nomos* est la forme immédiate rendant visible l'ordre politique et sociale d'une communauté. Or, reprenant cette image conceptuelle, pour les Spirituels il n'y que l'espace du Ciel à occuper, donc il n'y a pas de *nomos* pour la vie mondaine, au plus des lois à mépriser; en revanche, pour les franciscains normativistes il y a d'une

---

27 C. Schmitt, *Le Nomos de la terre*, Paris 2001, (éd. orig., *Der Nomos der Erde im Völkerrecht des jus publicum Europaeum*, Cologne 1950).

part le *nomos* du Ciel, touchant à l'espace de la Patrie céleste envisagé par les vœux religieux, d'autre part il y a le *nomos* de la vie mondaine, avec sa pluralité de lois particulières. Pour ces derniers, le franciscain a choisi le *nomos* de la Patrie céleste, mais tous les autres vivent à l'intérieur du *nomos* mondain: en revanche les lois mondaines ne sont que de l'arbitraire inutile, comme elles paraissent dans la représentation (voire non-représentation) de la société offerte par les Spirituels.

En dépit de la comparaison du frère mineur touchant à l'argent à la mouche se posant sur des déjections – rapportée par les légendes hagiographiques de la vie de saint François, chacune d'elles exprimant une certaine conception de son message –, saint François n'a pas voulu faire de la méfiance à l'égard de l'argent un slogan politique contre la classe sociale des riches (à savoir que pour certains il était un marxiste-léniniste 'illuminé'). Il s'agissait aussi pour lui de dessiner la règle de vie d'une communauté agissant dans le réseau social sans aucune tentation de rébellion sociale et implantée dans la plus grande conformité au sein de l'Église catholique. Cette perspective ne pouvait pas être mise en œuvre sans une dialectique profonde, sans compter les inévitables tendances centrifuges (de rébellion sociale) et centripètes (de repli sur le mysticisme intimiste). Le dépouillement des biens mondains était simple pour des moines vivant dans un monastère hors de la société mondaine (tout en construisant une économie moniale dans les confins du monastère lui-même); le dépouillement des biens (de plus, absolument radical) était compliqué pour un franciscain voulant vivre au milieu de la société mondaine. En effet, l'injonction de 'rien avoir' ne peut être mis à l'œuvre que dans un monde normatif dissociant l'usage légitime et la possession du titre d'un droit d'usage légitime (le frère mineur utilise une chose – à titre légitime – et il n'a pas absolument aucun droit – humain – pour l'utiliser).

Reprenant l'*Apologie des pauvres* de saint Bonaventure, nous pouvons y lire que les lois civiles ne concernent pas la Règle des frères mineurs (chapitre XI): les franciscains, tout en restant au milieu de la société laïque, vivent dans une autre sphère de conformité au Christ, ce qu'ils aimeront appeler 'droit du ciel', *ius poli*. Ce n'est pas le monde normatif du juriste classique Jean XXII, né à Cahors et Pape de 1316 à 1334, en ce sud de la France où même les franciscains les plus radicaux dans l'approche à l'Évangile étaient imprégnés par une formation juridique (c'est le cas de Hugues de Digne, 1256†): selon la tradition du droit romain, acceptée par le droit médiéval et par un théologien de la renommée de saint Thomas (1274†), tout acte légitime renvoie à l'existence d'un droit dont est titulaire l'auteur de l'acte. A défaut de ce droit, l'action est illégitime: donc, si le franciscain n'a pas le droit d'utiliser une église, il ne doit pas l'utiliser. Mais s'il l'utilise, il doit avoir quelque droit pour le faire. La règle de vie de 'rien avoir' comporte nécessairement la possession de quelque droit: les intellectuels de l'Ordre franciscain, plus fidèles à l'idéal de leur père fondateur qu'aux catégories conceptuelles du droit romain, préféreront inventer une nouvelle catégorie juridique, le droit subjectif, déjà bien formé dans la pensée de Duns Scot (1308†), et entrer en litige avec le Siège apostolique plutôt que de renoncer à la nature radicale et complète du 'rien avoir'. C'est le cas de la dissidence intellectuelle (les *fraticelles* justement dits *de opinione*): le procureur général de l'Ordre des franciscains, Bonagratia de Bergamo (1343†), juriste raffiné, et les autres partisans du ministre général rebelle Michel de Cesène (1342†), parmi lesquelles le fameux Guillaume d'Ockham (1347†) et François de Marchia (post 1341†), aussi ponctuel et acharné que son plus notoire confrère. C'est aussi le cas de la dissidence sans aucune prétention juridique et fixée sur la pratique factuelle et quotidienne du renoncement le plus absolu (les *fraticelles* justement dits *de paupere vita*): Pierre de Jean Olivi (1298†), subtil analyste de la réalité économique et féroce nominaliste du phénomène juridique, Ange Clareno (1337†), chantre des persécutions souffertes par les Spirituels proches du Pape Célestin V (1296†), Ubertin de Casale (1330†), fidèle à la pauvreté radicale franciscaine jusqu'à préférer la sortie de l'Ordre mineur pour rejoindre un Ordre monastique. La raison affichée du différend est juridique et politique, les uns penchant pour une nouvelle conception du droit, les autres pour un refus du phénomène juridique en lui-même. Mais les raisons implicites touchent aussi à la classification des images (parfois radicalement alternatives) de saint François produites par ses confrères et partisans. Tout le monde chez les franciscains reconnaît que saint François est un 'autre Christ', *alter Christus*: mais pour certains frères franciscains ce n'est pas une hyperbole pour souligner la grandeur immense de saint François, c'est le fait à la lettre que François est comme le Christ, et vice-versa. Ici ne s'ouvre pas une question d'appartenance fidèle à l'Église catholique: il s'agit en revanche du phantasme de l'oubli de la référence au Texte instaurant l'ordre de la civilisation, ce Texte censé trancher dogmatiquement entre les poussées humaines vers les rêves et la réalité. Il s'ouvre aussi un creuset délirant de la raison, mieux exprimé par le délire mystique ou iconographique, ce même creuset que le catholicisme veut renfermer pour évacuer le fantasme nihiliste de la dénégation de la mort personnelle. Je ne vous propose qu'un exemple: je songe à la gravure ouvrant l'ouvrage de Pedro de Alva y Astorga, intitulé *Naturae Prodigium, Gratiae Portentum*, publié à Madrid en 1651. L'ouvrage met en parallèle des références à la vie de saint François et de Jésus, même typographiquement car la page est imprimée sur deux colonnes, l'une consacrée aux références à saint François et l'autre aux références à Jésus. La gravure, due à Juan de Noort, prolonge le parallèle du livre: au milieu un homme en posture de crucifié, avec le visage voilé par des ailes d'ange (Isaïe 6, *et duabus velabant faciem eius)*, la moitié droite du corps nu et la moitié gauche enrobée par une bure de nuage. Derrière, sur la droite le mont Calvaire et Nazareth et sur la gauche le mont Alvernia et Assise. Sous les pieds cloués de l'homme ayant trois couples d'ailes, l'agneau pascal sans drapeau. L'image renvoie au livre et le livre à l'image, tout en étant l'image l'emblème d'une signification riche et difficile à exprimer par les mots. Dans la piété populaire on conserve les dépouilles des saints, préservées par intervention miraculeuse, à la ferveur de la dévotion des pèlerins; dans la piété du socialisme réel on conserve les dépouilles des chefs du peuples, préservées par intervention biochimique, à la ferveur de la dévotion du peuple. Le gnosticisme politique, comme nous l'enseigne Eric Voegelin, réduit la toute-puissance du Dieu transcendent à la toute-puissance du leader politique.[28] la première stratégie peut-être assume une donnée fausse (pour ceux qui ne croient pas au Dieu transcendent), mais sûrement la deuxième stratégie manifeste le délire de l'évacuation de la mort. Le Siège apostolique ne pouvait pas contrer la ferveur morale des nouveaux imitateurs du Christ, mais il se devait, en tant que pouvoir organisé, de rappeler le principe de l'autorité normative et de son exercice dans le contexte d'un Théâtre non-délirant de la Raison, selon l'expression de Pierre Legendre.[29]

III. Les frères mineurs et la société médiévale

La présence des frères mineurs au milieu de la société produit une réponse sociale visant à leur permettre de vivre

---

[28] E. Voegelin, *Modernity without Restraint*, in: M. Henningensen (éd.), *The Collected Works of Eric Voegelin*, V, Columbia – London 2000; E. Voegelin, *History of Political Ideas. The Middle Ages to Aquinas*, in: P. von Sivers (éd.), *The Collected Works of Eric Voegelin*, XX, London 1997; E. Voegelin, *History of Political Ideas. The Later Middle Ages*, in: D. Walsh (éd.), *The Collected Works of Eric Voegelin*, XXI, London 1998.

[29] P. Legendre, *Law and the Unconscious. A Legendre Reader*, New York 1997; Idem, *Sur la question dogmatique en Occident*, Paris 1999; et la deuxième partie, Idem, *Nomenclator*, Paris 2006.

leur vocation, fixée par la réflexion autour de l'identité franciscaine, selon les lois de la cité. Ainsi, la normativité sociale essaie de faire une place juridique à la présence franciscaine pour en recevoir en retour leur pastorale et leur enseignement pratique. Dans la pensée franciscaine, dès la Règle de saint François, il est question notamment de ne pas juger ceux qui choisissent les règles du monde plutôt que les règles de l'état adamique; c'est un choix 'inférieur', dans un sens, mais aussi 'supérieur' dans un autre – l'exercice social du pouvoir, nécessaire pour régir une société chrétienne et donc méritoire, demande l'acceptation des règles du monde. Or, la notion chrétienne de 'personne' maintient une unité dans la perspective franciscaine excluant la moindre dévalorisation des règles mondaines, qui pourtant ne seront jamais les règles choisies par un frère mineur (elles sont des règles, non des non-règles comme dans la perspective thomiste). Le Péché originel est dans l'anthropologie franciscaine l'emblème d'une double normativité, celle mondaine et celle céleste, ne pouvant retrouver son unité que par l'action du Tiers, le Dieu personnel, juge suprême et aimant après la fin du monde, le jour venu du Jugement dernier.

La personne est une unité métaphysique caractérisée par sa nature de non-communication et pourtant son premier acte est la communication: elle réalise de la sorte une identité relationnelle. La personne humaine répète le mystère de la Trinité: déjà saint Augustin avait affirmé que l'homme est image de Dieu, mais les franciscains poussent cette idée dans le contexte des subtilités d'une philosophie analytique scolastique prétendant expliquer la rationalité de la Trinité, à savoir trois personnes qui n'en sont qu'une. En ce sens, la personne humaine, en tant qu'ultime réalité, possède la même nature que la personne divine, sauf qu'elle n'est qu'unité et non pas trinité. Le mystère associant la personne humaine et la personne divine est dans le fait que la réalité ultime de la personne se place dans l'absence de communication avec l'extérieur (à défaut, la personne se confond avec l'extérieur) et en même temps dans la communication de la personne avec la réalité extérieure (chacune des personnes divines communique avec les deux autres, ensuite Dieu a créé le monde actuel). L'homme est une individualité car sa personne métaphysique ne peut se confondre avec toute autre individualité: nous avons là l'affirmation philosophique d'une valeur sacrée de la personne humaine, et le mépris de toute forme d'utilitarisme en tant que dénégation de la valeur fondamentale. Mais le mystère se manifeste dans le fait que la notion même de vie sociale renvoie à la communication entre personnes incommunicables. Les franciscains peuvent accepter que dans notre monde actuel les personnes se définissent comme individus caractérisés par certaines propriétés, mais à la différence de la pensée politique moderne, de Machiavel à Hobbes, ils refusent que la personne puisse se réduire à l'individu, car la personne nous renvoie à la vie éternelle, tandis que l'individu nous renvoie à l'existence (limitée) dans notre monde actuel.

Ainsi, il n'y a aucune confusion entre les franciscains et les mouvements hérétiques contemporains (à savoir, début treizième siècle et décennies suivantes), très souvent associés à des poussées sociales, économiques, et politiques: le 'perfectisme', l'aspiration à la réalisation de la perfection en cette vie mondaine, est radicalement étranger à la pensée franciscaine, car la perfection de la personne se joue dans la vie éternelle, et non pas de la vie dans le monde actuel. La dualité de la nature avant le péché originel et de la nature après le péché originel est résolue dans l'unité de la personne humaine, toujours la même en tant qu'image de Dieu, tout à fait différente en tant qu'individu mondain. De même, la co-présence d'ascétisme et de lassitude morale typique des mouvements rigoristes dans les contextes religieux les plus différents est absent dans l'expérience franciscaine (je songe à des cas comme le frankisme dans le monde juif, ou bien le quiétisme sectaire dans le monde protestant, en passant par le catharisme - dérive manichéenne du christianisme). En effet, l'unité primaire de la personne empêche de s'abandonner au fatalisme laxiste d'un salut qui vient de l'extérieur et rend vaine la rigueur morale sans l'intervention des 'parfaits', des 'illuminés', des 'initiés' ou autres. Il n'y a que la personne, par sa libre volonté, pouvant coopérer par l'aide divin à son salut: à défaut de cette coopération, Dieu ne peut contraindre personne au salut. Il ne s'agit pas ici d'un débat théologique autour de l'efficacité de la Grâce divine, comme c'est en revanche le cas pour le différend entre Luther et l'Église catholique. Il s'agit en revanche de souligner qu'en dépit des similitudes de surface entre les mouvances paupéristiques du douzième et treizième siècles et les franciscains il y a des différences essentielles entre les franciscains (orthodoxes) et les mouvements hérétiques prêchant la pauvreté absolue. La conception de la personne métaphysique dotée d'une volonté absolument libre comporte une unité morale souvent absente des mouvements hérétiques, où la pureté s'associe avec le passage à l'acte des perversions – le cathare, méprisant le mariage car impur, peut coucher avec la femme d'autrui, action à ses yeux indifférente pour atteindre la pureté. Le normativisme est l'autre rempart contre la transformation en une mouvance de contestation sociale.

Le succès de la présence franciscaine dans le monde social est lié à leur conceptualisation dans la sémantique catholique des structures profondes de l'anthropologie humaine: ils transportent les processus mentaux normalement confinés dans le confessionnel de leur action quotidienne au milieu des gens ordinaires. Dans le sacrement de la confession, il y a une structure ternaire: le pénitent, le ministre de l'Église, Dieu. La confession est une procédure liturgique assurant l'intervention libératoire du Tiers sans générer de situations anarchiques par une évocation individuelle, parcellisée et fragmentée, du Tiers. Le pardon des péchés s'opère grâce à la repentance du pénitent, à l'intervention du ministre habilité par la règle, à la miséricorde et à l'amour gratuit divin – le Tiers. Or, la confession ne peut qu'avoir lieu dans une procédure normative, elle n'est pas une action sans règles; et pourtant, les franciscains amènent l'amour gratuit divin au milieu des gens ordinaires, n'ayant pas été amenées à des gestes réglementés, par leur imitation de la vie du Christ et des Apôtres. Des gens ordinaires peuvent se confesser s'ils sont sollicités par leur propre conscience et par leurs propres croyances; des gens ordinaires peuvent connaître l'amour divin en voyant directement d'autres personnes vivant la miséricorde divine. L'évangélisation franciscaine ne pardonne pas les péchés, mais montre d'une façon spéciale, par l'imitation du Christ, la voie du pardon divin.

L'image sacralisée des origines de l'Ordre a une importance essentielle: saint François est le Père fondateur, il est pour certain un Père auquel vouer une obéissance directe sans passer par le Père céleste (l'expression *alter Christus*, anesthétisée par le discours orthodoxe, peut sonner hérétique dans une signification au pied de la lettre). Tandis que l'institution vivante, le Siège apostolique, peut se tromper dans son activité pastorale, saint François ne se trompe plus, car il est tout banalement mort: il n'y a pas de rébellion envisageable contre saint François, car il devient le Tiers assurant contemporainement l'identité du franciscain et la légitimité de son action. En revanche, l'erreur peut être reconnu dans l'action du Siège apostolique, et seule la présence effective du Tiers divin peut bloquer la contestation de l'autorité: mais si le Tiers peut être identifié parfois en Dieu, parfois en saint François, en face de l'erreur du Siège apostolique, le franciscain radical peut finalement briser sa fidélité directe et immédiate au Tiers par une contestation du Siège apostolique. Poussant la contestation jusqu'au bout, le

Siège apostolique devient la perversion du vrai Tiers: les *fraticelles* voient sur le trône de Pierre non pas le chef de la Chrétienté, mais l'Antéchrist, justement la perversion absolue. Dans un dialogue de saint Jacques de la Marchia (1476†), *Dialogus contra fraticellos*, rapidement traduit en langue italienne de l'époque, le fraticelle, héritier du schisme de Michel de Cesène contre Jean XXII, proclame d'obéir à la 'sainte église', mais il ajoute tout de suite que l'église est constituée par 'nous et les autres fidèles avec nous'.[30] Le refus de la source normative du Siège apostolique est ainsi explicitée, lui préférant l'accès direct et subjectif à la normativité de la Règle franciscaine, sans médiation d'aucune sorte, à l'exception de ceux qui se rangent à côté de moi, le fraticelle. En ce sens, les fraticelles soi-disant apologistes de la pauvreté évangélique et d'une Église pure et incontaminée ne sont que très peu différents de Mgr. Lefebvre et de sa fraternité schismatique contre le Vatican II. Les uns et les autres ne reconnaissant pas l'existence d'un Pape sur la Chaire de Pierre, les uns et les autres se considèrent dans le plein droit de bâtir eux-mêmes la véritable Église. Il n'y a pas de révolutionnaires – au moins dans le sens contemporain – dans la pensée chrétienne, car sa structure est par vocation réactionnaire, à savoir 'réagir' pour revenir au 'vrai' passé. Tout simplement, les Lumières nous ont appris que le 'vrai' passé, celui nous menant à la félicité, est le futur, donnant vie à la chimère du chrétien illuminé. L'un des passages de la réplique de Jacques de Marchia est fondamentale: saint François a commandé à ses frères d'obéir à l'Église catholique, et non pas à eux-mêmes, car 'obéir' renvoie à la différence entre l'assujetti et celui qui commande. La fonction du Tiers est explicité dans le langage le plus simple et le plus immédiat: il n'y a pas de Tiers sans échange relationnelle, obéir à soi-même est la dénégation du Tiers.

---

30 D. Lasic (éd.), S. Iacobus de Marchia, *Dialogus contra fraticellos*, Ancona, 1975 96-7.

Mais en dépit d'éventuelles dérives contestataires, cette grande fidélité à la mémoire de saint François donne une grande force de témoignage missionnaire aux franciscains, peu importe si ils obéissent ou non à l'Évêque universel de Rome. Il leur donne tout d'abord la force psychologique d'être au milieu du monde sans tomber dans les règles du monde, et notamment il leur donne la force convaincante de communiquer aux gens ordinaires l'intégralité du message évangélique, dans sa force étonnante de l'amour que la raison ne peut pas exprimer. Le succès du frère franciscain dans l'imaginaire collectif des populations européennes, américaines, africaines ou asiatiques est dans cette force spéciale, entre d'une part l'explosion de l'amour gratuit, du pardon et de la miséricorde, mais d'autre part aussi le délire fantasmatique de la suppression de toute norme en tant que négation de l'amour.

Ainsi, pris dans leur souci d'évangélisation, les frères mineurs en Angleterre contribuent à l'évolution de la réalité normative sociale, et par conséquent au développement du *trust*.[31] Ancrés dans les sociétés urbaines, sur les vagues d'un monde s'éloignant lentement de la quotidienneté du monde féodal, ils contribuent partout ailleurs à une nouvelle conception de la machine juridique. La société occidentale médiévale ne sera jamais une société franciscaine, et récemment un historien (K.B. Wolf) a formulé la thèse selon laquelle l'apologie franciscaine de la pauvreté est une apologie à l'usage exclusif des riches (donc, dans un sens spécifique, conservatrice du *statu quo*). Or, la pensée franciscaine a contribué à donner une nuance spécifique à l'influence du droit canonique – dont est tirée la notion fondamentale de hiérarchie pour notre civilisation occidentale – dans la société occidentale, et plus en général elle a influencé sur deux niveaux l'histoire de l'Occident

---

31 L. Parisoli, 'Théorie et pratique de la pauvreté. Les Franciscains au Royaume-Uni', *Antonianum* 78 (2003) 627-650.

chrétien: au niveau de l'élaboration des catégories conceptuelles, et au niveau de la pastorale populaire.

IV. Justifications des pratiques économiques

Les partisans de la pauvreté absolue produisent au Moyen Âge une théorie de l'utilité sociale de la richesse, notamment pour tous ceux voulant vivre dans la sphère d'une communauté mondaine. Scot proclame, à la suite du franciscain Richard de Mediaville, la nécessité pour le gouvernement de disposer de personnes concernées par la mise à disposition aux citoyens des biens de consommation. Un moine au onzième siècle, vivant dans le microcosme de l'économie du monastère placé au beau milieu d'un monde féodal, ne pouvait même imaginer l'importance de la mise à disposition des biens de consommation pour les gens. Tout simplement, autour de lui il n'y avait que des paysans vivant à l'intérieur d'une économie de subsistance, ou bien des aristocrates pour lesquelles l'argent était viable pour le luxe et le faste, la gloire de Dieu et l'aide aux pauvres, mais surtout pas pour ce qui sera appelé la capitalisation. Mais Olivi ou Duns Scot, appartenant à un Ordre religieux enraciné dans la vie urbaine, vivait directement les exigences logistiques des habitants d'une ville. Les marchands n'étaient pas seulement les messagers de biens ne pouvant être produit localement par la transformation agricole, donc touchant au luxe et à l'exotique. Ils sont les rouages indispensables pour assurer les besoins fondamentaux d'une population vivant dans une zone très concentrée, la ville justement. Aux habitants des villes il fallait assurer la distribution des biens alimentaires et de première nécessité, ou de tout autre bien ne pouvant être produit à l'intérieur de l'espace urbain. Il fallait des personnes fournissant ce que l'économie de la ville, marquée par les corporations artisanales, renonçait *a priori* à produire. Ces personnes à titre privé sont les marchands, et la licéité de leurs gains est montré selon Scot par le fait que – des marchands étant absent dans une communauté –

la collectivité se devrait de rémunérer des fonctionnaires publiques (*ministri rei publicae*) assurant les mêmes fonctions.[32] Il pousse jusqu'au but, dans une exaltation du pouvoir normatif de la volonté de la personne humaine, la notion de capital déjà tracée par Olivi – dans son univers conceptuel mais aussi dans son choix des mots – et l'idée olivienne que grâce aux opérations commerciales visant le gains les acteurs économiques produisent un bien commun pour toute la communauté. En dépit des différents essais de placer la pensée économique occidentale dans la lignée exclusive du droit romain et de ses techniciens à défaut de toute connotation religieuse chrétienne, il est manifeste que c'est l'univers symbolique d'un franciscain comme Olivi qui établi la persuasion fondatrice du capitalisme pour une communauté humaine. A ceux qui doutent que la théologie morale puisse avoir influencé l'essor du capitalisme occidentale, il convient de rétorquer qu'il ne s'agit pas tout simplement d'une pensée académique (théologie morale, ou théologie sacramentelle, ou géographie, ou physique etc.)[33]. Le discours des franciscains, et des autres penseurs scolastiques les ayant suivi, a modelé un nouvel univers de symbolisme dogmatique, le transmettant à la société par le

---

32 Cf. dans l'édition Wadding *Opus oxoniense*, IV, d. 15. q. 2, nn. 22-23.

33 Je me borne à évoquer Julius Kirshner, infatigable adversaire de la reconnaissance de l'existence d'une pensée franciscaine ayant contribué à l'essor du capitalisme occidentale, dès 'The Moral Theology of Public Finance', *Archivum Fratrum Praedicatorum* 40 (1970) 46-72, à 'Peter John Olivi's Treatise on Contracts of Sales, Usury, and Restitution: 'Minorite Economics or Minor Works?', *Quaderni fiorentini* 13 (1984) 233-86. Il lui faut opposer les brillants travaux de Todeschini sur la spécificité de la pensée franciscaine en tant que source de l'essor du capitalisme, jusqu'au récent G. Todeschini, *Ricchezza francescana: dalla povertà volontaria alla società di mercato*, Bologne 2004. Il y a aussi l'historien de l'économie Oscar Nuccio qui minimise la contribution franciscaine, mais le notaire Albertano da Brescia, mort en 1270, dont Nuccio souligne la rationalité économique, était très proche de la spiritualité franciscaine.

biais de la prédication, et non pas par les salles de cours universitaires. Ce n'est pas un hasard si la plus grand notoriété de penseur économique revient dans les siècles passés à saint Bernardin de Sienne, ayant vécu au quinzième siècle, penseur nullement original ayant retenu les analyses d'Olivi et Scot, mais étant en revanche un grand prédicateur réputé d'une sainteté indiscutable. Les juristes romanistes et canonistes n'étaient point prédicateurs, ils ne pouvaient s'imposer comme des 'prêtres de la normativité économique' dans une société puisant dans bien d'autres sources son symbolisme dogmatique. De fins juristes canonistes comme Innocent IV ou Jean d'Andrée ne saisissent pas le phénomène social menant vers la monétarisation du manque à gagner dans l'intérêt pour le prêt; les juristes romanistes utilisent un symbolisme émanant de la société païenne romaine en décalage avec la société chrétienne médiévale, et ils leur faudrait étirer les deux pour trouver un terrain de compromis. Ils vont devenir des maîtres absolus de la normativité bientôt, au fur et à mesure du déclin de la confiance dans le droit naturel, mais il ne faut surtout pas regarder le Moyen Âge avec les lunettes du totalitarisme du droit positif du vingtième siècle. De plus, les juristes romanistes n'avaient pas les outils pour façonner la construction sociale du marché et du bien commun: il s'agit là d'une construction puisant dans l'anthropologie religieuse, comme le montre aussi le fait que le partisan du libre marché économique aujourd'hui, même s'il est désormais loin d'une anthropologie religieuse, est un adversaire de l'intervention législative de l'État, monstre biblique, Léviathan ou Béhémoth, produit par la 'romanisation' de l'Europe occidentale à défaut de sa 'canonisation' par une normativité enracinée dans la chrétienté. Enfin, la contribution franciscaine est tout à fait capitale parmi les analyses d'autres penseurs chrétiens, car la lignée thomiste n'a pas marqué l'évolution d'une pensée économique dans la société, même s'il y a bien sûr des dominicains – et d'autres penseurs religieux – qui ont participé à cette contribution, tout simplement car ils ont laissé tomber l'orthodoxie mathématicienne du juste prix thomiste pour embrasser l'approche franciscaine. C'est le cas de saint Antonin de Florence, contemporain de saint Bernardin de Sienne, et de tous les (rares) dominicains ayant trahi au Moyen Âge les consignes de la plus grande fidélité au penseur de référence de leur Ordre. Je dis au *Moyen Âge* car au seizième siècle la trahison de saint Thomas de la part des penseurs dominicains est en train de s'accomplir au grand jour, notamment par Domingo de Soto et ses alliés jésuites, Molina et Suarez: il faudra attendre la fin du dix-neuvième siècle pour assister à la renaissance du thomisme, ainsi que de tout jugement que l'on puisse porter sur celle-ci.

Or, le grand canoniste cardinal Hostiensis s'était bien interrogé sur la licéité de la réparation du *lucrum cessans*, la dimension du préjudice concernant le gain éventuel venant à manquer après l'évènement (se révélant) dommageable. Dans sa *Summa Aurea*, en ouverture du cinquième livre consacré à l'usure, il accepte la réparation du *lucrum cessans*, un passage très important pour justifier le prêt à intérêt sans le qualifier d'usure. L'argent que je te donne, en effet, je ne peux le faire fructifier comme j'aurai pu, donc tu dois me rendre le montant prêté plus l'équivalent de mon *lucrum cessans* pour la durée du prêt. A la même époque saint Thomas refusait formellement toute réparation du manque à gagner déterminé par le montant concédé en prêt (*Summa theologica*, IIa IIae, q. 78, a. 2, ad 5um). Pour saint Thomas, l'intérêt était le paiement d'un manque à gagner probable, donc non-réel: l'intérêt était donc illicite, un peu comme la vente d'une licorne. Un changement du statut des choses probables pourra contribuer à modifier cette position: pour Scot, les choses probables sont non-existantes, mais elles sont quand même réelles. Mais même un nominaliste comme Olivi ne peut accepter la position de saint Thomas, tout simplement à cause de son excès d'abstraction et de son incapacité à comprendre l'esprit de l'échange commerciale, visée ultime de l'approche franciscaine, visant toujours à comprendre les hommes plutôt qu'à leur dicter ce qui est mieux. Olivi affirme que le manque à gagner du préteur doit être compensé par un intérêt payé au moment de la restitution du prêt si et seulement si le préteur avait vraiment envisagé d'utiliser l'argent pour la suite prêté dans une entreprise commerciale. L'intérêt est en ce cas là une *valor superadiunctus* – une valeur survenante, et le gain éventuel est assuré au préteur[34]; le capital est ici défini comme la *seminalem rationem lucrosi* – la cause originaire du gain, et l'argent prêté est plus qu'un ensemble de monnaies, il est un capital voué en soi – par la volonté de son possesseur – à produire un gain. Duns Scot, plutôt que de parler d'une stérilité de l'argent (argument classique, l'argent se consomme comme le pain à la limite), parle de la nécessité de coupler l'argent au travail et aux capacités, de manière à ce qu'il puisse produire son utilité. La manipulation licite de l'argent est celle de l'argent en tant que capital: un vignoble produit quelque chose même mal travaillé, en revanche l'argent sans un travail soigné ne peut rien produire, sauf en violation de la justice (*Reportata parisiensia*, IV, d. 15, q. 4, n. 26). La manipulation financière de l'argent est moralement inacceptable, en revanche la manipulation capitaliste de l'argent est moralement acceptable. La volonté de défendre la séparabilité de l'usage (sans droit) de la propriété (ou tout autre droit juridique) a amené les franciscains à comprendre d'une façon nouvelle la notion classique de stérilité de l'argent. Finalement, pour défendre leur style de vie de 'rien avoir' ils ont fait émerger la notion d'argent-capital et ils en ont justifié la licité à défaut de tout autre usage.

---

34 Giacomo Todeschini a édité le *Tractatus de emptionis et venditionibus, de usuris, de restitutionibus*, d'Olivi à Rome en 1980, sous le titre *Un trattato di economia politica francescana* (voir à page 85).

L'argent est un fait institutionnel: il n'a pas la même réalité qu'une chaise (la pièce de monnaie ou les billets-papier ne sont pas de l'argent, ils représentent l'argent), mais l'argent est une réalité sociale (notamment au vingtième siècle où triomphe le Management). Les franciscains, par leur analyse de l'argent, proposent de considérer que l'argent-capital est un fait qu'il vaut la peine de façonner par la normativité sociale, grâce à la volonté pouvant constituer son ontologie, tandis que l'argent-financier est un fait qu'il ne faut pas façonner, il faut en revanche l'évacuer de la normativité sociale grâce à une volition contraire.

D'autres auteurs franciscains ne développent pas la même notion complète d'argent-capital: par exemple, Alexandre d'Alexandrie (mort en 1314) dans son traité *De Usuris* (écrit en 1302)[35] limite la notion de *lucrum cessans* à celle d'indemnisation, car pour lui il n'y a que le défaut de paiement à la date préétablie pour la restitution du prêt qui peut faire partir le droit à une réparation pour le manque à gagner. Évidemment, cette conception est débitrice d'une vision de l'illicéité de tout intérêt, sauf à le requalifier de dédommagement dans le cadre de la responsabilité contractuelle. Donc, la concession du prêt ne peut faire partir le droit à la compensation pour le manque à gagner, car il ne s'agit pas d'un acte illicite; en revanche, le défaut de paiement est un acte illicite, donc on peut songer à la compensation du manque à gagner. La notion d'argent-capital n'a pas la même centralité chez Alexandre que chez Olivi ou Duns Scot, car il accepte explicitement la notion de stérilité de l'argent, complètement mise dans l'ombre par Olivi et Scot. Alexandre d'Alexandrie peut justifier la pratique de la lettre de change, à savoir l'outil des changeurs d'argent d'une devise à l'autre (de Roover a proposé une histoire de cet outil économique au Moyen

---

35 A.-M. Hamelin (éd.), *Un Traité de morale économique au XIVe siècle. Le Tractatus de usuris de maître Alexandre d'Alexandrie*

Âge dans *L'évolution de la lettre de change*)[36], et sa position est consacrée par la *Summa astesana*, véritable *vulgata*, opinion très majoritaire, de la pensée normative au début du quatorzième siècle. En dépit du fait que la tradition chrétienne n'aimait pas un métier qui transformait une devise dans une autre en tirant un profit substantiel, Alexandre conserve le principe de la stérilité de l'argent et affirme tranquillement que l'Église a toujours approuvé le métier de changeur de monnaie. Mais il ne s'agit pas d'un prêt pour lui, il s'agit en revanche d'une vente, ou à la limite d'un troc, notamment car le paiement est immédiat, donc il n'y a pas de spéculation sur le temps-délai: il n'y a pas que l'argent qui soit stérile, il y a aussi le temps. Le changeur achète des monnaies-pièces contre d'autre monnaies-pièces d'une autre espèce. Peut-être qu'Alexandre a eu connaissance des stratégies utilisées dans le monde juif pour justifier la pratique de la lettre de change, mais il convient de souligner que la doctrine rabbinique a toujours suivi une différence entre des rapports commerciaux personnels et de rapports commerciaux impersonnels. En effet, ce qui dérangeait l'approche rabbinique n'était pas l'achat-vente de devises – en tant que rapport direct entre vendeur et acheteur, mais l'existence d'un titre de crédit autorisant le porteur (sans précision de son identité) à encaisser chez un autre sujet (sans précision spécifique de son identité, par exemple un banquier lambda à la foire d'automne de Troyes) une certaine quantité de monnaies-pièces dans un pays différent de celui où un autre sujet lui a délivré ce titre de crédit en échange d'une quantité de monnaie-pièces d'une autre devise.

Le prêt est en effet considéré par Alexandre à l'instar de la tradition plus ancienne de l'Église comme absolument gratuit, mais toute autre opération différente peut être

---

(Analeca mediaevalia Namurcensia, 14), Louvain 1962.

36 R. de Roover, *L'évolution de la lettre de change: XIVe-XVIIIe siècles*, Paris 1953.

licitement rémunéré, car chaque travailleur mérite son salaire. C'est dans cette espace que l'ancien de la tradition catholique trouve la possibilité de faire éclore le nouveau concept de capital, alimenté par l'anthropologie franciscaine. Or, comment se faisait-il que le prêt devait être absolument gratuit? Il faut ici comprendre l'argent en tant qu'ensemble de pièces de monnaie, considérées comme des objets qui tirent leur valeur de leur consommation (comme une poire), de manière à ce que le prêt d'une chose consommable renvoie à la restitution d'une chose consommable équivalente sans être la même (en l'usant, la chose consommable prêté a disparue). Tandis que la charrue (chose inconsommable) prêtée peut être louée, la chose consomptible ne peut pas être louée, car la chose elle-même ne peut pas être rendue après usage, mais seulement par équivalent. En effet, la *Summa astesana*, un recueil visant à former les confesseurs dans leur pratique datant entre 1314 et 1317, le dit explicitement quand parle de l'argent prêté (contrat de *mutuum*) comme de *moneta* – monnaie, à savoir *pecunia numerata* – pièces d'argent (III, 10, 2). Un vocabulaire pareil permet de faire la différence entre le prêt qui ne concerne que les pièces en tant que telles – et qui par ailleurs n'a aucune importance commerciale, et toute autre opération commerciale concernant l'argent-capital, où le principe de la stérilité de l'argent ou du temps ne marchent pas car les pièces de monnaie ne sont pas l'objet de l'analyse. Évidemment, le contrat de société est un moyen d'évacuer toute soupçon d'illicéité à l'égard d'une activité commerciale où un sujet apporte l'argent et un autre le travail: même la *Summa astesana*, beaucoup plus prudente d'Olivi ou Scot dans la mise à l'écart des considérations les plus moralistes contre la pratique commerciale des intérêts, reconnaît la pleine licéité d'un contrat de société où les apports sont les plus différents parmi les participants (III, 12). Les partages des avantages et des risques rend légitime un rapport qui sous la forme du prêt à intérêt serait simplement usuraire.

Alexandre d'Alexandrie, source de la *Summa astesana* est repris massivement par des traités franciscains au quinzième siècle comme le *Tractatus de Restitutionibus* de François de Platea, avait déjà précisé que toute forme de partage de la contribution à l'activité sociale (1 – l'un donne le capital, l'autre le travail; 2 – l'un et l'autre donnent et le capital et le travail; 3 – l'un donne le capital et le travail, l'autre confère ou le capital ou le travail) est une forme équitable de l'activité économique. Ici la réflexion franciscaine rejoint et justifie la pratique du contrat de *commenda*, une forme de contrat développée dans le domaine des transports maritimes, notamment dans la ville communale de Gênes où le mot *commenda* devient synonyme de bourse des affaires maritimes. Il s'agit d'une relation où le prêteur concède au transporteur par mer un capital sans assumer aucune responsabilité à l'égard des tiers (par exemple, vis-à-vis de l'acheteur de la marchandise livrée avec un défaut de qualité) mais en partageant les risques et les avantages entre fournisseur du capital et agents commerciaux.

On est amené à penser que la réflexion franciscaine a d'une part suivi les développements de l'activité commerciale méditerranéenne des grandes villes communales italiennes comme Gênes et Venise ayant interagi avec les pratiques des populations orientales, islamisées – plus ou moins – et judaïques. Mais d'autre part, elle a aussi contribué à faire préférer la *commenda* à d'autres formes contractuelles en indiquant aux marchands chrétiens qu'il s'agissait d'un rapport licite à préférer aux autres usuraires. En se débarrassant de cette idée patristique de la stérilité de l'argent (en tant que monnaie), pour se concentrer sur l'association argent-travail-capacités, le panorama intellectuel du catholicisme s'actualise avec les réalités sociales de l'époque, tout en restant fidèle à sa textualité dogmatique de la croyance centraliste du Père absolu. Par exemple, on arrive à justifier les obligations étatiques, très courantes dans des villes communales comme Gênes ou Venise, sans contorsions mentales visant à les requalifier comme étant autre chose qu'un prêt. Alexandre d'Alexandrie devait les qualifier d'opérations d'achat-vente du 'droit au remboursement' ou de dépôt ou encore de contrat de société, afin de pouvoir les approuver, au niveau privé comme au niveau public sans trop de distinctions, notamment dans la forme de rentes viagères, un peu comme l'assurance-vie d'aujourd'hui (avant lui, le franciscain Richard de Mediaville, *Quodlibet*, II, 23, emploie la même argumentation). En revanche, la notion d'argent-capital, reprise par ailleurs par le frère mineur Jean de Saxe (ou d'Erfurt, mort en 1325) dans sa *Tabula utriusque juris* – véritable encyclopédie normative pour les confesseurs – , conduit à qualifier ces obligations finançant la dette publique comme des investissements en capital pour le bien commun, celui-ci était bien différencié du bien individuel de chacun. Pour souligner l'importance de ces obligations, il convient de rappeler avec Jacques Heers que la dette publique à Gênes du quatorzième au quinzième siècle était intégralement gérée par les individus achetant les parties des *comperes*, les obligations finançant les opérations d'économie publique.

Dans la perspective de souligner l'utilité sociale des commerçants, la manipulation de l'argent-capital n'est plus conçue comme visant l'obtention du superflu, elle est en revanche la condition de la satisfaction d'un besoin primaire d'une communauté. Les marchands ne sont pas du tout nécessaires pour une communauté d'ermites, mais ils le sont pour une communauté urbaine. Évidemment, le discours des Pères de l'Église doit être mise à jour à l'époque des villes communales médiévales. Il s'agit d'une nouvelle conception de la vie économique dépourvue de tout moralisme: le marchand n'est pas consciemment au service de la communauté, il produit un avantage à la communauté en réalisant son intérêt individuel. Mais elle est aussi ancrée profondément dans une conception en même temps théologique et anthropologique de la normativité humaine, beaucoup plus propre à la mouvance franciscaine qu'à la culture ecclésiastique en général. Un élève de Duns Scot, François de Meyronnes, produit une brève mais fulgurante apologie de l'activité mercantile. Il le fait presque en passant, dans son commentaire au Sentences traitant du sacrement de la pénitence. Il invoque à plusieurs reprises l'utilité de la communauté (*utilitate rei publice*) assurée par l'activité mercantile (IV, d. 16, q. 3), dont il affirme la licéité tout d'abord par le droit naturel et ensuite par le droit divin. En effet, l'activité commerciale permet de dépasser les bornes de la localisation géographique des ressources et garantie les besoins fondamentaux des hommes (IV, d. 16, q. 4), elle peut aussi assurer le salut éternel en étant exercée par le respect de la justice commutative. Meyronnes utilise le mot *usura* sans aucune connotation négative, en le rendant équivalent à notre 'intérêt': comme le disaient les canonistes tels que Raymond de Peñafort, son commentateur Guillaume de Rennes, ou encore le cardinal Hostiensis, et comme l'avaient répété Olivi et Scot, le contrat prévoyant des intérêts dès le départ est licite. Le pacte valable selon les dues formes n'empêche nullement la rémunération de l'argent prêté. L'argent n'est pas du tout stérile, et même le temps n'a pas à être ainsi qualifié sans confusion: l'argent est *multum utilis*, notamment associé à l'*industria humana* – l'argent-capital n'est pas simplement justifié, Meyronnes il en fait l'apologie. Il dit même que la règle d'or évangélique justifie l'usure, car chacun veut recevoir des prêts à intérêt, donc pratiquer l'usure est une activité licite. Par ce renversement de l'opinion patristique Meyronnes exerce une ironie typiquement scotiste, mais il se débarrasse aussi du passage de l'Évangile de Luc (6, 30), employé pendant des siècles pour affirmer la gratuité absolue de tout prêt. Meyronnes, au contraire, interprète le même passage en relation aux seuls biens spirituels, et il n'y voit aucune condamnation des pratiques commerciales à intérêt. Nous ne pouvons pas ranger Meyronnes comme un franciscain standard, mais sa position presque anarco-capitaliste à la manière de Robert Nozick montre comment un franciscain avec le goût de l'extrémisme intellectuel pouvait produire une justification de l'activité capitaliste extrêmement poussée, tandis que la culture ecclésiastique dans son intégralité devait combattre pendant des siècles les vestiges moralistes de la Patristique dans le domaine économique, pour s'en débarrasser finalement avec l'ouvrage du penseur scolastique du seizième siècle, Léonard Lessius (1554-1623).

En effet, par la notion d'une sphère juridique divine supérieure à toute autre sphère juridique humaine, et par une anthropologie philosophique fondée sur la rupture essentielle introduite par le péché originel dans la nature humaine, les frères mineurs se donnent les moyens d'étudier les phénomènes de la vie mondaine (dans l'état de nature déchue) sans leur donner une justification positive autonome. Leur travail se dégage et se déploie de façon précise car il les concerne directement: l'utilité sociale de la richesse concerne les hommes ayant choisi de vivre selon les lois du monde, parmi lesquelles ils trouvent leur espace du plaisir du luxe et de la gourmandise, le plaisir de l'accumulation des propriétés foncières et de l'honneur social. Les franciscains, eux, refusent ces règles du jeu, donc ne doivent pas faire l'effort de s'en détacher pour mieux en comprendre les rouages. Tandis que le moraliste catholique ne peut pas vraiment comprendre la machinerie économique car il veut moraliser l'homme le cas échéant au prix de la destruction de cette machinerie, les franciscains n'ont pas l'intention de moraliser ces rouages, car il va de soi que l'homme choisissant la perfection évangélique doit refuser ces rouages mondains. Mais il s'agit là de l'issu d'un vœu solennel engageant à un changement de statut anthropologique, tandis que l'homme ordinaire, tout en ayant le salut éternel comme but ultime, n'est pas du tout engagé à ce changement anthropologique. Evidemment, le fait de l'obtenir est un bien capital, mais il n'y a que les franciscains à s'être engagés à réaliser immédiatement un pareil changement. Les moralistes catholiques peuvent bien proposer un modèle de conception de l'usage de la richesse, c'est bien la doctrine sociale de l'Église: la misère empêche la satisfaction des besoins fondamentaux, le luxe empêche le salut de l'âme car il détourne de la vertu. Donc, pas de misère, pas de luxe; on pourrait dire que la condition idéale pour cette doctrine est une modeste aisance, éloignant les soucis contraignants qui touchent celui qui est pauvre (il ne dispose nullement du superflu) et éloignant aussi les tentations du luxe, ancrant l'homme à la recherche du bien matériel comme fin en soi. Or, cet enseignement n'est pas une théorie économique, car elle ne dit pas comment on obtient le bien-être collectif, à savoir la modeste aisance de chacun: il s'agit d'un modèle adressé au riche pour le détourner du matérialisme éthique et au pauvre pour viser la prévoyance du demain et non pas la recherche du simple plaisir matériel. Les franciscains ne disent pas des choses différentes. Ils se proposent en plus de ne pas accepter les règles mondaines de la société marquée par le péché originel, et finalement de vivre la perfection évangélique. En revanche, l'homme vivant dans le monde renonce *a priori* à la perfection évangélique, mais il doit quand même aspirer à la rencontre avec Dieu. En conseillant l'homme qui n'est pas capable d'abandonner les règles mondaines, les franciscains essayent de comprendre la machinerie économique, afin de lui montrer la route pour rejoindre Dieu après la mort. Il est vrai, comme le répètent les 'parfaits', qu'on ne peut pas servir Dieu et Mammon, à savoir l'argent, mais Jésus Christ a exhorté l'homme à utiliser les ressources du monde pour gagner la vie éternelle. Il n'y a aucun paradoxe dans le fait que les partisans de la pauvreté absolue aient produit une théorie de l'utilité sociale de l'activité économique capitaliste. Au contraire, c'est justement en tant que détaché *a priori* par choix (choix normatif, n'empêchant pas à ce franciscain-là d'être gourmand ou avide en violation de ses voeux) que le frère mineur a pu s'intéresser à l'activité économique sans parler de ses passions apparement en forme impersonnelle. Aujourd'hui, certains reprochent à l'Église catholique d'enseigner une morale sexuelle et familiale tandis que ses ministres, célibataires, n'ont aucune expérience du sexe et de la famille. Ces mêmes personnes pourront voir dans la contribution franciscaine à la pensée capitaliste un paradoxe. Ces mêmes personnes sont beaucoup plus proches du nominalisme matérialiste d'Engels et de Marx qu'à une doctrine de la valeur objective de la philosophie réaliste. En effet, pour évaluer le gâteau, il faut le goûter: or, la morale humaine est-elle formellement équivalente à un gâteau? Le champion du matérialisme Feuerbach le croyait, les franciscains pas du tout. En réalité, comme le dit l'historien du christianisme médiéval Lester Little, il est vrai que «des frères désargentés justifièrent le commerce et l'acquisition d'argent»[37]: il convient de souligner que «les hommes cherchent toujours une solution aux problèmes qui les tourmentent et il le font de diverses façons qui ne sont toutes raisonnables ni mêmes conscientes» – j'ajoute que très souvent les contraintes de la pensée produisent des contributions 'involontaires' à la façon de penser et de dire le monde autour de nous. Little instaure une comparaison et une différence entre les moines et les franciscains: tous les deux «cherchaient à suivre le Christ qui, de riche, s'est fait pauvre (2 Cor. 8, 9). Mais, étant donné que 'riche' et 'pauvre' avaient des significations différentes dans les deux sociétés différentes, rurale et urbaine, les deux formes de pauvreté volontaire qui en sont sorties furent inévitablement différentes l'une de l'autre. Les moines ont d'abord rejeté, puis transformé et finalement sanctifié la force, et les frères

---

37 L. Little, 'L'utilité sociale de la pauvreté volontaire', in M. Mollat (éd.), *L'histoire de la pauvreté*, Paris 1974.

en firent autant à l'égard de l'argent». Dire que les frères mineurs ont sanctifié l'argent est tout à fait une suggestion trompeuse, mais en le comprenant comme une boutade elle montre qu'il n'y a aucun paradoxe dans la contribution des franciscains aux fondements du capitalisme.

Finalement, les outils théoriques du capitalisme sont déjà ainsi affinés dans un contexte d'éthique catholique, bien avant la Réforme protestante. Il s'agit par exemple de la différence entre une richesse socialement utile et une richesse socialement stérile: les franciscains élaborent une notion de bien commun très concrète, absolument pas abstraite, et le bien-être économique tombe dans cette réflexion concernant la sphère du bien commun. Tandis que la détermination du juste prix dans le discours aristotélicien et thomiste de proportionnalité mathématique et d'analogie peut se révéler assez lointain des pratiques effectives des sujets économiques, même le discours théorique de Duns Scot est assez concret. Je dis que le discours aristotélico-thomiste *peut* se révéler détourné de la pratique courante des acteurs économique, car on peut toujours en tirer une interprétation riche de signification économique. Notamment, Raymond De Roover, s'opposant à la thèse selon laquelle pour saint Thomas et plus généralement pour la pensée médiévale le juste prix est un prix idéal, soutient que le juste prix n'est rien d'autre que le prix du marché pour les penseurs scolastiques.[38] Le catholique De Roover est ici en train de défendre la pertinence de la philosophie scolastique, conçue comme un bloc unitaire avec très peu de nuances, pour l'histoire de la réflexion économique occidentale. Partageant l'avis d'un grande économiste comme Schumpeter, il peut affirmer que «Thomas considérait comme juste prix le prix courant du marché». Il n'y a pas de passage explicite de saint Thomas, mais la thèse découle de sa réflexion autour de la justice. Or, ce qui

---

38 R. de Roover, *La pensée économique des scolastiques: doctrines et méthodes*, Montréal 1971.

nous importe de souligner, c'est que la scolastique n'est pas un bloc unitaire, car il y a une philosophie chrétienne aristotélisante et intellectualiste parallèlement à une philosophie chrétienne méfiante envers Aristote et volontariste. Dans le cadre de cette dernière, l'équivalence entre le juste prix et le prix de revient est tout à fait explicite, car la volonté est le fondement ontologique des actes humains, à savoir qu'elle leur confère une existence absolument réelle. Donc, sans vouloir rentrer dans le débat thomiste sur la meilleure interprétation de saint Thomas, il convient de souligner qu'une philosophie volontariste, comme la philosophie franciscaine, fournit les meilleurs instruments pour fonder la licéité des pratiques commerciales en expansion au treizième siècle, sans pour autant renoncer à séparer par une rigueur moraliste l'activité économique licite de celle illicite. Critique à l'égard de saint Thomas[39], Scot fonde le juste prix, librement déterminé par les acteurs de l'échange, dans la loi de nature «fait aux autre ce que tu veux les autres faisant à toi»[40], de manière à ce que chacun dans l'échange 'donne' à l'autre une partie de la valeur subjective de l'objet échangé. Scot utilise le mot latin *donatio*, mais il ne s'agit pas d'une donation au sens d'un cadeau, il s'agit de la juste rétribution du travail et des capacités de soi-même et de l'autre impliqués dans l'échange. Celui qui vend un bien 'donne' son travail et ses capacités ayant permis la formation du bien, celui qui achète 'donne' – payant par l'argent disponible en liquidité – le capital symbolisant son travail et ses capacités. Les évaluations des différentes capacités de travail de l'un et de l'autre peuvent être contrastées, et le prix retenu n'est que le point d'équilibre des évaluations des sujets concernés. Il s'agit de la composition des volontés des acteurs du marché, le lieu de l'échange, et non pas de l'issu de formules mathématiques touchant aux

---

39 Cf. la critique de Scot à une approche mathématicienne au juste prix, *Opus oxoniense*, IV, d. 15, q. 2, n. 15.
40 Cf. *Opus oxoniense*, IV, d. 15, q. 2, n. 15.

quantités matérielles en jeu. Le discours du franciscain Scot est ce qu'on peut imaginer comme étant le plus lointain de toute forme de marxisme économique, et plus généralement de toute forme d'objectivisme et de déterminisme social.

'In the last days at the end of the world': Roger Bacon and the Reform of Christendom

Amanda Power

(The University of Sheffield)

The 1250s were heady and difficult years for the Franciscan order. To its eschatologically-minded visionaries, their age was the dark evening of human history when every kind of crisis and danger would beset a Christendom lying under the shadow of Antichrist's imminence. Yet contained within this sense of impending doom was the hope that made the whole vast world shimmer with the beckoning mirage of evangelical triumphs.[1] From their earliest days, the Franciscans had felt acutely conscious of having a unique role to play in Christian society based on their dedication to apostolic poverty and their promotion of spiritual reform and renewal. Their sense of purpose evolved rapidly as the order expanded, produced its own histories and propaganda, and became more closely identified with the papacy. It took a markedly eschatological direction in some circles through the 1240s and more generally through the order under the leadership of John of Parma (1247-57), who was much influenced by the prophetic writings of Joachim of Fiore.[2]

---

1 This century has been identified as one of outstanding optimism about the prospect of conversion, especially of Muslims, and especially among Franciscans and Dominicans. See R.W. Southern, *Western Views of Islam in the Middle Ages*, Cambridge (Mass.) 1962; B.Z. Kedar, *Crusade and Mission: European Approaches towards the Muslims*, New Jersey 1984; E.R. Daniel, *The Franciscan Concept of Mission in the High Middle Ages*, Kentucky 1975.

2 On these developments see D. Burr, *The Spiritual Franciscans: From Protest to Persecution in the Century after Saint Francis*, Pennsylvania State University 2001, 1-41. On propaganda see A. Power, 'Franciscan Advice to the Papacy', *History Compass*, 5.5 (2007), 1550-75.

It had long been thought that two 'witnesses' [Revelation 11] would come forth to proselytise in the time of Antichrist. In the eleventh century, an increasingly important role was assigned to them, most influentially by Adso of Montier-en-Der, who wrote: 'they will defend the faithful of God against the attack of Antichrist with divine weapons and will instruct, comfort and prepare the elect for war, by teaching and preaching'.[3] From the late twelfth century, these 'spiritual men' were interpreted in a Joachite light, not as two individuals, but as two religious orders. By the mid-thirteenth century, some people were hypothesising that these orders were already active in the world as the Franciscans and Dominicans.[4] This apocalyptic role was made virtually official when, in 1255, John of Parma and the Dominican minister general, Humbert of Romans, issued a joint encyclical that attempted, among other things, to heal the breaches between the two orders. 'In the last days at the end of the world,' they announced, Christ: 'raised up our two orders in the ministry of salvation, calling many to himself and enriching them with celestial gifts... These orders are – to speak to God's glory and not our own – two great luminaries which by celestial light shines upon and ministers to those sitting in darkness and the shadow of death.'[5]

---

3 *Qui contra impetum Antichristi fideles Dei diuinis armis premunient et instruent eos et confortabunt et preparabunt electos ad bellum, docentes et predicantes*, Adso Dervensis, 'Epistola adsonis monachi ad gerbergam reginam de ortu et tempore antichristi' in *De ortu et tempore antichristi necnon et tractatus qui ab eo depenunt*, ed. D. Verhelst (CCCM, 45), Turnhout 1976, 27-8.

4 See M. Reeves, *The Influence of Prophecy in the Later Middle Ages: A Study in Joachimism*, Oxford 1969, 133-90; Eadem, 'Opponents of Antichrist: A Medieval Perception', *Consilium*, 200 (1988), 105-8. For the case that only some among those Franciscans interested in the apocalypse were specifically Joachite in their interpretations, see B. Roest, 'Franciscan Commentaries on the Apocalypse' in: M. Wilks (ed.), *Prophecy and Eschatology* (Studies in Church History, Subsidia, 10), Oxford, 1994, 29-37.

5 'The joint encyclical of 1255' in: B. McGinn, *Visions of the End: Apocalyptic Traditions in the Middle Ages* (Records of Civilisation: Sources and Studies, 96), New York 1998, 164. For the full text see L. Wadding (ed.), *Annales minorum*, 30 vols., Quaracchi 1931-1951, III, 380-1. On the Dominican involvement see: E.T.

These were strong and controversial assertions of a kind that are generally only articulated publicly in times of extreme strain and polemical combat.[6] In this case, a complex political situation lay behind and provoked their publication. Growing internal dissensions among the Franciscans, rivalry between the two orders and bitter, damaging conflicts with the secular clergy made the world a demanding and uncertain place for its would-be saviours. The most dangerous and complicated clashes of the decade were with a powerful alliance of secular clergy and university masters in the city of Paris who threatened to discredit both orders and the whole concept of apostolic mendicancy and poverty.[7] The main protagonists on both sides made escalating use of apocalyptic rhetoric, and some of them came to grief when they overstepped the limits that the papacy would tolerate and found themselves condemned for heresy. Amid this debacle, John of Parma was forced to stand down and the order took steps to disassociate itself from the most controversial trends in eschatological thinking.[8] One of the main tasks of Bonaventure, who became the new Minister General, was to create and maintain a *via media* between conflicting interpretations of the Franciscan Rule. Although vocal advocates of radical Joachite perspectives were suppressed, society was saturated in

---

Brett, *Humbert of Romans: His Life and Views of Thirteenth-Century Society* (Studies and Texts, 67), Toronto 1984 26-8.

6   The same sort of rhetoric was, for example, employed on both sides during the papal-imperial conflicts of the preceding decades. R.K. Emmerson / R.B. Herzman, *The Apocalyptic Imagination in Medieval Literature* (Middle Ages Series), Philadelphia 1992, 32-3.

7   B. Roest, *A History of Franciscan Education (c. 1210-1517)* (Education and Society in the Middle Ages and Renaissance, 2), Leiden 2000, 51-8; Brett, *Humbert of Romans* (cf. note 5), 12-40; Y.M. Congar, 'Aspects ecclésiologiques de la querelle entre mendiants et séculiers dans la seconde moitié du XIIIe siècle et le début du XIVe', *Archives d'histoire doctrinale et littéraire du Moyen Âge* 28 (1961), 35-151.

8   On the scandal of the *Liber introductorius in evangelium aeternum*, which caused the condemnation and its outcome, see: D. Burr, *Olivi's Peaceable Kingdom: A Reading of the Apocalypse Commentary*, Philadelphia 1993, 14-21; Daniel, *Franciscan Concept of Mission* (cf. note 1), 76-82.

apocalyptic expectation, and many Franciscans continued to understand both history and their vocation in eschatological terms. Bonaventure himself reissued the 1255 encyclical in the year that he became Minister General and went on to produce the official biography of Francis, in which he identified the saint as the angel of the sixth seal.[9]

It was probably at some time between the two issues of this apocalyptic mission statement that an English scholar called Roger Bacon entered the Franciscan order.[10] Bacon is today one of the most famous medieval intellectuals, renowned for his much-discussed role in the development of science. Despite, or perhaps because of, this, aspects of Bacon's life and thought have not been entirely well-served by the ways in which he has been studied. In particular, his Franciscan vocation has been

---

9   Reeves called Bonaventure 'a Joachite *malgré lui*'. *Influence of Prophecy* (cf. note 4), 181. After J. Ratzinger's study, *Die Geschichtstheologie des heiligen Bonaventura*, Munich 1959, it was generally accepted that Bonaventure had been deeply influenced by Joachim's thought. See also Emmerson / Herzman, *Apocalyptic Imagination* (cf. note 6), ch. 2; G. LaNave, *Through Holiness to Wisdom: the Nature of Theology according to St. Bonaventure* (BSC, 76), Rome 2005.

10 The dating of this event rests on fragile evidence, but the consensus of historians puts it at ca. 1257. The most authoritative biographical studies of Bacon are: J. Hackett, 'Roger Bacon: his life, career and works', in: *Idem* (ed.), *Roger Bacon and the sciences: commemorative essays* (Studien und Texte zur Geistesgeschichte des Mittelalters, 57), Leiden 1997, 9-23; A.G. Molland, 'Roger Bacon', in: *Oxford Dictionary of National Biography* (2004); D.C. Lindberg, Introduction to *Roger Bacon's Philosophy of Nature: A Critical Edition, with English Translation, Introduction, and Notes, of* De multiplicatione specierum *and* De speculis comburentibus, Oxford 1983, updated in the Introduction to his *Roger Bacon and the Origins of Perspectiva in the Middle Ages: A Critical Edition and English translation of Bacon's* Perspectiva, Oxford 1996. Older, but still useful are: S.C. Easton, *Roger Bacon and His Search for a Universal Science: A Reconsideration of the Life and Work of Roger Bacon in the Light of His Own stated Purposes*, Oxford 1952 and T. Crowley, *Roger Bacon: the Problem of the Soul in his Philosophical Commentaries*, Louvain 1950.

underestimated and even overlooked.[11] This has had two important consequences. One is a certain difficulty in grasping Bacon's mind in its totality and in particular, the nature, effects and power of his spirituality. The other is a wariness in exploiting the very great value of his writings for shedding light on thirteenth-century society, especially as many historians are rightly conscious of the pitfalls into which their predecessors fell while using Bacon as a witness to his age.[12] In this article, I hope to address both by investigating his programme for the reform of learning in the specific context of the apocalyptic expectation that he repeatedly expressed.[13] The fact that his response to the threat of Antichrist was to suggest reform that was primarily practical and intellectual rather than moral reveals a great deal about how some Franciscans thought about their role in the Church during the crucial evolutionary period of the 1260s.

Bacon became a Franciscan when he was in his early forties. He had been educated in Oxford, where he was among the first to make a thorough study of the recently-translated philosophical and scientific works of Aristotle and his Muslim commentators. During the 1240s, he taught arts and natural philosophy at the

---

11 For a justification of these claims see: A. Power, 'A Mirror for Every Age: The Reputation of Roger Bacon', *English Historical Review* 121 (2006), 657-92.

12 Concerns about Bacon's reliability as a witness have their origin in the series of critical articles by L. Thorndike, initiated in his 'Roger Bacon and Experimental Method in the Middle Ages', *Philosophical Review* 23 (1914), 271-92.

13 The important links between apocalypticism, astrology and Bacon's wider programme have been considered recently in H. Carey, *Astrology and Antichrist in the Later Middle Ages*, Time and Eternity: the Medieval Discourse (International Medieval Research, 9) Turnhout 2003, 515-35; J. Hackett, 'Aristotle, *Astrologia*, and Controversy at the University of Paris (1266-1274)', in: J. Van Engen (ed.), *Learning Institutionalized: Teaching in the Medieval University* (Notre Dame Conferences in Medieval Studies, 9) Notre Dame 2000, 69-111; J. Hackett, 'Astrology and the Search for an Art and Science of Nature in the Thirteenth Century', in: G. Marchetti *et al* (eds.), *Ratio et Superstitio: Essays in Honour of Graziella Federiei Vescovini* (Textes et Études du Moyen Âge, 24) Louvain-la-Neuve 2003, 117-36.

University of Paris. Towards the end of that decade, when he was perhaps in his mid-thirties, he grew frustrated with the limitations of the curriculum and environment and abandoned the formal world of the university to devote himself exclusively to the pursuit of *sapientia* – wisdom. He spent the next twenty years of his life studying languages, especially Greek and Hebrew; various branches of mathematics including astronomy, astrology and geography; the science of optics; arcane and occult arts such as alchemy and forms of magic; the moral philosophy and rhetoric of the classical world, and much else.[14] It was during this period that he entered the order. He never, in his extant works, told the story of how he came to do so, but it was probably not a very surprising decision. There is some risk involved in tracing his spiritual development on the basis of his major works, which were all written after he had been a friar for some years.[15] Nevertheless, it is certainly the case that by this date, the Franciscans and Dominicans were increasingly ubiquitous and influential in Christian society and especially in the intellectual sphere. They had succeeded in creating a notional divide between those secular scholars who chiefly sought personal glory and therefore achieved little and the mendicants whose personal humility and virtue enabled them to touch higher truths.[16] The belief in a necessary and fundamental connection between moral and intellectual endeavour enabled both orders to take, on the

---

14 For his account of these years, see *Opus tertium*, in *Fr. Rogeri Bacon Opera Quaedam Hactenus Inedita*, ed. J. S. Brewer (RS, 15) London 1859), 59.

15 I have attempted to construct such a narrative in my forthcoming *Roger Bacon and the Crisis of Christendom*. For other attempts at explanation see: Daniel, *Franciscan Concept of Mission* (cf. note 1), 66, 55-7; Lindberg, *Roger Bacon's Philosophy of Nature* (cf. note 10), xx; Lindberg, *Roger Bacon and the Origins of* Perspectiva (cf. note 10), xviii; Crowley, *Roger Bacon* (cf. note 10), 34-42, 67-71; Easton, *Roger Bacon and His Search* (cf. note 10), 124-6.

16 Evidence of the success of this conceptualisation – which had its roots in antiquity – can be found in the extensive recruitment among university masters by preachers using such arguments. See for example those of Jordan of Saxony, edited in A.G. Little / D. Douie, 'Three Sermons of Friar Jordan of Saxony, the Successor of St. Dominic, Preached in England, A. D. 1229', *English Historical Review* 54 (1939), 1-19.

whole, a practical view of the roles of *scientia* and *sapientia* in their wider mission of *renovatio*. These concepts were absolutely central to Bacon's own view of learning and can, I think, be assumed to have predated and therefore played a role in his decision to enter the order.[17]

Despite the apparently secular and even unorthodox nature of many of the subjects that he had devoted his life to studying, he conceived them to be organic parts of the divine wisdom unfolded by God through the ages. '[O]ne God has given the whole of wisdom to one world, for a single purpose,' he wrote, 'for wisdom is the way to salvation. Every consideration of man that is not to do with salvation is full of blindness and leads in the end to the blackness of hell'.[18] These remarks should not be read in isolation from the difficult, complex and evolving debate about education in the order, but they certainly indicate that he shared the fundamental ideas of Bonaventure and other leading Franciscans even if his was to some extent a novel voice.[19] The main common ground among those Franciscans committed to education was that the only possible justification for scholarship, as for anything else in life, was to assist the individual in serving the needs of Christendom and finding personal salvation. The

---

17 Bacon had admired since boyhood the moral philosophy of antiquity, which emphasised the connection between virtue and philosophy, and the application of morality to civic life. *Rogeri Baconis, Moralis Philosophia*, ed. E. Massa (Thesaurus mundi), Turin 1953 [hereafter *MP*], III.v.proemium, 133.

18 Roger Bacon, *Opus maius*, ed. J.H. Bridges, 3 vols., Oxford 1897 [hereafter *OM*], VII.iv, 2:376-7, II.1, 3:36. *ab uno Deo data est tota sapientia et uni mundo, et propter finem unum ... sed sapientia est via in salutem. Omnis enim consideratio hominis, quae non est salutaris, est plena caecitate, ac ad finalem inferni deducit caliginem.*

19 On the disputes about the place of the arts in mendicant *studia* see Roest, *A History of Franciscan Education* (cf. note 7), esp. 137-52 and M.M. Mulchahey, *"First the Bow is Bent in Study..." Dominican Education Before 1350* (Studies and Texts, 132), Toronto 1998, esp. 219-77. On Bacon and Bonaventure specifically, see: C. Bérubé, *De la philosophie à la sagesse chez St Bonaventure et Roger Bacon* (BSC, 26), Rome 1976; C. Bérubé, 'Le dialogue de S. Bonaventure et de Roger Bacon', *CF* 39 (1969), 59-103.

Church had wide responsibilities in a time when the rising Mongol empire and a broadening strategy in the conflict with Islam led to both the expansion of horizons and opportunities, and multiple threats to Christian security. Bacon did not merely share the views of his brothers in this regard, but he went further and argued that new types of knowledge were required to meet new demands. Essential areas of scholarship in which he was expert were being neglected because they seemed unorthodox, yet the Church could simply not afford to go on ignoring them.

In July 1266, Bacon had the opportunity to put these opinions to the highest authority in Christendom when, as a result of some prior exchanges, Pope Clement IV wrote to him asking him to explain: 'the remedies that you think we should adopt to address that great danger which you communicated to me on a recent occasion'.[20] In his main response, the *Opus maius*, he covered a range of areas in which he thought reform was necessary. His intention was to inform Clement about new developments in Latin scholarship – chiefly those resulting from the recent, rich fertilisation by Greek and Arabic learning – and to persuade the Pope of their utility to the Church. Running through the whole was his concern with the impending appearance of Antichrist and the sort of knowledge that would be required by religious men for the spiritual fortification and practical defence of the souls of the faithful during the subsequent time of tribulation.

Bacon's expectations of Antichrist appear to have been conventional. '[I]t is an article of faith,' he wrote, 'that one should believe that Antichrist will come'.[21] The salient points of this 'article of faith' were that the coming of Antichrist was inevitable and probably imminent. His appearance would be heralded by a terrifying onslaught of savage armies, unleashed

---

20 *Et per tuas nobis declares litteras quae tibi videntur adhibenda remedia circa illa, quae nuper occasione tanti discriminis intimasti, Fr. Rogeri Bacon Opera*, ed. Brewer (cf. note 14) 1. The early contact between Bacon and Clement remains obscure, but the available evidence is thoroughly scrutinised in E. Massa, *Ruggero Bacone: etica e poetica nella storia dell''Opus maius'* (Uomini e dottrine, 3), Rome 1955.

21 *Ideo annexum articulis fidei est, quod credatur Antichristus venturus. MP* (cf. note 17), I.3 (6), 15-16.

from long centuries of imprisonment by Alexander the Great in the distant wildernesses of the world. After his arrival among Christians, Antichrist would use every possible weapon at his disposal to destroy their faith. Particularly dangerous was his capacity to seduce the faithful with false miracles and other illusions and to exercise a hypnotic power over human minds. Although his reign would be short, he would bring destruction and despair to Christianity.[22] Bacon thought carefully about each element of this complex threat, considering how best to prepare and protect Christian society during every stage of Antichrist's campaign.

To begin with, the coming of Antichrist was certain, but the date and the direction from which he would appear were unknown. It was vital to discover them as nearly as possible, and there were a number of ways in which this might be done. 'I do not want to sound as though I am above myself,' he wrote cautiously, 'but I know that if the Church would look again at the sacred text and holy prophecies, as well as the prophecies of the Sibyl, Merlin, Aquila, Seston, Joachim [of Fiore], and many others, as well as the histories and the books of philosophers and would command that the techniques of astronomy be considered, a sufficient suspicion or even a greater certainty about the time of Antichrist could be acquired'.[23] Despite St Augustine's discouraging remarks about trying to find exact dates for future events, Joachim had ushered in a new and very specific way of reading the Apocalypse which sought intimations of the end in current affairs and personalities. It seems that Franciscans who were interested in Joachite and other apocalyptic literature in

---

22 On medieval expectations of Antichrist see B. McGinn, *Antichrist: Two Thousand Years of the Human Fascination with Evil*, New York 2000.

23 *Nolo hic ponere os meum in coelum, sed scio quod si ecclesia vellet revolvere textum sacrum et prophetias sacras, atque prophetias Sibyllae, et Merlini et Aquiliae, et Sestonis, Joachim et multorum aliorum, insuper historias et libros philosophorum, atque juberet considerari vias astronomiae, inveniretur sufficiens suspicio vel magis certitudo de tempore Antichristi. OM* (cf. note 18) IV.iv.16, I, 268-9.

these decades were mainly concerned with discovering exactly this information.[24] Bacon himself felt that although many hints could be drawn from prophetic material, information was usually veiled in colourful, symbolic language or it was imprecise on the subject of dates which was why it needed to be combined with the second, more empirical, method for determining the pattern of future events: astronomy.

Astronomy, especially in the predictive form now called astrology, had always been regarded with considerable unease or downright hostility by Christians, as Bacon knew well. Nevertheless, he was convinced that it posed no risk if done responsibly with due regard for the exercise of free will and that the Latin West could not afford to reject the vast amount of information that it was capable of providing. Everything that was true had its origin in God, who had good reasons for sharing it. '[T]he sun rises on the wicked and the seas lie open to pirates,' pointed out Bacon, 'so how much more is God bound to give useful knowledge of things to the good!'[25] Not only did celestial bodies influence all sublunary activity in ways that could be explained mathematically, but God permitted their movements and configurations to reflect the unfolding of the great drama of salvation history. Careful observation of the heavens could therefore reveal past, present and future alike: 'for God has willed to order his affairs so that certain future events which he has foreseen or predestined can be shown to rational people by means of the planets'.[26]

---

24 *Sancti Aurelii Augustini, De civitate dei libri XI-XXII* (Aurelii Augustini Opera Pars 14.2. CCSL, 48), Turnhout 1955, XVIII.53; M.W. Bloomfield / M.E. Reeves, 'The Penetration of Joachism into Northern Europe', *Speculum* 29 (1954), 772-93.

25 *Nam et sceleratis sol oritur et pirates patent maria; quapropter longe magis Deus debet bonis utilem cognitionem rerum*, *OM* (cf. note 18) IV.iv.16, I, 286. See Carey, 'Astrology and Antichrist' (cf. note 13); P. Adamson, 'Abū Ma'šar, Al-Kindī and the Philosophical Defense of Astrology', *Recherches de Théologie et Philosophie médiévales* 69 (2002), 245-70.

26 *Voluit ergo Deus res suas sic ordinare, ut quaedam quae futura praeviderit vel praedestinaverit rationabilibus per planetas ostenderentur, OM* (cf. note 18), IV.iv.16, I, 267.

Knowledge obtained from the writings of *sapientes* and the study of the heavens needed to be further supplemented by close observation of what was going on in the wider world. It had long been thought that a particular sequence of events would usher in the Apocalypse. The first indication would be the destruction of Islam. Shortly afterwards, the ferocious tribes of the North – Gog and Magog – would emerge and ravage the whole world. Amid these tribulations, Antichrist himself would appear. Bacon pointed out that, at the time of writing: 'already the greater part of the Saracens has been destroyed by the Tartars together with the capital of their kingdom, which is Baldac [Baghdad], and the Caliph, who was just like our Pope'.[27]

The apparent impending doom of Islam was a sign reinforced by the possibility that the second part of the sequence might already have begun. Bacon was not alone in wondering whether the Mongols ought in fact to be identified with the tribes of Gog and Magog, 'due to issue forth in the days of Antichrist, who will first lay waste to the world and then will meet Antichrist and call him God of Gods'.[28] By this time, it was clear that it was the same people who had, within the last thirty years, so shockingly devastated the kingdoms along the north-eastern frontiers of Christendom and made such drastic inroads into the Islamic world. Recent events certainly seemed to fulfil the ancient prophecies, but Bacon remained cautious: 'since it is true that other races have in the past come forth from those places and have invaded the world as far south as the Holy Land, just as the

---

27 *Et jam major pars Saracenorum destructa est per Tartaros, et caput regni quod fuit Baldac, et Caliph qui fuit sicut papa eorum. OM* (cf. note 18), IV.iv.16, I, 266.

28 *Exitura in diebus Antichristi, qui mundum primo vastabunt et deinde obviabunt Antichristo, et vocabunt eum Deum Deorum, OM* (cf. note 18), IV.iv.16, I, 365. On Latin responses to the Mongol threat see: D. Bigalli, *I Tartari e l'Apocalisse: Ricerche sull' escatologia in Adamo Marsh e Ruggero Bacone*, Firenze 1971; G.A. Bezzola, *Die Mongolen in abendländischer Sicht, 1220-1270: ein Beitrag zur Frage der Völkerbegegnungen*, Munich 1974; J. Fried, 'Auf der Suche nach der Wirklichkeit: die Mongolen und die europäische Erfahrungswissenschaft im 13. Jahrhundert', *Historische Zeitschrift* 243 (1986), 287-332; P. Jackson, *The Mongols and the West, 1221-1410*, Harlow 2005.

Tartars are now doing ... therefore the activity of the Tartars is not sufficient to certify the time of the coming of Antichrist, but other things need to be considered'.[29] He particularly recommended the careful study of geography and detailed attention to all activity in the northern regions.[30] He was eager to emphasise the considerable range of knowledge upon which Christians ought to draw to evolve an early-warning system for the approach of Antichrist.

A greater preoccupation for Bacon was the fortification – physical and mental – of the Latin West against Antichrist during the two stages of his assault on Christians. The Church must consider ways to strengthen the defences of Christendom, focusing on the moment when Christians would find themselves faced with the armies of Antichrist on the battlefield. Bacon's priority here, as so often in his writing, was to come up with ways of avoiding actual confrontation and bloodshed by using advanced scientific methods: 'so that without a sword and without touching anyone, [our army] could destroy everyone who resists'.[31] His most famous suggestion was to set up different types of mirrors, convex, concave or fractured so that invading forces would be intimidated by their own reflections turned into giants, multiplied, or monstrously distorted. They could be made to see and attack things that did not exist. They could be driven to the point of madness by the manipulation of their environment: 'we could make the sun, moon, and stars appear to descend to the terrestrial realm and appear over the heads of enemies. And we could perform many similar feats, so that the mind of a mortal ignorant of the truth could not withstand them'.[32]

---

29 *Verum enim est quod alias exiverunt gentes de locis illis et mundum invaserunt meridianum usque ad terram sanctam, sicut nunc Tartari faciunt ... Et ideo discursus Tartarorum non sufficit certificare tempus de adventu Antichristi, sed alia exiguntur,* OM (cf. note 18) IV.iv.16, I, 16-17.

30 *OM* (cf. note 18), IV.iv.16, I, 302-4.

31 *Ut sine ferro, et adsque eo quod tangerent aliquem, destruerent omnes resistentes,* OM (cf. note 18), VI.xii, 2:217.

32 *Et sic faceremus solem et lunam et stellas descendere secundum apparentiam hic inferius et super capita inimicorum apparere, et*

In addition to their capacity to confuse, mirrors could be used more directly as weapons. Concave mirrors could be used to focus the sunlight into concentrated rays of such power that they would burn whatever they touched. Certain branches of knowledge, particularly *scientia experimentalis*, could assist in the creation of a range of technologies for saving Christian lives by killing at a distance. Some would be imperceptible to the senses, or perhaps could only be smelled, while others would work by mysteriously infecting the enemy. There were some that would require some physical contact, such as malta, which was a kind of bitumen, easily found, that would burn up a soldier if it landed on his skin. Yellow petroleum would have a similar effect, and could not be extinguished by water. Other inventions could produce such a loud noise that, if they were set off suddenly at night, armies or cities might be overthrown by the shock of the sound and the accompanying light and cloud.[33] While most of these methods foreshadow the excesses of modern warfare, they were designed to save Christian lives from the violence of those who could not be converted and those who could not be stopped, such as long-prophesied armies with an eschatological role to play.

However successful these weapons might prove, Antichrist himself could not be dealt with on the battlefield. His most dangerous and terrifying aspect was his capacity to deceive and fascinate good Christians, seducing them to evil, snatching salvation from them in the bitter turbulence of the last days of the world.[34] He would, wrote Bacon, 'infatuate the world through the art of magic and his lies'. This, then, was the nature of the deadliest threat. Christians who were killed in battle against

---

multa consimilia, ut animus mortalis ignorans veritatem non posset sustinere. Perspectiva, ed. Lindberg (cf. note 10), III.iii.4, 334-5.

33 *OM* (cf. note 18), VI.xii, I, 217-8.

34 Bacon's contemporaries feared that Antichrist might come as both Emperor and Pope; might pretend to be Christ, using the powers of demons to simulate the workings of the Holy Spirit, even enacting a false Pentecost so that Antichrist's disciples might appear to be speaking in tongues, and many other such horrors of deception and parody. See Emmerson / Herzman, *Apocalyptic Imagination* (cf. note 6), esp. 14-31; N. Morgan, *The Douce Apocalypse: Picturing the End of the World in the Middle Ages* Oxford 2006.

Antichrist's forces might prove to be the fortunate ones. Christians who fell into the spiritual snares of Antichrist would suffer eternal torment.

Bacon explained to the Pope something of the mechanics of how Antichrist would use fascination, magic and illusion on humanity. He wrote in a guarded, often oblique, manner, for despite wide popular use of various forms of magic, these matters lay, for clerics, in the shadows beyond the safe circles of approved and institutionalised knowledge. Yet he maintained that even ordinary, unlearned Latins needed to know how such arts functioned, how to recognise them, and how to turn them against those same enemies who would use them remorselessly to destroy Christianity. 'They will be absolutely necessary to the Church of God against the fury of Antichrist,' he wrote.[35] He had given hints in the early chapters of the *Opus maius* about the enigmatic power of words: the words of the sacraments, which could transform bread into the flesh of Christ, and the words of the saints, which had suspended the very laws of nature. He believed that the days of miracles were not over: 'we should believe that if, through the authority of the Church and with right intention and steadfast desire, many true and wise Christians were to utter holy incantations for the propagation of the faith and the destruction of lies, a great number of good things, by the grace of God, would be possible'.[36] For, noted Bacon, Avicenna had taught that: 'the soul sanctified and purified of its sins is able to change the universe and the physical elements, so that rains, tempests and all alterations of bodies in the world are made by its virtue'.[37] Such words, he believed, would be even more powerful

---

35 *Ecclesiae Dei sit omnino necessarium contra furiam Antichristi*, *OM* (cf. note 18), IV.iv.16, I,392.

36 *Credere debemus quod si auctoritate Ecclesiae et ex recta intentione et forti desiderio multi veri et sapientes Christiani voces sacras proferrent ad pro[pagationem] fidei et destructionem falsitatis, quod multa bona possint Dei gratia provenire*. *OM* (cf. note 18), III.xiv, III, 123. Similar ideas were common enough in medieval Europe. See D.C. Skemer, *Binding Words: Textual Amulets in the Middle Ages* (Magic in History), Pennsylvania 2006.

37 *Anima sancta et munda a peccatis potest universale et elementa alterare, ut ejus virtute fiant pluviae, tempestates, et omnes alterationes corporum mundi*. *OM* (cf. note 18), IV.iv.16, I, 403.

if spoken at the proper time, under the most advantageous constellations of the heavens.

A particular part of magic was the ability to fascinate and manipulate people. Bacon explained: 'By this extraordinary method, [Antichrist] will achieve what he wants to achieve without war, and men will obey him just like beasts, and he will make kingdoms and states fight each other for him, so that friends will destroy their friends, and in this way he will make what he likes of the world.'[38] It therefore seemed obvious to Bacon that: 'Unless the Church hurries to meet [these threats] by using exactly the same methods for impeding and destroying such works, it will be intolerably oppressed by these scourges of Christians'.[39] He concluded: 'the Church ought to consider employing [them] against *infideles* and rebels so that Christian blood might be spared, and especially because of the future dangers which will come in the times of Antichrist, which, with the grace of God, it would be easy to oppose, if prelates and princes were to promote study and investigate the secrets of nature and of art.'[40]

Beyond these specific suggestions for turning arcane arts and sciences against the very enemies who would employ them, Bacon's whole programme was aimed to strengthen and spread the Christian faith. This was obviously the best possible defence against Antichrist. He looked for ways to prove the truth of Christianity through reason rather than through scriptural citation. 'For we can have great consolation in our faith,' he wrote, 'since the philosophers who have been led solely by the

---

38 *Et per hanc viam magnificam faciet sine bello quid volet, et obedient homines ei sicut bestiae, et faciet regna et civitates pugnare ad invicem pro se, ut amici destruant amicos suos, et sic de mundo faciet quod desiderabit.* OM (cf. note 18), IV.iv.16, I, 399.

39 *Et nisi ecclesia occurrat per facta consimilia ad impediendum et destruendum opera hujusmodi, aggravabitur intolerabiliter flagellis Christianorum.* OM (cf. note 18), IV.iv.i16, I, 402.

40 *Et hoc deberet ecclesia considerare contra infideles et rebelles, ut parcatur sanguini Christiano, et maxime propter futura pericula in temporibus Antichristi, quibus cum Dei gratia facile esset obviare, si praelati et principes studium promoverent et secreta naturae et artis indagerent.* OM (cf. note 18), VI.xii, II, 222.

exercise of their reason agree with us ... not because we require reason before faith, but after faith, so that rendered certain by a double confirmation we may praise God for our salvation which we possess without doubt. And through this method ... we are fortified in advance against the sect of Antichrist.'[41] If preachers could be trained in the rhetorical arts of the classical world, so that they could speak more effectively, their power to inspire ordinary people with spiritual joy would be greatly enhanced. If the widespread doubts about the Eucharist could be obliterated by careful, scientific arguments, the grace of that sacrament would uplift the whole population and greatly empower Christendom. Internal wars could be avoided by keeping a watchful eye on the movements of Mars and working especially for peace when that bellicose planet was in ascendance.[42] In these, and in many other ways, improved knowledge within the Church would promote moral reform and unity in society and protect the faithful through the coming trials.

This massive and controversial programme clearly demanded work and commitment from scholars of the highest moral calibre. Bacon did not say explicitly that such people would have to be members of religious orders, but considering that absolute rejection of worldly temptations was a preliminary step on the way to wisdom, it seems unlikely that it could be achieved by anyone outside the orders. Indeed, such a high standard of personal sanctity was required that very few people even within the orders could have achieved it.[43] It would be necessary to train pure young men to the task from their earliest years. Bacon wrote enthusiastically to Clement about one in particular of his students, John, a boy of twenty years, poor and untaught before he came to Bacon, and not of really outstanding intellectual

---

41 *Magnum enim solatium fidei nostrae possumus habere, postquam philosophi qui ducti sunt solo motu rationis nobis consentiunt...non quia quaeramus rationem ante fidem, sed post fidem, ut duplici confirmatione certificati laudemus Deum de nostra salute quam indubitanter tenemus. Et per hanc viam ... praemunimur contra sectam Antichristi, OM* (cf. note 18), IV.iv.16, I, 253-54.

42 *MP* (cf. note 17), V, 247-63 [on rhetoric]; *MP*, IV.iii, 223-43 [on the Eucharist]; *OM* (cf. note 18), IV.iv.16, I, 385-86 [on war].

43 *OM* (cf. note 18), I.iii-iv, III, 6-11.

ability. Yet because of the extraordinary innocence and virtue of his soul, he had been able, with God's grace, to surpass all other students. In the course of just one year, he had learnt everything that it had taken Bacon thirty or forty years of intensive study to master. Nor was he the only one. Bacon had trained a number of virtuous young men so that they might be: 'useful vessels in the Church of God, that they may reform the whole academic curriculum of the Latins through the grace of God'.[44]

Bacon entered the order at a time when its leaders were committed to a profoundly eschatological vision of their role in society. Even after the formal suppression of extreme versions of such ideas, it is clear that many prominent Franciscans continued to understand their role in such a light. Bacon was discreet and avoided making any specific claims in this direction for the order, but taken as a whole, the underlying sense and unifying purpose in his writing seems clear enough. As John of Parma and Humbert of Romans had gone on to say in their encyclical, those of the orders would be like: 'the two cherubim full of knowledge … spreading out their wings to the people while they protect them by word and example, and flying about on obedient wing over the whole people to spread saving knowledge …' Bacon envisaged the reform of learning within Christendom being led by a group of exceptional young friars for the purpose of defending the community of the faithful against the most terrible threat it would ever face: the coming of Antichrist.

---

44 *Vasa utilia in Ecclesia Dei, quatenus totum studium per gratiam Dei rectificent Latinorum, OM* (cf. note 18), VI.i, II, 170-1.

Late Medieval Franciscan Statutes on Convent Libraries and Education

Eva Schlotheuber

(Universität Münster)

When the Observant Franciscans met at the Council of Constance in 1414 to discuss their reform concerns, they also addressed the important problem of replenishing their ranks[1]. Their remarks allow us a clear recognition of the order's struggle to recruit new members: 'Although they [the non-reformed Franciscans] are allowed under certain conditions to take in children – that is, when they are donated by their parents – with regard to this activity the brothers nonetheless commit an abuse, because they do not simply leave it to parents or the children (*parvulos*) themselves to volunteer. Instead, when on their journeys they see children who display any sign of dexterity, they flatter them and try as hard as they can to convince them to enter the order. By promising to let them study, to give them the necessary books and to support them in their search for knowledge, those brothers tell them that it will be easy to become bishops or even greater men in the church. They give them fruit and everything they like, until they

---

[1] See for the council in general W. Brandmüller, *Papst und Konzil im Großen Schisma (1378-1431)*. Studien und Quellen, Paderborn 1990. Idem, *Das Konzil von Konstanz (1414–1418)*, 2 vols. (Konziliengeschichte. Reihe A. Darstellungen, 8, 11), Paderborn 1991-1997. J. Miethke, Kirchenreform auf den Konzilien des 15. Jahrhunderts. Motive–Methoden–Wirkungen, in: *Studien zum 15. Jahrhundert*. Festschrift für E. Meuthen zum 65. Geburtstag, 2 vols. (eds.) J. Helmrath / H. Müller, Munich 1994, I, 13–47.

have caught them in their snare, and moreover, they make sure that those children stay with them.'[2]

The critical remarks of the reform-minded Franciscans on their brothers' practice of taking in new members reveal several themes relevant for our subject[3]. First, this quotation suggests that even at the beginning of the fifteenth century, the order's attraction depended on its internal educational offerings[4]. This social acceptance was based on the

---

2 *Et licet permissum est conditionaliter iuvenes recipi, videlicet si ap*[!] *parentibus suis oblati sint, de hoc tamen fratres abutuntur, quia non dimittunt parvulos de se vel ap* [!] *parentibus offerri ex sua libera voluntate. Sed quando ambulantes per mundum vident pueros aliquid principium habilitatis habere, ipsos verbis blandis alloquuntur et quantum possunt inducunt ad huius religionis ingressum, promittentes eos ad studia promovere et libros necessarios dare et ad acquirendam scienciam iuvare, dicentes eis, quod de levi semel poterunt esse episcopi et adhuc maiores in ecclesia; dant illis poma et omnia placentia usquequo eos alligaverint vinculis suis, et etiam secum tales pueros manere procurant* (Singulare opus ordinis seraphici Francisci a spiritu sancto approbati [...] quod Speculum minorum seu Firmamentum trium ordinum titulatur. Bonifatius de Ceva, 5 T., Venice 1513, Bayerische Staatsbibliothek Munich, 4 H. Mon. 494, III, fol. 157[rb]). The Observants regarded this method of recruiting novices as noxious because the will to be devoted to a spiritual life was lacking: *Et quia tales spiritus dei instinctu non inducuntur sed spiritu humano et inflante bonum fructum non faciunt in religione cum adhuc bene inspiratis in principio sit satis arduum donec amor divinus advenerit, quod iugum Christi facit suave et onus suum leve* (ibid.).

3 Cf. B. Roest, 'Franciscans between Observance and Reformation, the Low Countries (ca. 1400–1600)', *FS* 63 (2005) 409–44; for the non reformed branch cf. P. Weigel, *Ordensreform und Konziliarismus: der Franziskanerprovinzial Matthias Döring (1427–1461)* (Jenaer Beiträge zur Geschichte, 7) Frankfurt am Main 2005. See the review by B. Roest, 'Ordensreform und Konziliarismus: Der Franziskanerprovinzial Matthias Döring (1427-1461)', *The Catholic Historical Review* 93 (2007) 161-3.

4 See E. Schlotheuber, 'Bildung und Bücher. Ein Beitrag zur Wissenschaftsidee der Franziskanerobservanten', in: *Könige, Landesherren und Bettelorden. Konflikt und Kooperation in West-*

particular curriculum of the order, which guaranteed a good education of preachers and pastors while offering opportunities for social advancement at the same time.[5] Libraries, too, belonged to the 'profile' of the Franciscans – they facilitated access not only to pastoral works, but also to the expensive scholarly and theological literature as well.[6] Secondly, we can conclude from the remarks of the Observants at the periphery of the Council of Constance, that in many cases, Franciscans assumed responsibility for the elementary education of their order's future members as well. Since the fourteenth century in particular, they had opened their doors to younger adolescents who would otherwise have had no opportunity of a literate education. Although the higher education of the Franciscans has frequently been the object of research, their role in offering elementary instruction has often been ignored. Of fundamental importance for this task was the friars' access to literature, the different book collections in the late

---

und Mitteleuropa bis zur frühen Neuzeit, (ed.) D. Berg, (Saxonia Franciscana, 10) Werl 1998, 419 – 34; see in general for the Franciscan education system an excellent overview on the research of the last decades B. Roest, *A History of Franciscan Education: (c. 1210-1517)* (Education and Society in the Middle Ages and Renaissance, 11) Leiden 2000. D. Berg, *Armut und Wissenschaft: Beiträge zur Geschichte des Studienwesens der Bettelorden im 13. Jahrhundert* (Geschichte und Gesellschaft, 15) Düsseldorf 1977. Recently T. Ertl, *Religion und Disziplin: Selbstdeutung und Weltordnung im frühen deutschen Franziskanertum* (Arbeiten zur Kirchengeschichte, 96) Berlin 2006. D. Berg, *Armut und Geschichte. Studien zur Geschichte der Bettelorden im Hohen und Späten Mittelalter*, Kevelaer 2001.

5   Roest, *History* (cf. note 4) 272–6; Idem, '*Ignorantia est mater omnium malorum*: the validation of knowledge and the office of preaching in late medieval female Franciscan communities', in: *Saints, Scholars and Politicans. Gender as a Tool in Medieval Studies. Festschrift in Honour of Anneke Mulder-Bakker on the occasion of her Sixty-Fifth Birthday*, (eds.) M. van Dijk / R.I.A. Nip, Turnhout 2005, 65–83.

6   See Roest, *History* (cf. note 4) 197–200.

medieval convents and profile and organization of the libraries.

I. Book possession and libraries in the Franciscan Convents

Dieter Berg has suggested that 'The supervision of the order's superiors, concerned not only the quality of the education but also its contents, so that Dominicans and Franciscans standardized the knowledge of their clerics and at the same time developed a theology specific to the order that became binding for the brothers and which they were required to teach.'[7] This centralizing orientation, which superseded the authority of individual convents, affected the structure of studies as well as the basis of their education – in the convent libraries and books in the private use of the brothers.[8] Normative sources such as the general and provincial chapter statutes give evidence of the care the Franciscans took in dealing with their books. In his *History of Franciscan Education*, published in 2000, Bert Roest emphasizes that most researchers assumed the Franciscan order took a similar development to that observed among the Dominicans – who from the very beginning incorporated libraries into their communities.[9] Nonetheless, the Franciscans did follow their own path in this regard, one justified via their understanding of apostolic life. An analysis of the order's statutes reveals a development that

---

7 D. Berg, ‚Bettelorden und Bildungswesen im kommunalen Raum. Ein Paradigma des Bildungstransfers im 13. Jahrhundert', in: *Zusammenhänge, Einflüsse, Wirkungen*, Symposion Tübingen 1984, (eds.) J.O. Fichte / B. Schimmelpfennig, Berlin / New York 1986, 414–26, here 424.

8 B. Roest, *Franciscan Literature of Religious Instruction before the Council of Trent*, (Studies in the History of Christian Traditions, 117) Leiden 2004. M. Robson, 'The growth of the libraries of the Greyfriars in England (1224-1539)', *Il Santo. Rivista francescana di storia, dottrina e arte* 2 (2003) 493–521.

9 Roest, *History* (cf. note 4) 198.

differs on a basic level from that of the Dominican order. Francis of Assisi rejected acquisitions and possessions of books, and the Franciscan understanding of religious poverty was not set up to accommodate the accumulation of valuable book collections in the order's houses.[10] They knew very well about the dangers embedded in precious books for the life of evangelical perfection. Even when the structure of the order began to be formed they sought to avoid a firm connection between individual brothers and a particular convent. The friars were convinced, that sooner or later, such arrangements would end in the involvement of the religious community in the economic and social interests of the lay people – as could easily be seen in the case of the older orders. As a consequence the order preferred to equip the brothers individually with the necessary books, which were granted to them for lifetime. Although Gregory IX's bull *Quo Elongati* of 1230 permitted the Friars to use books, the order remained conscious of the danger that the possession of valuable books caused for *the life of evangelical perfection*.[11] Each book was regarded as belonging to the entire order, and as a result, in principle, each educated member of the order had the same right to the use of any particular book.[12] For this reason, the selection and treatment of books was discussed at provincial and general chapters.[13] Their decisions were

---

10 Thomas de Celano, Vita Secunda S. Francisci (AF 10), 127–268, c. 23 (*Contra curiositatem librorum*).

11 H. Grundmann, 'Die Bulle Quo elongati Papst Gregors IX.', *AFH* 54 (1961) 3–25.

12 At the general council of Narbonne 1260 the *patres* stated: *Nullus libros aliquos retineat sibi assignatos, nisi sint totaliter in ordinis potestate, quod libere per ministros dari valeant et aufferri*, Narbonne, 1260, Assisi, 1279, Paris, 1292; clause 27, 74.

13 See for the early legislation of the order C. Cenci (ed.), 'De Fratrum Minorum Constitutionibus Praenarbonensis', *AFH* 83 (1990) 50–95, clause 70, 90; clauses 76–79, 92. M Bihl (ed.), 'Statuta generalia Ordinis edita in capitulo generali. Anno 1354 Assisii celebrato communiter Farineriana appelata', *AFH* 35 (1942) 35–112.

incorporated into the statutes as binding upon the entire order.

The method of equipping the individual brothers with books was accommodated to the mobility of the order's members and may have been related to the still relatively manageable number of Franciscans with a literate education in the first half of the thirteenth century. There already existed some shared book collections but they were few. The library of the Portiuncola, which probably took shape between 1212 and 1220, is perhaps the oldest of them.[14] Even the statutes that predate the Narbonne general chapter in 1260 suggest that the superiors of the order intended to regiment the access to books.[15] The were specially anxious that books should eventually be returned to the province which had payed for them. Expensive bibles were to be sold and cheaper ones purchased to supply a larger number of brothers.[16] In Narbonne, the order enumerated the rules of the use of books according to systematic principles of access. For the possession of biblical texts, the permission of a superior was required; this could only be given to individuals able to undertake higher academic studies who would be suitable as preachers.[17] The examination of *libri*

---

14 G. Abate, 'Manoscritti e bibliotheche francescane del medio evo', in: *Il libro e le biblioteche*. Atti del primo congresso bibliologico francescano internazionale, 20-27 febbraio 1949, 2 vols. (Bibliotheca Pontifica Athen, 6) Rome 1950, II, 77–126, here 93–7.

15 *Et nullus minister provintialis audeat habere vel retinere aliquos libros absque licentia generalis ministri; nec etiam alii fratres accipiant vel habeant absque licentia suorum provintialium ministrorum.* Cenci, De Fratrum Minorum Constitutionibus (cf. note 13) clause 79, 92.

16 *Omnes libri, qui de cetero pretio scribuntur vel emuntur, remaneant in provintiis, in quibus empti sunt vel scripti [...]. Ibid.*, clause 76, 92.

17 Narbonne, 1260, Assisi, 1279, Paris, 1292, clause 28 p. 74. For this cf. already the Constitutiones Praenarbonensis, Cenci (ed.), 'De Fratrum Minorum Constitutionibus' (cf. note 13) clause 80, 92f.

curiosi was forbidden.[18] As a consequence new writings were to be examined before being distributed more widely.[19] If somebody published a non examined work he lost it and had to suffer three days of water and bread. No special reference in 1260 in Narbonne is made to convent libraries, they continued to play only a marginal role. The basic attitude of the order toward a self-imposed limitation of possession of books became even more recognizable in 1279 in Assisi: No Franciscan was allowed to own a duplicate copy of a book or two commentaries on the same subject. The minister provincial was to ensure compliance with this provision during the visitation of the convents.[20] If a brother did own books – for example, from gifts –, which he did not necessarily need, they were to be redistributed at the next provincial chapter to brothers who needed them more urgently. Despite the increasing clericalization of the order, particularly after the deposition of Elias of Cortona in 1239, studies and scholarship were not meant to take on the most important role among the brothers' activities.

Naturally, the order's houses owned smaller collections of books like the liturgical texts for their offices and masses which were kept in the sacristy or in a room above it. But these collections were connected with practical usage and it is unlikely that they constituted the nucleus of the convent libraries which then simply increased over the course of time. It is much more likely that the development of the order's educational system in the second half of the

---

18 Narbonne, 1260, Assisi, 1279, Paris, 1292, clause 20, 73.

19 *Item inhibemus, ne de cetero aliquod scriptum novum extra ordinem publicetur, nisi prius examinatum fuerit diligenter per generalem ministrum vel provincialem et definitores in capitulo provinciali. Et quicumque contrafecerit, tribus diebus tantum in pane et aqua ieiunet et caret illo scripto.* Ibid. clause 21, 73.

20 Narbonne, 1260, Assisi, 1279, Paris, 1292, (Assisi 1279) clause 24a, 81.

thirteenth century was the turning point.[21] Custodial and provincial schools were founded everywhere. Here brothers suitable for university studies or preaching activity were prepared for work in a *studium generale* or university. Over the course of the thirteenth century the order grew enormously, so that an educational substructure had to be created for the training of priests, preachers, confessors and convent teachers.[22] The Aristotelian-influenced scholarly and methodological foundation of theology training had increasingly prevailed. The order embraced this form of theological education. Thus its curriculum was systematized and standardized, its education system following the scholastic subject divisions of the arts, philosophy and theology, for the pursuit of which a broad spectrum of special literature was necessary.

The *Ordinationes*, confirmed by Pope Benedict XII in 1336 responded to this new situation.[23] These ordinations now demanded the organization of libraries in all Franciscan settlements for the first time.[24] Texts on grammar, logic, philosophy and theology were to be available to all members of the Franciscan communities. Libraries were to include duplicates or even triplicates of important works depending on the *conditio* and *status* of the house. Even so, normative regulations reveal an equally important economic consideration: the equipment of the

---

21 E. Schlotheuber, 'Büchersammlung und Wissensvermittlung. Die Bibliothek des Göttinger Franziskanerklosters', in: *Schule und Schüler im Mittelalter. Beiträge zur europäischen Bildungsgeschichte des 9. bis 15. Jahrhunderts*, (eds.) M. Kintzinger / S. Lorenz / M. Walter, Cologne / Weimar/ Vienna 1996, 217–44, here 222.

22 Roest, *History* (cf. note 4) 65f.

23 M. Bihl (ed.), 'Ordinationes a Benedicto XII pro fratribus minoribus promulgatae per bullam 28 novembris 1336', *AFH* 30 (1937) 309–90.

24 *Ibid.* XI, 4–6, 356.

libraries was connected to the status of a convent, and unnecessary or superfluous items were to be avoided. This basic systematizing feature can also be clearly seen in practice: from the size and composition of a library we can determine whether a house had a convent school, a custodial or provincial school or even *studia solemnia*.[25] More important houses often possessed two separate collections, a public library and a secret collection. The custody or rather the province retained control over the administration, for 'extra' books according to these ordinances were to be redistributed to other houses in the same province.[26] Two different libraries appear to have existed in the Cambridge convent.[27] One was the school library of the convent and the other was the library for the custody, from which the order equipped brothers who went on to university studies and supplied convents or new settlements with less generous collections.[28]

The transition of the libraries to the status of mandatory constituent parts of the convent around the turn of the fourteenth century seems at first an accommodation of the Franciscans to the practices of the older orders or the Dominicans. At second glance, however, clear differences can be found in the circumstances that prevailed for example in the largely autonomous Benedictine or

---

25 E. Schlotheuber, 'Die Franziskaner in Göttingen. Die Geschichte des Klosters und seiner Bibliothek' (Saxonia Franciscana, 8) Werl 1996, 116–32.

26 Roest, *History* (cf. note 4) 202.

27 *Ibid.* n. 22: See more detailed A.G. Little, 'The friars and the foundation of the Faculty of Theology in the University of Cambridge', in: *Idem, Franciscan Papers, Lists and Documents*, Manchester 1943, 122–43, here 142f.

28 The libraries of the custody were also mentioned by the *Ordinationes* of Benedict XII: *Libri vero ad communitatem custodiae pertinentes distribuantur in provinciali capitulo fratribus eiusdem custodiae tantum* (…). Bihl, Ordinationes (cf note 23) XI, c. 8, 356f.

Cistercian abbeys. As in the past, the order continued to supersede convent control of the selection of the literature and the collection. In this way, the brothers could generally be assured that wherever they landed, the necessary literature would await them. This centralizing concern for training and teaching as seen in the *Ordinationes* also left its mark in an organized system of scrutinizing the texts read, taught and reproduced in the order. Every new work, each theological, legal or philosophical treatise, no matter which author wrote it, was subject to examination. Only when the text received the approval of four of the order's masters of theology, permission was given for its further distribution within the community.[29] Acceptance or rejection was noted in writing to the custodian or guardian in a so-called *epistola approbatoria.* Thus notes of approbation are found in some codices, as late as the *Kannemannkodex*, which found its way into the convent library at Lüneburg in 1461 from the estate of the Franciscan Johannes Hagen. On its flyleaf, we find the entry: 'This material has been approved by four scholars of the law, confirmed by signature and seal.'[30] The Franciscans were reluctant to trust the copying skills of the secular clergy – their Latin was too poor and their

---

29 *Ne autem nova cuiusvis doctrinae opera per fratres ipsius ordinis incaute et periculose communicari aut publicari contingat, districte praecipimus, quod novum opus theologicum, iuridicum vel philosophicum, scilicet librum seu libellum, (…) a quocumque fuerit editus vel edita seu editum, nullus frater sine subscripto examine ac ministri et capituli generalis prius obtenta licentia speciali, intra vel extra ordinem publicare, communicare vel copiare praesumt.* Bihl, 'Ordinationes' (cf. note 23) IX, c. 34, 352.

30 *Hec materia per multos utriusque doctores est approbata, subscripta et sigillis roborata, qui doctores nominatim habentur in libraria Luneburgensi in libro, qui intitulatur Sompnium pauperis.* Manuscript formerly kept in the Münster, Studien- und Zentralbibliothek der Franziskaner Ms OFM 20, fol. 225vb. The manuscript is today in the Diözesanbibliothek Münster. See for a

carefulness limited.[31] Thus the brothers were to copy necessary texts themselves, which in turn increased the need for members of the order with a sufficient standard of literacy.

The library was just one of several places where books relevant for the friars' spiritual life were stored. Thus it is worthwhile to undertake a sort of tour through a Franciscan convent in order to consider the size and composition of these different book collections: in the choir and sacristy of the church, in the chapter room, in the cloister court and refectory, and in the dormitory or cells, which housed private collections. Size and types of these collections depended on the daily use. Most of these books we usually do not find in library inventories. The most expensive books which were necessary for every spiritual community were those meant for the service of the *choir* and thus for liturgical use. They were kept in the choir on lecterns or in the sacristy in wall cabinets. Often, they were richly embellished volumes with representative decorations; the sorts of volumes included in this category were relatively fixed: Missals and graduals, lectionaries, epistle books, legends and an Evangelistar. As an exception the library catalogue of Youghal also includes the choir books and refers to five choir psalters (*psalteria chori*).[32] Additionally there were antiphonaries for responsive singing of

---

description of the codex Schlotheuber, *Franziskaner* (cf. note 25) 115.

31 Roest, *History* (cf. note 4) 66.

32 The book inventory of the observant Irish convent in Youghal had been careful edited by C. O'Clabaigh, *The Franciscans in Ireland 1400–1534; from Reform to Reformation*, Dublin 2002, 223–58, here 226. It was a rather small house that possessed a book collection in the choir in 1481 consisting of five parchment Missals, a Legendary of the Saints in two volumes, nine Graduals, a *collectorium*, two *martirologia*, *unum grande antifonarium* and two other antiphonaries. The two bibles – one was a representative big one – probably also belonged to the choir.

antiphons, hymns and the psalms. Legends and martyrologies or saints' calendars were also indispensable for the choir library. These choir collections should not be thought of as scanty: the Franciscan convent of Göttingen was not particularly significant and only housed its own local *studium conventuale*. But here alone, as the dissolution inventory of the house in 1533 revealed, forty-seven volumes were partly not chained partly chained to lecterns in the choir.[33]

The *sacristy*, in contrast, held books for more complex liturgical celebrations: further missals, *plenaria*, and additional breviaries. Since the sacristy was typically a stone construction and thus protected against fire, the convent archive was traditionally found here or in a room located above it. It is possible that – like the Benedictines – the Franciscans also marked special liturgical places in the convent church with their own literature. At the end of the fifteenth century the observant Augsburg monk Leonhard Wagner, called 'Wirstlin', wrote a *Legendam et historiam de sancto Simperto ad corpus eius in sepulcro* – a special *legendarium* for readings at the graves of the saints, which occurred in context with memorial celebrations.[34]

In the hierarchy of sacred spaces, the church choir was followed by the *chapter room*. The convent met there daily for readings of excerpts of the rule or statutes – the *scripta ordinis* were found here – to which visitation minutes also belonged.[35] Since the monastic reforms of the fifteenth

---

33 Schlotheuber, *Franziskaner* (cf. note 25) 78. For the chained books in the choir cf. K. Löffler, *Deutsche Klosterbibliotheken*, Cologne 1918, 22.

34 *Mittelalterliche Bibliothekskataloge Deutschlands und der Schweiz.* III, 1 (Bistum Augsburg), (ed.) P. Ruf, Munich 1932, 46. Here are also listed special *liturgica* for the chapels in the church.

35 An example of a late-medieval chapter book from a Cistercian abbey has recently been edited by Guido Cariboni: G. Cariboni (ed.), *La via migliore Pratiche memoriali e dinamiche istituzionali nel "liber" del capitolo dell'abbazia cistercense di Lucedio*, Berlin

century were always connected to liturgical – or in a broader sense to a ceremonial reform, brothers and monks often had to consult written directions in order to conduct the new and often abbreviated sequence of their prayers. Therefore they needed a current ceremonial or *ordinarium*. A heavily-used copy of such a work in the German language from the Regensburg convent of the Poor Clares has survived.[36] In it, one could look up details for the day's liturgical order of service: such as which bells were to be rung at what point, how long matins should run – measured by the number of prayers – or even which prayers were to be selected for which days to precede the day's readings in the refectory. Since departed members of the convent were remembered in the chapter room on the anniversaries of their deaths, special necrologies also found their place there.

The actual location for meditation and silent reading, however, was the cloister, located to the north of the church, the so-called *Kollations-* or *Lesegang*. Many cloisters were specially equipped and provided with opportunities to sit. We cannot prove definitely that the Franciscans placed texts here for meditation, as we know for certain in the case of Cistercian monasteries. Cistercians typically provided a wall chest for books or *armarium* in the northeast corner of the cloister, where the north went over into the east passage. It offered monks books for private reading and meditation.[37]

2006. A chapter book was probably also the *Liber in quo continentur scripta ordinis videlicet regula, declaraciones, statuta, speculum disciplinae ad novicios* from the Franciscan convent in Youghal, see Clabaigh, *Franciscans* (cf. note 32) 228.

36 A.E. Schönbach, *Mitteilungen aus altdeutschen Handschriften*, Hildesheim / New York 1976, 1–54 (vernacular rule of the Poor Clares of Regensburg) and at 55–58 (Ordinarium). Both were probably used in the chapter room.

37 Cf. M. Mersch, ‚Gehäuse der Frömmigkeit – Zuhause der Nonnen: zur Geschichte der Klausurgebäude zisterziensischer Frauenklöster

In comparison, a small library was certainly maintained for daily reading aloud during meals in the *refectory*. This state of affairs persisted into modern times, as Christian Plath has shown for the Thuringian Franciscan province.[38] This collection included items such as the Golden Legend, Lives of the Fathers, writings of Bonaventure, exegetical writings of the Church Fathers, sermons, or *exempla* collections. In Göttingen the refectory collection consisted of fifty-three books. We know from other convents that these volumes often bore library signatures and were seen as belonging to the main library.[39] Literature for daily reading aloud during meals was of special meaning for the communities. In fifteenth-century observant convents we find specific types of literature, among them the works of Jean Gerson († 1429) or Johannes Nider († 1438). Following a general custom, on Sundays the *Rationale divinorum* of Guillaume Durand († 1296) was read which transmitted basic knowledge of the liturgy and its spiritual meaning.

As we have seen *private use of books* was the original means of supplying the clerical brothers with literature. And even after the *Ordinationes* of Benedict XII in 1336 demanded the creation of libraries in all convents, *private*

---

im 13. Jahrhundert', in: *Studien und Texte zur literarischen und materiellen Kultur der Frauenklöster im späten Mittelalter: Ergebnisse eines Arbeitsgesprächs in der Herzog August Bibliothek Wolfenbüttel, 24. - 26. Februar 1999*, (eds.) F. Eisermann / E. Schlotheuber / V. Honemann (Studies in Medieval and Reformation Thought, 99) Leiden 2004, 45–102.

38 C. Plath, 'Die Bibliotheken der Thüringischen Franziskanerprovinz bis zur Säkularisation', *Jahrbuch für Mitteldeutsche Kirchen- und Ordensgeschichte* (forthcoming).

39 See the study on table readings of the female Dominican convent St Katharina in Nuremberg, B. Hasebrink, 'Latinität als Bildungsfundament. Spuren subsidiärer Grammatikunterweisung im Dominikanerorden', in: *Schulliteratur im späten Mittelalter*, (ed.) Klaus Grubmüller (Münstersche Mittelalter-Schriften, 69), Munich 2000 49–76.

possession of books was still usual. Benedict XII decreed that first the library of a convent should be sufficiently supplied, but that remaining works could be distributed among the brothers.[40] The allocation was conducted by the guardian with the agreement of the convent and normally remained in force *ad vitam* – so that these books could be taken along in the case of transfer to another convent or during a study sojourn. In such cases, there was a risk that books could be lost over time, so that around 1360 the Florentine guardian Bernhard Guascone mandated that books granted for life should be produced annually for the examination of the custodian, the guardian or librarian.[41] In addition to books distributed by the superiors, brothers could keep books they had copied for themselves as their own possession. Their collections grew from both sources.[42]

---

40 *Postquam vero quilibet conventus fuerit libris praemissis hoc modo munitus, de aliis libris fiat distributio, primo fratribus eiusdem conventus habilibus et indigentibus, deinde, si facta distributione huiusmodi libri superfuerint (...) distribuantur aliis fratribus ex eadem custodia tantum, cuius erit ipse conventus. Distributiones autem huiusmodi fiant per guardianum, de consensu conventus et de licentia ministri.* Bihl, 'Ordinationes' (cf. note 23) XI, c. 4, 365.

41 *Item quod omnes fratres de custodia florentina et extra custodiam, qui habent libros armarii ad vitam, teneantur semel in anno custodi, guardiano et amariste presentialiter demonstrare.* M. Bihl, 'Ordinationes fratris Bernardi de Guasconibus, Ministri Provincialis Thusciae pro bibliotheca conventus S. Crucis, Florentinae (1356–1367)', *AFH* 26 (1933) 141–64.

42 In 1510 the library of the convent of Fribourg in Switzerland contained about ninety manuscripts. Over half of them had been collected by two friars, Friedrich of Amberg and Jean Joly, P. Ladner, 'Zur Bedeutung der mittelalterlichen Bibliothek des Franziskanerklosters Freiburg', in: *Zur geistigen Welt der Franziskaner im 14. und 15. Jahrhundert. Die Bibliothek des Franziskanerklosters in Freiburg/Schweiz. Akten der Tagung des Mediävistischen Instituts der Universität Freiburg vom 15. Oktober 1993*, (eds.) R. Imbach / E. Tremp (Scrinium Friburgense, 6) Fribourg 1995, 11–24.

Observants everywhere attempted to limit private property, but this was an arduous venture. At the end of the 1460s the Vicar-General of the Observants, Johannes Philippi (1467–1470), emphatically invited the reform convents to place books for private use – including those that had been copied by their owners – in the common library.[43] But we should doubt the success of this directive, no matter how energetically proclaimed. In 1498 a Franciscan provincial chapter in Kempten mandated that the brothers should not let their private book collections expand to the point that money would need to be paid for their transport in the case of transfer to another cloister.[44] And literature for private use was even found in the brothers' cells in the Franciscan house of Göttingen in 1533, although the brothers had taken along all of the books they could carry at their departure.[45]

A good example of the extent and composition of such a private collection is the book bequest of the two Franciscans Hermann and Johannes Sack from the years about 1440.[46] The careers of the Sacks, who were also biological brothers, are typical for those of educated Franciscans: Hermann became custodian of the Franciscan convent in Munich at the beginning of the fifteenth century

---

43 *Chronica fatris Nicolai Glassberger Ordinis Minorum Observantorum (ca. anno 1508), sive Chronica aliaque varia documenta ad historiam Fratrum Minorum* edita a Patribus Collegii S. Bonaventurae, (AF, 2) Quaracchi 1887, 438.

44 F. Landmann, 'Zum Predigtwesen der Straßburger Franziskanerprovinz', *FS* 13 (1926) 337–66, here 359.

45 Schlotheuber, *Franziskaner* (cf. note 25) 70f.

46 B. Kraft, 'Der Bücherrücklass der Minderbrüder Hermann und Johann Sack', *AFH* 28 (1935) 37–57. Another instructive example is the private book collection of Nikolaus Lakmann, who taught theology about 1446 in Erfurt. In 1461 he was elected Minister Provincial for Saxony; L. Meier, 'De schola Erfordensi saeculi XV', *Antonianum* 5 (1930) 157–73. Some of his manuscripts have survived. See also the collection of the observant Irish lector Maurice Hanlan, O'Clabaigh, *Franciscans* (cf. note 32) 246–50.

and went later to Regensburg as confessor to the Poor Clares there. We encounter him for forty years copying books of theology and spiritual care. Johannes Sack studied at first in Erfurt and afterwards became lector in Speyer.[47] In 1431 he resumed his studies in Vienna and then went to the Regensburg convent as lector. Shortly before the end of his life, he was invested with the office of custodian of Bavaria. At his death in 1438 he bequeathed his books to his brother Hermann, who in turn left the entire collection (forty-three volumes of diverse content) to their mother house in Munich.[48] Over time, such legacies allowed the development of splendid collections in convent libraries.

From their detailed wills, the literary profiles of each man can be discerned. Confessor Hermann Sack owned, in addition to liturgical books (missals and breviaries) mostly books for use in the *cura animarum*: he apparently preferred Bonaventure, but also possessed the *Speculum humanae salvationis*, the pericopic moral sermons of Konrad of Waldhausen who died as an influential preacher 1369 in Prague, sermons by Jacobus de Voragine († 1298), a *Quadragesimale* by Jordan of Quedlinburg († 1380), as well as saints' lives he had copied himself. In contrast, Johannes Sack copied natural science and moral texts that he used in his activities as lector, as well as lexical works and grammars. In addition, he also collected astronomical, mathematical and physical science works: The *Naturalia bona moralisata,* as well as historical works like the *Flores temporum* or the *Historia* of Flavius Josephus († about 100). Beside that he had a small collection of Canon Law.

---

47 Kraft, 'Bücherrücklass' (cf note 46) 41.

48 *Hii sunt libri relicti a fratribus germanis Johanne Sack, custodi* [!] *Bawarie, et Hermanno Sakch, qui multis annis fuit guardianus Monacensis. Qui libri omnes pertinent ad eorum conventum nativum Monacensem. Ibid.* 57. For the edition cf. *Mittelalterliche Bibliothekskataloge Deutschlands und der Schweiz,* (ed.) Bayerische Akademie der Wissenschaften, Munich 1918–1979, IV/2, 691–95.

Here we recognize the literary horizon of an active, scholarly lector who also taught the *Quadrivium*. And it is certainly no coincidence that Johannes Sack was not a member of the reform branch of the order, for such a large collection with decidedly scholastic, academic texts did not follow the spirit of the dictates of the Observants. The testament tells us that the books of Hermann and Johann Sack were then 'prepared' for the library of the Munich convent.[49] That is, they were covered with title and signature labels and attached to a chain and iron buckle so that the bindings would not be damaged on the reading desk.[50] The books themselves should be simple and low-cost – for the use of the brothers not for representation.

An invaluable source for our knowledge of the size and composition of the medieval Franciscan *libraries* – and thus for the intellectual horizon of their brothers – are the library inventories.[51] In his *Ordinationes*, Benedict XII had

---

49 *Hii libri omnes sunt in asseribus et preparati ad liberariam Monacensem. Ibid.* 695.

50 A good example with the original binding, title and signature labels is the already mentioned *Kannemanncodex* (cf. note 30), Münster, Diözesanbibliothek Ms OFM 20.

51 See in general A. Derolez, *Les Catalogues de Bibliothèques* (Typologie des sources du moyen âge occidental, 13), Turnhout 1979. J. Duft, 'Bibliothekskataloge als Quellen der Geistesgeschichte', in: *Die Abtei St. Gallen: ausgewählte Aufsätze in überarbeiteter Fassung von Johannes Duft*, herausgegeben zu seinem 75. Geburtstag, 3 vols. (eds.) P. Ochsenbein / E. Ziegler, Sigmaringen 1990-94, I, 192–202. For the medieval book inventories of the Franciscan Friars (beside Roest) K.W. Humphreys, *The Friars' Libraries* (Corpus of British Medieval Library Catalogues) London 1990; Idem, *The Book Provisions of the Medieval Friars*, Amsterdam 1964. For special research O'Clabaigh, *Franciscans* (cf. note 32), 223–58. A. Schmitt, 'Die ehemalige Franziskanerbibliothek zu Brandenburg an der Havel: Rekonstruktion, Geschichte, Gegenwart', *Archiv für Geschichte des Buchwesens* 60 (2006) 1–175. Schlotheuber, *Franziskaner* (cf. note 25). L. Camerer, *Die Bibliothek des Franziskanerklosters in Braunschweig*. (Braunschweiger Werkstücke Reihe, A 18, der

required each guardian to produce an inventory of all books upon assumption of his office. This inventory was to be verified each year, while the books themselves were to be shown to the librarian.[52] Most of the inventories are probably lost but some survive and they allow us often to glimpse the old organization of the libraries according to subject groups.[53] In certain respects, the library of the Göttingen Franciscans is typical for a simple convent

---

ganzen Reihe, 60), Braunschweig 1980. K.W. Humphreys, *The Library of the Franciscans of Siena in the Late 15th Century*, Amsterdam 1978. H. Döring, 'Rekonstruktion der Franziskanerbibliothek in Freiberg', in: *Studien zur Buch- und Bibliotheksgeschichte. Festschrift für Hans Lülfing zum 70. Geburtstag*, (eds.) U. Altmann / E.-H. Teitge, Berlin 1976, 128–42. K. W. Humphreys, *The Library of the Franciscans of the Convent of St Antony Padua at the Beginning of the 15th Century*, Amsterdam 1966. O. Clemen, 'Reste der Bibliothek des Franziskanerklosters Zwickau', *FS* 17 (1930) 228–45. H. Mertens, 'Die alte Franziskanerbibliothek in Hannover', *FS* 17 (1930) 97–105. J. Schmidt, 'Die Bibliothek des Franziskanerklosters Weida', *FS* 17 (1930) 90–6. W. Dersch, 'Zur Geschichte der Franziskanerbibliotheken zu Fulda und Salmünster', *FS* 10 (1923) 346–50. G. Abb, 'Die ehemalige Franziskanerbibliothek in Brandenburg. Ein Beitrag zur Geschichte des märkischen Buchwesens im Mittelalter', *Zeitschrift für Bibliothekswesen und Bibliographie* 39 (1922) 475–99. W. Dersch, 'Die Bücherverzeichnisse der Franziskanerklöster Grünberg und Corbach', *FS* 1 (1914) 438–78.

52 *Ut autem libri in ipso ordine melius valeant conservari, ordinamus quod guardiani in sua novitiate infra unum mensem, postquam officium guardianatus assumpserint, et in conventu suo fuerint, teneantur in praesentia conventus sui facere fieri inventarium de omnibus libris qui in ipso conventu tunc fuerint, eisdem libris dicto conventui realiter demonstratis.* (…) (12) *Et huiusmodi inventaria renoventur annis singulis et legantur in praesentia conventus, libris ipsis tunc etiam realiter demonstratis.* (14), Bihl, 'Ordinationes fratris Bernardi' (cf. note 41) XI, c. 12 / 14, 357. T. Grassmann, 'The Librarian' Role in Franciscan Research', in: *Librarianship and Franciscan Library of the Franciscan. Educational Conference* Santa Barbara, California June 23–26, Washington 1947, 280–342.

53 Roest, *History* (cf. note 4) 206–09.

library of smaller dimensions. I have compared it with that of several other late-medieval Franciscan convents.[54] A basic collection specific to the order and common to these libraries emerges clearly, but apart from that, each library had its own particular profile, depending on its size or the presence of a *studium*, or on whether a reform had taken place in the particular convent.

At the dissolution of the house in 1533, the Göttingen collection included almost five hundred volumes. About a third were incunabula or early imprints. The books lay on double-sided lecterns, each of which housed between twenty and thirty volumes. Labels with signature and title were affixed to the front book cover, as it was typical for medieval chained books. Signature labels consisted of a combination of letters in red and numbers in black, the letters indicating the lectern on which the book was stored and the number, its specific position on the lectern. As libraries grew, the series of signatures could be expanded with an additional numeration of lecterns with opposite colors or a combination of letters.[55] Signature and title labels were usually protected with a thin, transparent plate of horn in an iron frame. Today those frames and the horn plates are often lost. The title label reproduced in key words the contents of the volume. The titles named in the inventories were drawn from title labels, so the inventories do not necessarily reproduce the entire contents of a manuscript, but are intended instead to describe each individual volume.

The Franciscans were able to produce the book binding and book cover by themselves just as they needed them. In the Göttingen Franciscan convent not only the dissolution

---

54 Schlotheuber, *Franziskaner* (cf. note 25) 116–28.

55 See images 21 and 22 in E. Schlotheuber, 'Die Auflösung der Bettelordensklöster in der Reformation', in: *700 Jahre Paulinerkirche. Vom Kloster zur Bibliothek.* Ausstellungskatalog, (ed.) E. Mittler, Göttingen 1994, 35–40, 71–4, here 55f.

inventory, but also archaeological discoveries in the convent's cesspit, testify to the existence of a small bookbinding workshop in the house.[56] In this way texts copied by the brothers during studies in Erfurt, Bologna, Oxford or Paris could be made suitable for use in the convent's library. In the Magdeburg convent the Franciscans even printed books! The *Speculum discipline* attributed to St Bonaventure (probably written by his secretary Bernard de Besse), an introduction to the religious life, was printed here by the brothers. It is a unique bookprint with its low-cost book cover, taken from an old manuscript. It still imitates the appearance of a manuscript and has two written texts bound to the printed section.[57]

In their systematic order the Franciscan libraries obeyed the general organization of medieval libraries. Complete or partial copies of the Bible, Bible concordances and glosses filled the first lecterns A and B, accompanied by esteemed exegetical works by authors such as Hugh of St-Cher († 1263), Hugh of St-Victor († 1142), Nicolas of Gorram († 1295) and above all of Nicolas of Lyra († 1349).[58] They were followed by the Church Fathers, especially Jerome and Gregory the Great, but also by other influential

---

56 The dissolution inventory of the Göttingen convent mentions: an *ahneboth* [ambos] *ton boyk to bynden nodig, I cleyne thogerickelte dehnen lade mit allerleye boykbyndes gheraide, schrifftfuege* [a letter plunger], *viff boykpressen* and a *klophamer tom boykbynden gehorik*. Schlotheuber, *Franciscaner* (cf. note 25) 78. See G. Laurin, 'Der Binder mit dem Arma-Christi-Stempel. Zur Geschichte der Franziskanerbuchbinderei in Graz', *Gutenberg-Jahrbuch* 45 (1970) 359–70; in general: P. Lehmann, 'Inventare klösterlicher Buchbindereien', *Jahrbuch der Einbandkunst* 3/4 (1929/1930) 38–40.

57 *Speculum discipline*. Printed in Magdeburg, in the Franciscan convent St. Andreae, 1504. Munich, Bayer. Staatsbibliothek, Res P.lat. 1685 b.

58 See for the text edition: Schlotheuber, *Franziskaner* (cf. note 25) 138–84. The first folio of the inventory with lectern A today is missing.

theologians such as Bernard of Clairvaux and the great reform theologian Jean Gerson. To this basic literature were added the exegetical works of Augustine, Isidore's *Etymologies*, Albertus Magnus († 1280) and the *Diadema monachorum* of Smaragdus of St-Michel († 825). On lectern F the Franciscan convents of Grünberg, Brunswick and Göttingen displayed theological *Summae* and sentence commentaries: the four-volume *Summa* of Alexander of Hales († 1245), the great *Summa* of Thomas Aquinas († 1274), Peter Lombard's *Sentences* († 1160), the sentence commentary of Peter of Tarantaise (Pope Innocent V., † 1276), the *Summa aurea* of William of Auxerre († 1231), Bonaventure's *Commentarii in quattuor libros sententiarum* and the *Quodlibeta* of William of Ockham († 1349). They were necessary insofar as such works organized the scholarly theological knowledge of the period systematically for readers.

In Göttingen, the theological *Summae* were followed by confessors' manuals: the *Summa* of the Franciscan Astesanus of Ast († 1330), the *Summa confessorum* of Johannes of Erfurt († 1340/50), the Summa of Raymund of Peñaforte († 1276) and of course the well known *Summa angelica* of the Franciscan Angelo Carletti de Clavasio († 1495)[59]. Lectern I housed the encyclopedias of Vincent of Beauvais († 1254), to which the moral *Summa* of Antoninus Florentinus († 1459) and the beloved *Pharetra doctorum*, a collection of sayings by classical philosophers and poets, were added. Sermon cycles, treatises on penance and confession, moral theology texts and penitential sermons were found on lecterns K and L. As a rule, a single lectern (N) was reserved for non-theological works and philosophy, beginning with Boethius and the *Consolatio philosophiae*. In Göttingen, the friars also possessed a couple of Aristotelian writings, among them the

---

[59] See for the Franciscan Confession Handbooks (Summae) Roest, *Franciscan Literature* (cf. note 8) 314–55.

Nichomachean Ethics, and a printed version of the *Margarita Philosophiae* of the Carthusian Gregor Reisch († 1525). These titles were accompanied in other convents by astronomical and natural science works that also belonged to a convent's typical equipment. This section was quite thin in Göttingen; in the convent of Grünberg, which housed a *studium philosophie/naturale,* one could examine significantly more classics. Lectern O offered a selection of historical and church-historical works: the *Summa historialis* of Antoninus Florentinus, the *Historia ecclesiastica* of Eusebius of Caesarea († 339/40), probably a printed version of the *Liber chronicarum* of the humanist Hartmann Schedel († 1514), the *Peregrinatio in terram sanctam* of Bernard of Breydenbach († 1497) as well as the historical works of Flavius Josephus. Here, too, the Legends and *Vitae* of St Francis could be found. Two further lecterns were filled with sermon *exempla* and smaller edifying texts. The last lectern of the Göttingen collection was filled with works of canon law; a solid collection of canon law was typical for late medieval Franciscan libraries. The convent had obtained copies not only of the papal decretals, but also of the most usual commentaries: Martin of Troppau's *Margareta decreti* († 1278), Innocent IV's († 1254) five books of commentaries on the decretals of Gregory IX, the *Novella* of Johannes Andree († 1348) and the *Summa Hostiensis* of Henry of Segusio († 1271). Such material was useful in confrontations with the secular clergy, controversies with Rome or in giving advice to members of the laity.

Organisation of the Franciscan library at Göttingen

Lectern A	Bibles
Lectern B	Exegetical works
Lectern C	Bible Concordances
Lecterns D and E	Church Fathers

Lectern G	Theological Summae (Thomas Aquinas, Bonaventure etc.)
Lecterns F and H	Sentences and confessors' manuals
Lectern I	Encyclopedias (Vincent of Beauvais)
Lecterns K and L	Sermon cycles, treatises on penance and confession
Lectern M	Praeceptoria (moral theology texts)
Lectern N	Classical and Christian Philosophy
Lectern O	History and Church History
Lecterns P and Q	Sermons, Exempla
Lectern R	Canon (and sometimes Roman) Law

On one hand, the book collections of the Franciscans reveal texts specific to the order, covering a wide range of subjects. Compared to other late medieval libraries the collection's content was conservative – shaped by the specific needs of the brothers. This state of affairs was due to the order's regulations concerning access to books – the community's most valuable property – and its system of scrutinizing texts. However, a closer examination often reveals individual features: We can trace thematic emphases originating from the integration of formerly private book collections made by individual friars during the course of their lives and studies. Whenever a convent was reformed, books that no longer fitted the profile of the Observants disappeared while others deemed important were added. Friends of the Nuremberg Franciscans for example donated numerous humanistic works to the brothers. And here Nikolaus Glaßberger, a friend of the humanists at the end of the fifteenth century, worked himself as a chronicler and helped filling the lecterns.[60] Thus the libraries tell stories, testifying to a thirst for knowledge and intellectual ambition as well as reflecting the industry of copyists and the needs of their readers.

The care the order invested in its libraries and the education of the friars had a considerable effect on the outside world. It increased the authority and attractiveness of the Franciscan communities. In the eyes of contemporaries the Franciscans were regarded as unmatched in giving reliable information on difficult theological questions. Since brothers returning to their original friaries from the universities or from other centres of education brought the most recent literature back with them, their libraries were often (comparatively) up to date. A fine example is here the library of the Franciscans in Fribourg, Switzerland.[61] Public collections were made accessible to a broader population by chaining books to the pulpits, and in many cases it was even possible to borrow the books. The secular clergy took this opportunity as long as any local competition with the mendicant brothers did not complicate the relationship.

Books could be loaned by the friars. Our Florentine guardian, Bernhard Guascone, himself certainly a book-lover, specified a lending period of fourteen days or a month at most for convent members.[62] Then, however, the

---

60 For his activities also towards the Poor Clares in Nuremberg see recently E. Schlotheuber, 'Humanistisches Wissen und geistliches Leben. Caritas Pirckheimer und die Geschichtsschreibung im Nürnberger Klarissenkonvent', in: *Die Pirckheimer. Humanismus in einer Nürnberger Patrizierfamilie*, (ed.) F. Fuchs (Pirckheimer Jahrbuch, 21), Nürnberg 2006, 75–104. See Roest, *History* (cf. note 4), Franciscan reform and humanism 168-71.

61 Ladner, 'Bedeutung' (cf. note 42) 11–24.

62 *Item quod libri qui fratribus ad studium commodantur semper de quindena in quindenam vel ad tardius omni mense pro dispositione guardiani, ad pulsatione campanelle, armariste fideliter resignentur. Et qui contrarium fecerit, sequenti die in prandio a*

book must be returned punctually, at the tolling of the bells. Anyone who failed to comply was made to abstain from wine at the next day's meal – apparently an effective punishment – and the tardy party lost his library access for a month. In 1467 the provincial statutes of Saxony allowed borrowing by non-members of the order (*seculares*), but provided for a 'loan slip' (*cedula recognitionis*).[63] Parish priests, burghers and members of the city council used the well-equipped libraries.[64] In the north and central German libraries I have researched, the legal section was noticeably rich, in Canon as well as Roman law. In the cities, people had a great need for just such resources as a means for resolving their various controversies. Not at least because of this state of affairs, Franciscan refectories were often seen by many German city councils as appropriate venues for their meetings. In this way, libraries enhanced the political and social significance of the Franciscans in their immediate surroundings. Nonetheless opening up the libraries' to secular readers could also be risky. In 1514 a provincial chapter of Dominicans published directives that readers who were not members of the order should put down a deposit. Besides a brother always had to be present to supervise the external reader – and the brother was to exit the library after the visitor![65]

---

vino abstinere firmiter teneantur et nichilominus per mensem libris armarii sit privatus. Bihl, 'Ordinationes fratris Bernardi' (cf. note 41) c. 8, 150.

63 *Et libri etiam fratribus sine cedula recognitionis non concedantur, multo minus secularibus, quibus sub cedula recognitionis poterunt de consensu vicarii et discretorum per guadianum ad tempus commodari.* B. Kruitwagen (ed.), 'Statuta Provinciae Saxoniae condita Brandenburgi anno 1467, immutata Luneburgi anno 1494', *AFH* 3 (1910) 8–114; 280–293, here 280.

64 Schlotheuber, Büchersammlung (cf. note 21) 242f.

65 *Eciam sub eadem pena prohibemus, ne aliquis liber cathenatus fratri vel seculari sine circographo et sufficienti pignore concedatur. (...) Insuper nullus fratrum quemcumque extra obedienciam ordinis constitutum, insignibus personis et non eorum*

II. The education of children

In some cases Franciscans even took the responsibility for the elementary education of future members of their order. The question of accepting children was a subject of particular interest in the fourteenth century. The demographic break in the religious communities caused by agricultural crisis and plague gave rise to the problem of recruiting new members in a completely new form. Giving children religious status, called *oblation* or donation, had already been a widely used method for replenishing a convent's membership among the older orders in the Early and High Middle Ages.[66] The reform orders and among them the Franciscans originally rejected it. The order did not need to be concerned with elementary education, because many highly educated men joined its ranks.[67] The general statutes of Narbonne (1260) could self confidently say that nobody was allowed to enter the order without

famulis exceptis, ad librariam nostram intromittat, nisi ipse vel alius cum eis in libraria maneat et ante ipsum de libraria exeat. G. Löhr, 'Die Kapitel der Provinz Saxonia im Zeitalter der Kirchenspaltung 1513–1540', *Quellen und Forschungen zur Geschichte des Dominikanerordens in Deutschland* 26 (1930) 1–260, here 110.

66 See M. de Jong, 'Growing up in a Carolingian Monastery: Magister Hildemar and his Oblates', *Journal of Medieval History* 9 (1983) 99–128. *Eadem, Kind en klooster in de vroege middeleeuwen. Aspecten van de schenking van kinderen aan kloosters in het frankische rijk (500–900),* (Amsterdams Historische Reeks, 8) Amsterdam 1986. *Eadem, In Samuel's Image. Child Oblation in the Early Medieval West,* Leiden / New York / Köln 1996. For the importance of the oblation in the late middle ages E. Schlotheuber, *Klostereintritt und Bildung. Die Lebenswelt der Nonnen im späten Mittelalter.* Mit einer Edition des ‚Konventstagebuchs' einer Zisterzienserin von Heilig-Kreuz bei Braunschweig (1484–1507), (Spätmittelalter und Reformation. Neue Reihe, 24) Tübingen 2004, 175–221.

67 Michael Robson named many of them in his fine history of the medieval custody of York, M. Robson, *The Franciscans in the medieval custody of York,* York 1997.

sufficient knowledge of Latin, Grammar and Logic, because 'we have to be an example to the people, having good advice and giving them salutary exhortation.'[68] The general statutes of Assisi (1279) and Paris (1292) repeat the austere regulations about the age of novices.[69] But the numerous newly-founded settlements and *Termineien* further on demanded great numbers of personnel. Despite the normative regulations some problems regarding the age of acceptance must have existed already in the middle of the thirteenth century. Pope Alexander IV (1254–1261), formerly cardinal protector of the order, forbade the Franciscans and the Dominicans to accept anyone who was not at least fourteen years old and the friars were equally prohibited to make profession before the year of probation was completed.[70] Bert Roest states that younger people were indeed accepted and that they were educated in the now established custodial and provincial schools.[71] The

---

68 Narbonne, 1260, Assisi, 1279, Paris, 1292, (n. 12) clause 1, 38 (Narbonne 1260).

69 *Ordinamus etiam, ut nullus recipiatur citra XVIII annum, nisi per robur corporis vel industriam sensus seu per excellentem aedificationem, a XV anno et supra, aetas secundum prudentium iudicium suppleatur Ibid.* clause 1, 40.

70 *Vobis de fratrum nostrorum consilio in virtute obedientiae et sub poena excommunicationis auctoritate praesentium districtius inhibemus, ne ante annum probationis elapsum, qui est maxime in subsidium fragilitatis humanae regulariter institutus, quemquam ad professionem vestri ordinis seu renunciationem in saeculo faciendam recipere, nec constitutum infra huiusmodi annum aliquatenus impedire, quo minus infra ipsum ad aliam religionem, quam maluerit, transeat, vel nisi, maior tamen quatuordecim annis exsistens, professus sit tacite vel expresse, aut evidenter constet, illum vitam voluisse mutare, quod tamen non praesumitur, nisi clara probatione vel competentibus indiciis ostendatur, omnino ad saeculum redeat, sicut de sua voluntate processerit, praesumatis. Corpus iuris canonici*, 2 vols., (ed.) E. Friedberg, Leipzig 1879–1881, II, Liber Sextus 3. 14. 2, 1051.

71 Roest, *History* (cf. note 4) 68. For the basic research see L. Oliger, 'De pueris oblatis in ordine Minorum', *AFH* 8 (1915) 389–447; 10

general statutes of Assisi (1316) did nor change the minimum age for novices (15 years) but made two remarkable exceptions: younger novices lacking the prerequisite of good knowledge of Latin should only be accepted if they were – according to the judgment of the senior members of the convent – capable of becoming literate 'or if you have to take someone (*oportet recipere*) in order to preserve the family's memory of the dead.'[72] These additions show that the Franciscans apparently saw themselves forced to assume responsibility for the elementary education of new members. They could also make an exception for younger individuals who were eager or willing to learn. Consequently most of these new arrivals needed to go through a basic education in Latin before the novitiate started. In a development corresponding to these changes we find basic works of grammar, logic and rhetoric, usually organized together on a separate reading stand for school literature in convent libraries for the first time.

The second exception made in 1316 can only mean that the order saw itself forced to take in candidates when certain families sought the entry of one of their members in order to cultivate the family's *memoria*. The general statutes of Lyon (1325) already treat the admission of children as a natural and accepted means of entry into the

---

(1917) 271–88.

72 *Statuimus in principio quod nullus recipiatur ad ordinem nostrum nisi quartumdecimum annum compleverit in etate. (...) Et nullus recipiatur pro clerico, nisi sit competenter instructus in gramatica 'vel alia facultate'. Quod si alicubi tales haberi non possunt, non recipiantur ad minus nisi qui sunt discretorum iudicio habiles ad predicta, aut nisi oporteat aliquos recipi pro familiaribus obsequiis exercendis.* A. Carlini (ed.), 'Constitutiones generales Ordinis fratrum minorum anno 1316 Assisii conditae', *AFH* 6 (1911) 269–302, 508–536, here clause 1, 277.

community.⁷³ The Franciscans had, in the interval since their founding, created their own connections and traditions. Via their work as confessors they cultivated close contacts with the nobility and the urban elite, many of whose members had chosen Franciscan churches as burial sites. In this way they developed the same network of relationships in which the older orders were already trapped. The most important connection in this framework was the presence of multiple generations of the same family in a convent.⁷⁴ These family members assumed the obligation of memorializing the deceased, thus maintaining the ties between the living members of the family and their relatives buried in the convent church. The connections of these families with their ancestors and with the convents in which they were buried could be best sustained through the oblation of relatives dedicated to this purpose. Religious communities had a difficult time refusing the requests of their frequently influential supporters in this regard. Decisions concerning this practice were often described with phrases like *oportet recipere*.

In the year 1430 the reform statutes approved by pope Martin V (*Constitutiones Martinianae*) were supposed to find a new basis for the two contending branches of the

---

73 *Statuimus in principio quod nullus recipiatur ad ordinem nostrum, nisi quartumdecimum annum compleverit in aetate, praeter illos qui a parentibus ordini offerentur, ita quod quando ad professionem recipitur annus XV sit completus.* Carlini, Constitutiones (n. 72) clause 1, 527 (Lyon 1325).

74 Schlotheuber, *Klostereintritt* (cf. note 66) 209f. The Latin written study of Livarius Oliger documents that oblation played an important role for the Franciscans in the late middle ages: *Rebus autem sic inspectis, apparet oblationis puerorum institutum, tum sensu stricto, tum latiore illo indicato, minime restringi ad ordines monasticos, sed – quod saepius negatur vel ad minus ignoratur – et apud Mendicantes, specialius apud Fratres Minores, de quibus hic principalius agimus, passim inveniri, et quidem, si eorum adversariis fidem licet praestare, non parva in mensura*, Oliger, Pueris (cf. note 71) 390.

order. Those statutes forbade the admission of anyone below the age of fourteen, even as an oblate.[75] But – probably as result of a compromise – they added an exeption: If the potential oblate happened to be the son of a powerful family and a refusal would create trouble for the community they could accept him as a child. The nobles apparently urged the convents to take their children. The regulation not to educate children in the convents has to be seen in this context.[76] Mediation failed and the Observants refused to follow the *Constitutiones Martinianae* after a short while. The reformed wing of the Franciscans categorically rejected oblation,[77] as we can tell from their complaints at the Council of Constance. They could afford this attitude because in the fifteenth century they were

---

75 *Statuimus insuper et ordinamus quod nullus recipiatur ad ordinem nisi annum quartumdecimum compleverit, eciam si oblatus fuerit a parentibus, nisi pro scandalo evitando, ut si forsan foret filius militis vel superioris dignitatis.* BF V, 736. See B. Neidiger, 'Die Martinianischen Konstitutionen von 1430 als Reformprogramm der Franziskanerkonventualen. Ein Beitrag zur Geschichte des Kölner Minoritenklosters und der Kölner Ordensprovinz im 15. Jahrhundert', *Zeitschrift für Kirchengeschichte* 95 (1984) 337–82.

76 *Per haec tamen nullus fratrum praesumat puerorum scholas regere in conventu, vel extra personarum saecularium, sub poena privationis actuum legitimorum.* BF V, 736.

77 The general statutes of the Observants 1451 make this point unmistakably clear. You can imagine the relevance of the subject when they start their regulations with the following statement: *Statuimus imprimis, quod qui venientem ad ordinem nostrum debet in fratrem recipere diligenter inquirat et attendat sollicite quod recipiendus, ut docet regula, sit fidelis et catholicus, de nullo errore suspectus, matrimonio non ligatus, corpore sanus, animo promptus, legitime natus, debitis expeditus, conditione liber, aetatem attingens XVI annorum ad minus, nulla infamia vulgari maculatus, competenter literatus, vel ad labores fratribus honestos et utiles aptus, aut talis condicionis existens quod eius receptio clero et populo non modicam aedificationem afferat*, Statuta generalia edita apud Barcinonam 1451, in: *Monumenta Francescana*, 2 vols. J.S. Brewer / R. Howlett (eds.), (RS, 4) London 1858-82, II, 81–123, here 83.

enjoying great popularity since they embodied the ideal of religious life in the sense of the *imitatio Christi*. They received support from princes and bishops, who frequently reformed convents according to the Observant rules even against the will of the brothers living in them. Although many highly-educated adults again found their way into the order as a consequence, above all in university cities, nonetheless the entry of minors into the order continued to remain relevant as a way to achieve educational and social advancement. A biography like that of Konrad Pellikan who entered the Observant Franciscan house of Rufach at the age of six towards the end of the fifteenth century is probably no exception.[78] He made his way through the order's entire curriculum and qualified for the important offices of lector and guardian. He was later considered an important scholar, famous for his knowledge of Hebrew and Greek.

Through their continuous and both systematic and professional approach to education and literature the Franciscans opened a path to the written word, to theology and to the Church to people from all social levels. Often the order's internal education system produced great scholars, men whose names are still known and who contributed significantly to the intellectual development of the medieval church and of society. At the same time they exercised a great influence on their immediate surroundings – by offering the opportunity of education with access to a spiritual and intellectual world to many people whose traces would otherwise have been lost to history.

---

78 H. R. Velten, *Das selbst geschriebene Leben. Eine Studie zur deutschen Autobiographie im 16. Jahrhundert*, Heidelberg 1995, 88–94. See E. Wenneker, 'Pellikan, Konrad', in: *Bio-bibliographisches Lexikon*, VII (1994) 180–3.

La Reforme en gestes et en textes. Autour de «l'Observance» Franciscaine

Ludovic Viallet

(Université Blaise Pascal, Clermont-Ferrand II)

À partir de la fin du quatorzième siècle, les ordres mendiants ont connu d'importants mouvements de réforme dont la diversité ne doit pas être masquée par le terme d'«Observance», souvent utilisé de façon générique par les historiens. Les frères Mineurs offrent le cas le plus spectaculaire d'un profond remaniement, qui déboucha sur la scission de l'Ordre en 1517 au moment même où apparaissait le terme de «franciscain», issu de la matrice qu'avait constituée, pour l'idéal d'une unité de plus en plus illusoire, le processus de fragmentation institutionnelle et de dissolution identitaire.[1] Celui-ci s'était indéniablement accéléré au milieu du siècle précédent. Jamais sans doute, en effet, les divergences de voies n'avaient alors été aussi importantes, en un phénomène généralisé à l'échelle de l'Ordre. Ainsi la «diversité de vie» (*diversitas vitae*) des frères est-elle mise en avant dans la *Chronica* de Nicolas Glassberger pour expliquer la décision du pape Eugène IV, à l'été 1443, d'instituer deux vicaires généraux de l'Observance.[2] La lettre *Fratrum ordinis Minorum* fut suivie trois ans plus tard, le 18 juillet 1446, de la *Ut sacra*,

---

1 Voir en particulier G.G. Merlo, 'Conclusion', in: F. Meyer / L. Viallet (dir.), *Identités franciscaines à l'âge des réformes*, Clermont-Ferrand 2005, 503, selon qui l'apparition de ce terme exprime la conservation de «l'ideal *unitario* di un'antica, se non mitica, ispirazione comune».

2 *Chronica Fratris Nicolai Glassberger Ordinis Minorum Observantium*, in: (AF, II), Quaracchi 1887, 308-9.

peut-être rédigée par Jean de Capistran lui-même. Elle fit prendre à la famille franciscaine un tournant essentiel, car le raidissement suscité chez les frères attachés à l'unité de l'Ordre plus qu'à une définition stricte de la pauvreté franciscaine déboucha sur la singularisation croissante de groupes et de réseaux réformés ou réformateurs.

Pour bien comprendre cette histoire complexe, il faut remonter plus haut dans le temps, au sortir des dramatiques décennies 1310 et 1320 au cours desquelles, après un siècle de tensions et de crises, l'ordre franciscain entra dans une nouvelle phase de son histoire. Tandis que s'ouvrait pour l'Occident une période dont il n'est pas besoin de rappeler les spécificités, les décisions de Jean XXII relatives à la pauvreté franciscaine donnent à bon droit le sentiment qu'une page était tournée: celle des «temps héroïques» marqués par l'extraordinaire expérience du fondateur et de ses compagnons, puis par les prolongements, jusqu'aux bûchers de Spirituels, de la lutte pour la fidélité à l'Évangile; celle de la fameuse «question franciscaine» chère aux «Franciscanisants» depuis Paul Sabatier. Passé le premier tiers du quatorzième siècle, l'histoire des Mineurs a souvent paru aux historiens, sinon moins «intéressante», à coup sûr moins fascinante, même si les grandes figures de prédicateurs du siècle suivant ont bien des atouts pour raviver la flamme. Il faut dire aussi que l'accumulation des textes législatifs ayant accompagné l'histoire de l'Ordre a de quoi décourager. Elle a incontestablement abouti, chez les historiens, à perdre de vue ce que pouvaient être les modalités du *vivre franciscain*, alors même que pour aucune autre famille régulière la nécessité d'en faire une véritable *anthropologie* ne paraît autant justifiée, tant ce genre de vie impliquait une véritable réflexion sur des pratiques, des postures, des gestes et le langage de ceux-ci.

Cette réflexion ne peut réellement s'effectuer qu'en levant un certain nombre de barrières, au premier rang desquelles se situe, d'un point de vue proprement méthodologique, l'insuffisante perméabilité entre des océans historiographiques qui trop souvent s'ignorent. Ce qui est vrai pour la production historique italienne l'est aussi pour celle des espaces germanique et d'Europe centre-orientale, français et ibérique.[3] Par ailleurs, il est nécessaire de prendre garde aux mots — rebattus et utilisés par facilité, ils finissent parfois par ne plus guère avoir de sens — et de ne pas raisonner avec des oppositions binaires trop tranchées ignorant que derrière les différences d'interprétation il y eut des fondements communs et que derrière les mouvements réformateurs il y eut des hommes, dont l'état d'esprit évolua avec l'âge, le parcours et les circonstances. Ainsi, par exemple, de la «stricte

---

3   Pour prendre un exemple récent, significatif me paraît être le cas du petit livre de F. Bolgiani / G.G. Merlo (éd.), *Il francescanesimo dalle origini alla metà del secolo XVI. Esplorazioni e questioni aperte. Atti del Convegno della Fondazione Michele Pellegrino, Università di Torino, 11 novembre 2004*, Bologne 2005, presque exclusivement centré sur la production des historiens de la Péninsule. Il rassemble, il est vrai, les interventions faites lors de ce qui fut davantage une présentation d'ouvrage qu'une véritable rencontre destinée à recenser les problématiques et stimuler la réflexion. Au centre de cet événement, le livre de G.G. Merlo *Nel nome di san Francesco. Storia dei frati Minori e del francescanesimo sino agli inizi del XVI secolo*, Padoue 2003, qui offre désormais une approche d'ensemble, remarquablement problématisée, de l'histoire de la famille franciscaine sans négliger le quinzième siècle. Il n'empêche, une figure aussi importante que celle de Matthias Döring, ministre de la vaste province de Saxe de 1427 à 1461, en est complètement absent. Sur ce personnage, on dispose désormais de la thèse de P. Weigel *Ordensreform und Konziliarismus. Der Franziskanerprovinzial Matthias Döring (1427-1461)*, Francfort sur le Main 2005, nouveau jalon dans une très féconde historiographie germanique du monde franciscain. Du côté de la péninsule ibérique, prodigieux terreau de la vie franciscaine, un important bilan thématique et historiographique est paru récemment sous l'égide de l'Asociación Hispánica de Estudios Franciscanos: M. del Mar Graña Cid (éd.), *El franciscanismo en la Península Ibérica. Balance y perspectivas. I Congreso Internacional. Madrid, 22-27 de septiembre de 2003*, Barcelone 2005.

observance»: au-delà de l'expression, a-t-elle jamais existé? Au milieu du quinzième siècle, les formes officielles de l'observance la plus stricte avaient intégré l'impossibilité de respecter *ad litteram* la Règle de saint François; il faudrait aller chercher dans des expériences extrêmes, notamment dans la péninsule ibérique de la seconde moitié du siècle, des exemples de volonté d'une *observantia strictissima*. En ce qui concerne l'un des principaux artisans de l'autonomie de l'Observance sous l'autorité des vicaires, Capistran lui-même, qui incarna dans les dix dernières années de sa vie un positionnement rigoureux, son parcours et son œuvre de législateur ne pouvaient lui faire renier toute *glossa* de la Règle, donc la totalité de ce que Grado Merlo a appelé le modèle franciscain «accumulatif»[4], défini par des textes pontificaux se fondant au début sur la connaissance de l'*intentio* de François. L'ancien juriste italien a probablement rédigé les Constitutions issues du chapitre général d'Assise et promulguées par Martin V en 1430: texte de consensus et de conciliation, après plusieurs décennies d'une floraison d'expériences réformatrices sans véritable coordination à l'échelle de l'Ordre; texte dont la postérité fut d'abord un retentissant échec, mais qui, par les refus et positionnements qu'il suscita dans l'immédiat, puis par la référence qu'il constitua au cours de la seconde moitié du quinzième siècle pour la réforme des Conventuels comme pour l'Observance «cismontaine», contribua à structurer le paysage franciscain. Toutefois, le *propositum vitae* que Capistran prôna dans les Constitutions de 1443, puis qu'il fit mettre en œuvre lors de sa grande tournée de 1451-1456 en Europe centre-orientale, était plus rigoureux. Le personnage, émancipé de la recherche du consensus, avait en effet évolué, le climat à l'intérieur de l'Ordre s'était durci et le contexte de la pastorale observante dans les villes germaniques et polonaises ne poussait pas à la modération.

---

4   Merlo, *Nel nome di san Francesco* (comme note 3), 306.

Corrélativement, il faut scruter attentivement, tout autant qu'on puisse le faire, ce qui se cache derrière les pratiques et les mots qui les désignent. Il ne suffit pas, par exemple, de placer comme poste-frontière entre «Conventuels» et «Observants» le maniement de l'argent, ou même, en affinant l'analyse, l'existence d'un procureur faisant office de *persona interposita* entre les frères et les biens matériels. Capistran ne bannit ni le premier ni le second de ses prescriptions réglementaires, notamment parce qu'il eut le souci de clarifier certains points restés ambigus dans les Constitutions de 1430 et qu'il tint compte des circonstances de l'usage nécessaire. En revanche, il est clair qu'au milieu du quinzième siècle, l'un des points d'achoppement principaux entre les «Conventuels», même favorables à certaines réformes comme le provincial de Saxe Matthias Döring, grand adversaire de Capistran, et ceux qui *se dicunt de observantia* — comme les désignent leurs adversaires dans les documents — réside dans la réception d'aumônes pécuniaires à l'autel et dans les troncs des églises. Pour les plus zélés des réformateurs, la vie des frères doit reposer sur le travail et sur la quête, qui ne se confond pas avec les offrandes récoltées lors de l'assemblée des fidèles, car la quête est effectuée en personne, sans aucune contrepartie et auprès d'une population, non d'un bienfaiteur déterminé — sur ce dernier point, l'ambiguïté n'est évidemment jamais loin. Accepter des dons dans le sanctuaire, notamment au moment des messes, est conçu comme une solution de facilité et de sécurité à proscrire absolument. Pour les tenants d'une vision plus souple, l'église est le lieu de l'indéterminé, du geste qui n'est pas adressé à un frère en particulier, a fortiori lorsqu'une personne extérieure à la communauté se charge de relever les offrandes, donc d'épargner aux frères tout contact direct avec l'argent.

Ce long préliminaire fournit d'ores et déjà quelques clefs essentielles pour cerner la réalité qu'a recouverte l'Observance. Afin d'en présenter les traits principaux dans une démarche «englobante», il faut avoir à l'esprit combien a été important le spectre couvert par *les* réformes franciscaines du quinzième siècle et replacer la question dans le cadre plus large d'une réflexion sur la *reformatio* de l'Église chrétienne. Ce sera l'objet du premier volet de ce propos. On soulignera ainsi, dans un deuxième et un troisième temps, combien le succès de l'Observance a résulté d'une tension, surmontée, entre le charisme et l'institution, et comment cette tension se confond en bonne partie avec une autre, entre «ouverture» et «fermeture», c'est-à-dire entre l'activisme de terrain — qui correspond surtout à la phase de conquête — et le *propositum vitae* — c'est-à-dire les textes réglementaires et la conception que l'on se faisait de la réforme. On concluera par l'évocation de quelques pistes de recherches qui concernent un autre défi posé à l'Observance, puisqu'elle appelait à un changement qui soit aussi remise en ordre: la conciliation des exigences de la *reformatio* et du lien avec les élites urbaines.

I. Réforme religieuse, contrôle social et entrée dans la «modernité»

On peut considérer que l'Observance franciscaine est née au milieu du quatorzième siècle, avec la petite congrégation formée autour de Jean de la Vallée et de l'ermitage de Brogliano, non loin d'Assise. Le relais y fut pris par Paul de Trinci, mort en 1391. L'essor de la réforme s'enclencha de façon concomitante, à la charnière des quatorzième et quinzième siècles, au couvent de Mirebeau (Poitou) et dans les provinces de Saint-Jacques de Compostelle, Aragon et Castille. En concédant, en 1415, une hiérarchie propre aux Observants de France, le concile de Constance ouvrit la porte à des affrontements qui allaient durer deux siècles. Au cours d'une large première moitié du quinzième siècle, la progression de l'Observance en Europe occidentale fut spectaculaire, par la réforme de communautés existantes ou la création de nouvelles maisons et grâce à l'action de personnages comme Colette de Corbie, Bernardin de Sienne et Jean de Capistran. Incontestablement, les deux principales sources ayant irrigué la dynamique réformatrice ont été méridionales, en Italie et en Espagne. Le va-et-vient fut fructueux entre les deux péninsules et contribua à façonner des choix de vie marqués par une observance extrême dans des milieux naturels propices à la fuite du monde. D'une façon générale, les années 1460-1470 marquèrent un tournant dans le conflit interne à l'ordre franciscain, avec l'intensification, sur le terrain, de la rivalité souvent violente entre les religieux. En 1517, la bulle *Ite vos* de Léon X entérina la scission de l'Ordre, mais la situation ne se stabilisa pas avant le début du dix-septième siècle.[5] Désormais majoritaires, les Observants étaient sortis vainqueurs du bras de fer.

---

5   Pour un panorama d'ensemble, indépendamment des actes de colloques, notamment ceux de la Société Internationale d'Études Franciscaines, on disposait jusqu'à une date récente essentiellement des «manuels» de H. Holzapfel, *Handbuch der Geschichte des Franziskanerordens*, Fribourg-en-Brisgau 1909, et L. Iriarte, *Storia del francescanesimo*, Rome 1982, issu de son *Manual de historia franciscana*, Madrid 1954 et traduit en plusieurs langues, notamment en français (*Histoire du franciscanisme*, Paris 2004) ainsi que, dans une optique plus «historienne» et problématisée, des synthèses de J. Moorman, *A History of the Franciscan Order from its Origins to the Year 1517*, Oxford 1968 et D. Nimmo, *Reform and Division in the Medieval Franciscan Order from saint Francis to the foundation of the Capuchins*, Rome 1987, qui consacre moins de dix pages aux années 1447-1528. Ce n'est pas le lieu, ici, d'aller plus loin dans la présentation de la bibliographie disponible. Je me contente de renvoyer à l'ouvrage de Merlo *Nel nome di san Francesco* (comme note 3), traduit récemment en français (*Au nom de saint François. Histoire des Frères mineurs et du franciscanisme jusqu'au début du XVIe siècle*, Paris, 2006), qui constitue désormais la référence pour toute approche générale de l'Ordre, ainsi qu'aux contributions publiées dans Meyer / Viallet (dir.), *Identités franciscaines à l'âge des réformes* (comme note 1), qui couvrent un espace très largement européen et la période allant de la fin du quatorzième au début du dix-septième siècle.

À la veille de la séparation, trois grands groupes de communautés existaient au sein de l'Ordre: la Conventualité, qui n'avait pas été et n'était pas étrangère à toute velléité de réforme; l'Observance, organisée en deux grands ensembles, cismontain et ultramontain, eux-mêmes divisés en différentes vicairies; entre ces deux pôles, une *via media*. Celle-ci était incarnée par l'Observance «colétane», dite à l'époque *sub ministris*, qui constituait un mouvement important dans les provinces franciscaines de France et Bourgogne, et par la réforme «martinienne», qui tirait son nom des Constitutions de 1430 et fut adoptée en particulier dans la vaste province de Saxe.[6] Cette voie moyenne était caractérisée par le refus de la rupture avec la hiérarchie de l'Ordre, mais aussi par des pratiques plus conciliantes, au cours du dernier quart du quinzième siècle, dans le rapport aux biens matériels. Les Constitutions de 1430, en effet, étaient un texte flou sur certains points essentiels — au sujet de la réception des legs et des fondations pieuses en particulier — dont l'interprétation divergea selon l'un ou l'autre camp.

Enfin, la province de Saxe offre à l'historien une situation encore plus complexe.[7] Le décret *Ad statum* du 28

---

6 Voir B. Degler-Spengler, 'Observanten ausserhalb der Observanz. Die franziskanischen Reformen *sub ministris*', *Zeitschrift für Kirchengeschichte* 89 (1978) 354-371 ; B. Neidiger, 'Die Martinianischen Konstitutionen von 1430 als Reformprogramm der Franziskanerkonventualen', *Zeitschrift für Kirchengeschichte* 95 (1984) 337-381.

7 Sur le cas de cette vaste province, qui s'étendait de la Baltique à la Bohême, la base de toute enquête est encore constituée par les travaux de F. Doelle, en particulier *Die Observanzbewegung in der sächsischen Franziskanerprovinz bis zum Generalkapitel von Parma 1529*, Münster 1918 et *Die Martinianische Reformbewegung in der Sächsischen Franziskanerprovinz*, Münster 1916. Bilan récent du projet de l'IFG de Münster dans B. Schmies, 'Die Geschichte der Sächsischen Franziskanerprovinz von den Anfängen bis zum Ende des 20. Jahrhunderts. Ein Werkstattbericht über das Forschungsprojekt des Instituts für franziskanische Geschichte,

août 1430 avait instauré une atténuation des Constitutions martiniennes, atténuation à laquelle le ministre provincial Matthias Döring était favorable, puisqu'il rédigea lui-même des Constitutions adoucies promulguées lors du chapitre général de Bologne en 1433. Les couvents ayant adopté cette modération connurent jusqu'au début du seizième siècle des processus de réforme d'après les Constitutions martiniennes, ce qui leur valut l'appellation de couvents de *Reformaten*. Dans la seconde moitié du quinzième siècle, certains d'entre eux choisirent d'appliquer le système du *visitator regiminis*, système qui visait à mener une vie plus stricte, mais conforme aux Constitutions martiniennes et qui permettait également une autonomie par rapport au custode sans soustraction à la juridiction du ministre provincial. Les autorités urbaines de Görlitz, en Haute Lusace, furent à la pointe de ce combat, dont l'enjeu était le contrôle du couvent local, qui était à son tour susceptible d'influencer d'autres maisons. Un levier d'action, pour Görlitz, fut la Ligue des Six Villes (Görlitz, Bautzen, Zittau, Löbau, Lauban, Kamenz), dont le refus de l'Observance était lié à la volonté de préserver l'autonomie de la Haute Lusace face à la Couronne de Bohême, dans un contexte de tensions ethniques — entre Allemands et Tchèques — et religieuses — entre le Catholicisme et les mouvements issus du Hussitisme.[8] Le paysage de la

---

Münster', in: J. Schneider (dir.), *Klosterforschung. Befunde, Projekte, Perspektiven*, Munich 2006, 119-126.

8 Pour une approche monographique du monde franciscain en Silésie et Haute Lusace, voir G. Wąs, *Klasztory franciszkańskie w miastach śląskich I górnołużyckich XIII-XVI wieku*, Wrocław 2000, auquel on ajoutera Idem, 'Religiöses und gesellschaftliches Bewußtsein. Stadträte und Franziskanerklöster im Schlesien des 15. und 16. Jahrhunderts', *Wissenschaft und Weisheit* 61 (1998) 57-97. Le cas de Görlitz, sur lequel je travaille également, est abordé dans S. Drexhage-Leisebein, 'Reformerisches Engagement städtischer Obrigkeit in der zweiten Hälfte des 15. Jahrhunderts. Die franziskanischen Reformbewegungen in der städtischen Kirchen- und Klosterpolitik am Beispiel ausgewählter Städte im Gebiet der

réforme est donc complexe. Pour mieux l'apprécier, il faut aussi s'intéresser à «l'arrière-pays» de la réforme, tant à l'échelle des espaces régionaux qu'à celle de l'Église tout entière, qui permet d'envisager une perspective et des dynamiques plus larges et «englobantes», donc de sortir des histoires de famille.

L'Église chrétienne, institution, a été dès l'origine travaillée par une contradiction fondamentale avec l'esprit de l'*agapè* — cette forme supérieure de l'amour qui, reliant les croyants entre eux, fait selon saint Jean l'appartenance à l'Église. Sur cette tension assumée, maîtrisée, reposa le succès de la christianisation médiévale, mais aussi une potentialité critique qui enfla avec l'institution ecclésiale et le contrôle social qu'elle prétendait exercer, ainsi qu'avec un certain nombre de mutations socio-culturelles touchant l'Occident à partir du douzième siècle surtout. La *reformatio* devint alors une véritable obsession que les historiens ont longtemps pensée en terme de réaction à une évolution négative, sans souligner combien il s'est davantage agi d'une sorte de «moteur interne» permettant à l'Église d'évoluer. Encore faut-il bien avoir conscience de certains caractères essentiels de la «réforme».

D'une part, il faut insister sur le fait que celle-ci participe d'un phénomène permanent, ou du moins récurrent, dans le Christianisme et dans d'autres religions; d'un véritable *travail* du champ religieux manifestant «le besoin d'expulser comme inauthentique une part des manières de faire et de penser autrefois reçues».[9] Phénomène dynamique que nous associons aujourd'hui à

Sächsischen Ordensprovinz', in: D. Berg (dir.), *Bettelorden und Stadt. Bettelorden und städtisches Leben im Mittelalter und in der Neuzeit*, Werl 1992, 215-22.

9   F. A. Isambert, *Rite et efficacité symbolique. Essai d'anthropologie sociologique*, Paris 1979, 61, qui souligne combien «unité du champ religieux et tension réformatrice doivent être tenues pour aspects complémentaires et sans doute inséparables» (*ibid.*).

un progrès, la réforme religieuse était en outre au Moyen Âge, comme toute réforme, associée à l'idée de restauration d'un ordre antérieur. Enfin, il convient de ne pas penser la réforme, désormais, en plaquant les outils avec lesquels la religion a été pensée par les anthropologues et les sociologues depuis la fin du dix-neuvième siècle. Je pense ici à Max Weber, dont la méthode de «l'idéal-type» semblerait facilement applicable à une lecture des dynamiques réformatrices tardo-médiévales si on oubliait, justement, qu'il s'agit... d'«idéaux» et de «types», qu'à ce titre on ne retrouve pas avec autant de netteté dans l'Histoire.[10] Devant les mutations et les phénomènes que connut l'*Ecclesia* aux onzième et douzième siècles, il est bien permis de distinguer deux versants de la *reformatio*: l'un, «institutionnel», «clérical», «grégorien»; l'autre «charismatique», «évangélique», «apostolique». La réalité historique paraît ici confirmer un schéma bi-polaire, celui des deux figures wébériennes du prêtre et du prophète, que l'on retrouve d'une façon ou d'une autre chez nombre d'auteurs ayant cherché à penser les diverses formes du fait religieux, par exemple Henri Bergson ou Maurice Halbwachs.[11] Or, l'évolution de la spiritualité de la fin du Moyen Âge fut dépassement du clivage — s'il a jamais existé — entre «religion des clercs» et «religion des mystiques», les Mendiants jouant un rôle essentiel dans ce dépassement qui fut enrichissement par l'intériorisation. En outre, l'Église sut utiliser les deux faces de la réforme en

---

10 On pensera aussi à E. Troeltsch, *Soziallehren der christlichen Kirchen und Gruppen*, Tübingen 1912. Sur les limites, et par là même les apports de la méthode «idéaltypique», voir ce qu'écrit Jean Séguy dans l'introduction de *Conflit et utopie, ou réformer l'Église. Parcours wébérien en douze essais*, Paris 1999, 47-56.

11 H. Bergson, *Les deux sources de la morale et de la religion*, Paris 1932; M. Halbwachs, *Les cadres sociaux de la mémoire*, Paris 1925 et *La mémoire collective*, Paris 1949 (nouvelle éd. critique Paris 1997).

s'appuyant constamment sur l'une, en combattant l'autre de façon sélective afin d'en absorber ce qui pouvait l'être.

On a suffisamment souligné combien la genèse de l'Ordre franciscain illustrait à merveille ce processus d'absorption par l'institutionnalisation d'un mouvement susceptible d'être rejeté dans les marges de l'orthodoxie catholique. Par la suite, si les Franciscains ont pu être proches de certains mouvements de «réveil» fondés sur l'enthousiasme des foules plus ou moins teinté d'anticléricalisme aux treizième et quatorzième siècles, il faut veiller à ne pas majorer l'importance du tropisme laïque et «populaire», davantage encore à ne pas en faire *le* trait caractéristique de la réforme chez les Mineurs.[12] Nombre des frères inquiétés par les autorités ecclésiales à la charnière des treizième et quatorzième siècles étaient des intellectuels (Angelo Clareno, Ubertin de Casale), fiers de leur cléricature, tentés par le désert et la clôture, et l'on aurait tort de considérer les «Spirituels» comme un mouvement populaire — quels qu'aient été les liens tissés par certains d'entre eux, comme Olivi, avec des milieux laïques. L'historiographie envisage désormais l'action novatrice de l'Ordre dans le domaine de *l'être chrétien*, dès les premières décennies, sous le double angle de la liberté individuelle et de l'intensification de la discipline sociale.[13] En première ligne au sein du vaste mouvement de rénovation de la vie régulière enclenché au tournant des

---

12 Ainsi le rapprochement entre les Mendiants d'une part, les phénomènes de *revival* et d'enthousiasme populaire d'autre part, comme l'effectue G. Dickson, 'Encounters in Medieval Revivalism: Monks, Friars, and Popular Enthusiasts', *Church History* 68 (1999) 265-93, doit-il être considéré avec nuance, en particulier pour l'Observance franciscaine.

13 Voir par exemple l'analyse récente de T. Ertl, *Religion und Disziplin. Selbstdeutung und Weltordnung im frühen deutschen Franziskanertum*, Berlin – New York 2006, à partir d'auteurs franciscains des treizième et quatorzième siècles dans l'aire linguistique allemande.

quatorzième et quinzième siècles, les réformes franciscaines ont ainsi tâché de prendre en compte un certain nombre des mutations caractéristiques de l'entrée dans notre *modernité* — dont les racines peuvent à bien des égards être qualifiées d'«inquiétantes»[14] — tout en œuvrant main dans la main avec les pouvoirs en place afin de créer «une religiosité du consensus et du contrôle social» et d'imposer une loi morale rigoureuse[15].

Au sein de ce mouvement de «restauration innovatrice»[16], faire la part entre les éléments de conservation et de renouveau ainsi que se demander comment s'est réalisée — par quel *modus vivendi* — la coexistence entre ces deux pôles est une démarche d'un intérêt relativement limité: une comptabilité à partie double classant les différentes manifestations de l'action des Mineurs en deux catégories se heurterait vite à bien des ambiguïtés, voire des contradictions, comme cela serait le cas si l'exercice était appliqué à l'action des élites urbaines de la Renaissance dont l'Observance fut si proche.

---

14 Selon le mot de J. Chiffoleau, 'Sur la pratique et la conjoncture de l'aveu judiciaire en France du XIIIe au XVe siècle', in: *L'aveu. Antiquité et Moyen Âge*, Actes de la table ronde de l'École française de Rome (1984), Rome 1986, 380. Marco Bartoli a récemment souligné, dans une note bibliographique consacrée à des travaux récents sur les prédicateurs observants italiens du quinzième siècle, combien ceux-ci «ne peuvent pas (…) être liquidés comme une pure survivance de la mentalité médiévale, parce qu'ils révèlent, au contraire, des aspects et des attitudes qui sont considérés comme étant à l'origine, pour le bien comme pour le mal, de la modernité occidentale» ('Nouvelles études sur l'Observance franciscaine', *Revue d'Histoire Ecclésiastique* 101 (2006) 149.

15 G. G. Merlo, *Nel nome di san Francesco* (comme note 3), 296.

16 Selon l'expression de G.G. Merlo, Observance, in: A. Vauchez (dir.), *Dictionnaire encyclopédique du Moyen Âge*, Paris 1997, II, 1095.

Assimilable en ses débuts à un «groupement volontaire utopique»[17], l'ordre franciscain a, comme tout ordre religieux, constitué l'incarnation d'un projet de vie spirituelle — plus ou moins déformé, rêvé, idéologisé — dans une construction sociale. Cette construction sociale, pour l'époque médiévale, s'est insérée dans les structures de la société globale, dont elle était dépendante, et trouva en face d'elle d'autres constructions sociales, en particulier les communautés urbaines. Dans ce cadre, l'Ordre a connu un phénomène corrélatif à la «routinisation du charisme» wébérienne et à la transformation du groupe charismatique en groupement hiérocratique porteur d'un charisme de fonction. À l'œuvre dans bien des groupes, sectes ou communautés religieuses, cette «socialisation aux valeurs dominantes», comme l'ont appelée les sociologues anglo-saxons, n'est jamais absolue dans les grandes religions et ne l'a pas même été dans le cadre du catholicisme médiéval, si l'on considère qu'un nécessaire écart doit exister entre le message porté par un groupement religieux et celui de la société, même quand le premier paraît pleinement légitimer le second.[18] Il n'empêche, le processus est essentiel à prendre en compte pour l'étude des villes tardo-médiévales, où les oligarchies en place ont travaillé au développement d'une discipline et d'un contrôle sociaux en s'appuyant sur

---

17 L'expression de «groupements volontaires utopiques» a été employée à propos des ordres religieux par J. Séguy, 'Pour une sociologie de l'ordre religieux', *Archives de sciences sociales des religions*, 57 (1984) 55-68, repris dans *Idem, Conflit et utopie* (comme note 10), 161-83. En tant que «système idéologique global visant, implicitement ou explicitement à transformer — de manière au moins optativement radicale — les systèmes sociaux globaux existants» *ibid.*, 170), l'utopie est ici conçue comme un «idéal-type». À ce titre, il est évident que l'expérience franciscaine des premiers temps s'en rapproche davantage que l'Ordre qui s'en est réclamé.

18 Voir J. Séguy, 'La socialisation utopique aux valeurs', *Archives de sciences sociales des religions*, 48 (1979), 187-212, repris dans *Conflit et utopie* (comme note 10), 209-232, en particulier 217.

un cadre, celui de la communauté des citoyens, qui n'était pas exempt de fondements utopiques et de processus de sacralisation — en témoignent le discours sur l'*universitas*, ses libertés et ses *secreta*, mais aussi la prégnance de l'image de Jérusalem dans la construction de l'identité urbaine.

En définitive, il faut se demander comment s'est traduite la conciliation des tendances de l'Observance au conservatisme et au renouveau, voire à l'innovation, dans un *propositum vitae* défini par les autorités de l'Ordre et mis à l'épreuve de l'insertion dans les sociétés urbaines du quinzième siècle. Scruter *les* réformes à l'œuvre dans la famille franciscaine implique ainsi d'essayer de cerner les influences, interactions et acculturations, dans une société donnée, entre les trois éléments que sont le *propositum vitae*, l'*ordo* et l'*universitas*.

II. L'Observance, ou les stratégies de la rupture

Le compagnon et successeur de Bernardin de Sienne, Jean de Capistran, acteur principal de la structuration de l'Observance et *wanderprediger* en Europe centre-orientale, incarne sans doute de la façon la plus spectaculaire la conciliation du charisme et de l'institution, puisqu'elle fut chez lui véritable fusion. Ce qui frappe, en lisant par exemple les chroniques urbaines relatant son passage en Silésie et en particulier à Breslau (Wrocław) en 1453, c'est l'usage qu'il faisait de la parole et du geste - je ne rouvre pas le dossier des massacres de Juifs perpétrés par les populations urbaines et dans lesquels il eut indéniablement une responsabilité. On rencontre aussi, sur certains terrains moins connus et avec des acteurs moins célèbres, au-delà de la seule prédication, une importante liberté de ton et de mouvement accompagnée d'une forme d'assouplissement, voire d'affranchissement de certains cadres essentiels de la vie religieuse et liturgique. Dans ces conditions, il faut tenter de cerner dans quelle mesure le renouvellement franciscain a pu être perçu comme une nouveauté.

En Silésie et en Pologne, les Franciscains réformés reçurent le nom de «Bernardins», qui exprime bien l'impact de la pastorale énergique menée par Capistran et ses disciples en faveur du culte du prédicateur siennois tout récemment canonisé, mais aussi la nouveauté que prit le mouvement aux yeux de fidèles pour qui il s'agissait quasiment du développement d'un nouvel ordre religieux. L'usage des mots n'est pas indifférent. Sous la plume du greffier municipal de Breslau Pierre Eschenloer, Jean de Capistran était un *frater ordinis s. Francisci de observancia* et il fonda *plura monasteria ejusdem ordinis de observancia*.[19] Le clerc de Breslau Sigismond Rosicz le présente également comme un professeur *ordinis fratrum minorum de observantia*.[20] Ces indices tendent à confirmer que le développement des Franciscains observants a été perçu, en Pologne, comme le «développement d'un nouvel ordre»[21]. Cela tient au fait que le mouvement a

---

19 P. Eschenloer, *Historia Wratislaviensis*, fo. 32b, éd. in: *Scriptores rerum silesiacarum*, éd. G.A. Stenzel, 16 vols., Breslau 1835-97, VII, 5: [Pour l'année 1453]: *Interea Wratislaviam venit devotus pater Johannes de Capistrano, frater ordinis s. Francisci de observancia, vite sanctimonia clarus, ab apostolica sede cum facultate magna contra hereticos Bohemos missus. Hic Ladislai licencia Bohemiam circumtransit predicando docendo scribendo contra heresiarcham Rockizanam, plura monasteria ejusdem ordinis de observancia hinc inde in urbibus erexit[...].*

20 S. Rosicz, *Gesta diversa transactis temporibus facta in Silesia et alibi*, éd. in: *Scriptores rerum silesiacarum*, (comme note 19), XII, 63: *Die 13 mensis Februarii dignus pater Johannes de Capistrano ordinis fratrum minorum de observantia professor intravit civitatem Wratislaviam [...].*

21 M. Derwich, 'Foyers et diffusion de l'Observance en Pologne et Lituanie dans la seconde moitié du XVe siècle', in: Meyer / Viallet (dir.), *Identités franciscaines à l'âge des réformes* (comme note 1), 276.

essentiellement progressé par la création de nouveaux couvents, non la réforme de maisons existantes, et qu'il s'est traduit par des pratiques et des codes visuels divergeant des usages franciscains traditionnels, en particulier dans le domaine de l'habit. Il est toutefois difficile de se fier à la seule expression «de l'ordre (de saint François) de l'Observance», car on la retrouve ailleurs qu'en Europe centre-orientale et, semble-t-il, assez fréquemment utilisée dans les actes. Le dossier documentaire disponible pour appréhender la façon dont les réformateurs franciscains s'implantèrent dans la petite ville française de Tournon, sur les bords du Rhône, le montre, tout en comportant des expressions qui confirment que les mots ne peuvent être négligés en tant que marqueurs d'une certaine perception de l'Observance. On dispose en effet de la procédure, avec enquête et audition de témoins, engagée en avril 1474 par le Chapitre de la Collégiale Saint-Julien et son vicaire afin de faire respecter les privilèges de la cure paroissiale[22]. Le frère Balthasar, meneur des «pionniers» observants, est mentionné dans le rapport du sergent royal comme faisant partie de l'ordre de saint François *sub Regula de observancia appellata*, avec quelques compagnons *sub eadem Regula*; puis, dans les Lettres exécutoires obtenues par les chanoines afin de faire citer les religieux à comparaître, tous sont présentés comme étant placés *sub secunda Regula beati Francisci vulgariter nuncupata de observancia.*[23] Voilà qui témoigne, à sa manière, de la façon dont pouvait être perçu le projet observant: comme l'application d'une seconde règle, plus dure que la première, et non comme la restauration dans la vie franciscaine de l'unique Règle de François. D'autres tournures utilisées dans les dépositions de témoins, plus loin dans le registre, semblent confirmer cette vision: *in*

---

22 Archives Départementales de l'Ardèche (Privas), G 402, registre de 106 feuillets papier.
23 *Ibid.*, fos.14r° et 21v°.

religione de observancia[24]; *secundum ipsorum Regulam de observancia*; *secundum Regulam ipsorum fratrum de observancia*; *juxta Regulam ipsorum de observancia.*[25] Il resterait à savoir, évidemment, si elle fut partagée, ou s'il ne s'est agi que de celle du scribe, et à cerner dans quelle mesure le fait que les réformateurs aient investi un terrain vierge de toute présence franciscaine antérieure a influé sur la perception du phénomène. Ce que l'on peut dire à la lumière de ce qui s'est passé ailleurs, c'est que dans un face à face entre «anciens» et «modernes», les premiers auraient probablement souligné auprès des fidèles et des séculiers, pour obtenir leur appui, ce qui les rapprochait des seconds; tenté d'atténuer, voire de gommer, en somme, le renouvellement dont se prévalaient leurs adversaires. Une expression telle que *in religione de observancia* montre combien le mouvement réformateur franciscain a pu, dans les esprits, être dissocié du reste de l'Ordre et constituer une véritable rupture — traduction, en définitive, de l'hostilité, voire de la violence ayant présidé aux relations entre Conventuels et Observants dans la seconde moitié du quinzième siècle et au début du seizième.

Sur ce point, les auditions de huit témoins éclairent de façon précieuse les modalités concrètes de l'installation des Observants. Elles nous montrent le début d'un travail de sensibilisation au moins trois ou quatre ans auparavant, par des prédications épisodiques du frère Gaspard Balthasar dans l'église paroissiale, et depuis un an, au plus tôt dix mois, le processus d'aménagement d'un «proto-couvent» pour trois religieux dans une maison pourvue d'une écurie donnée par un boutiquier. Dès son arrivée en ville pour ses prédications, le frère Balthasar aurait clairement choisi une stratégie de rupture, fondée sur une prédication «sauvage» et provocatrice, un véritable anticléricalisme face au clergé

---

24 *Ibid.*, fo. 79v°.
25 *Ibid.*, fos. 79v° et 92r° ; 83v° ; 88v°.

séculier, la célébration d'actes liturgiques en un lieu profane, y compris la communion pascale. Le succès de la greffe observante ne fut pas stoppé par une ordonnance favorable au Chapitre, car d'appels en appels la procédure s'enlisa tandis que le frère Balthasar et ses compagnons s'enracinaient chaque jour un peu plus dans la ville.

On pourrait citer maints exemples d'affrontements entre de nouveaux arrivants et le clergé déjà dans la place. Ils sont à insérer dans un enchaînement d'événements, enclenché en général avec la prédication d'une avant-garde de frère passés pour sensibiliser la population et évaluer les potentialités d'accueil: à leur tête, Jean Brugman aux Pays-Bas, Capistran en Europe centre-orientale, et d'autres demeurés moins connus.[26] Leur action fut souvent caractérisée par une parole excessive, débridée, sans doute aussi la plupart du temps intelligemment contrôlée, et des libertés prises avec les cadres coutumiers et séculaires de la vie religieuse locale, de ses institutions et de ses lieux. C'était là, d'ailleurs, un *modus operandi* redoutable, peut-être davantage encore que toute pastorale expressionniste, mais qui participait d'une même stratégie de violence, symbolique et matérielle, une stratégie de la provocation exprimant la volonté de rupture que cherchaient à afficher les réformateurs venus de l'extérieur. Cette stratégie visait en outre à déraciner pour mieux s'enraciner: les réformateurs, qui considéraient que les liens tissés par les Conventuels avec les communautés urbaines et les fondateurs étaient trop étroits, choisirent de peupler les couvents — au moins en partie — avec des religieux étrangers au «terreau social local».[27] Lorsqu'elle eut lieu

---

26 Sur le cas de Jean Brugman, voir M. De Smet / P. Trio, 'The Involvement of the Late Medieval Urban Authorities in the Low Countries with regard to the Introduction of the Franciscan Observance', *Revue d'Histoire Ecclésiastique* 101 (2006) 57-60.

27 Voir par exemple le cas du couvent auvergnat de Clermont, qui fit l'objet d'affrontement violents, dans L. Viallet, 'La lassitude de la réforme? Pouvoir royal et Franciscains de l'Observance à Clermont,

tardivement, dans le premier tiers du seizième siècle, cette coupure ne fut sans doute pas sans conséquence au moment où la Réforme protestante fit irruption dans les villes — je pense en particulier à celles du Royaume de France.[28]

Destiné à rappeler aux frères qu'ils ne devaient pas partager leur repas avec des laïcs, un passage d'une lettre de Capistran adressée au gardien du couvent de Nuremberg Albert Puchelbach en novembre 1452 me paraît révélateur d'une certaine conception de la réforme qui ne fut pas propre au prédicateur italien: «En vous voyant manger, ils [= les *saeculares, i. e.* les laïcs] croient que vous êtes des hommes, comme eux. Mais lorsqu'ils souffriront de votre absence, ils croiront que vous êtes des anges, et ils viendront alors nombreux vers vous, et votre famille sera florissante».[29] Du monde byzantin, dans lequel l'expression

---

au début du XVIe siècle', *Revue Mabillon*, n.s. 15 (2004) 175-89.

28 On connaît l'importance de cette thématique depuis les réflexions et discussions qui accompagnèrent la parution de l'ouvrage de R. Sauzet *Mendiants et Réformes. Les réguliers mendiants acteurs du changement religieux dans le royaume de France (1480-1560)*, Tours 1994. Pour des remarques sur ce travail par son auteur lui-même, avec une dizaine d'années de recul, voir *Idem*, Pour une nouvelle édition de l'ouvrage *Les réguliers mendiants acteurs du changement religieux dans le royaume de France (1480-1560)*, in: Meyer / Viallet (dir.), *Identités franciscaines à l'âge des réformes* (comme note 1), 463-70. Le dossier de l'implantation des Observants dans la ville de Romans (France, actuel département de la Drôme), à la faveur de la création de l'un des premiers Calvaires d'Occident, est révélateur des moyens utilisés par les réformateurs franciscains, notamment des libertés prises avec certains cadres liturgiques, et constitue aussi une page essentielle pour comprendre la «pré-histoire» des troubles socio-religieux du seizième siècle dans cette ville: voir L. Viallet, 'Autour du Calvaire de Romans. Remarques sur la pénétration de l'Observance au début du XVIe siècle dans la province franciscaine de Bourgogne', *Revue d'Histoire de l'Église de France* 88 (2002) 83-102.

29 Cette lettre du 15 novembre 1452 est insérée dans la *Chronica Fratris Nicolai Glassberger* (comme note 2), 343: *Nunc autem, videntes vos comedentes, putant vos eis similes homines. Quando*

d'«habit angélique» marquait bien le statut exceptionnel dont jouissaient les moines, jusqu'à l'Europe moderne et ses Capucins «frères des Anges», la comparaison utilisée par Capistran n'est pas originale. Elle en dit long sur la volonté de re-cléricalisation, et même plutôt de re-monachisation qui animait les réformateurs de l'Observance franciscaine.

III. L'Observance, ou le retour au cloître

Par-delà le caractère spectaculaire de cet activisme de terrain, ce qui frappe à la lecture d'une vingtaine de textes réformateurs du quinzième siècle et du début du seizième, c'est la façon dont ceux-ci «cadenassent» l'activité et surtout la mobilité des *religieux* — et ce terme prend alors toute sa signification. La limitation des mouvements des frères à l'extérieur du couvent et de leurs contacts avec le Siècle n'est pas une invention de l'Observance: l'interdiction de manger en ville ou chez des laïcs, dans les maisons des «séculiers» sans autorisation du gardien est ainsi une interdiction récurrente dans les textes depuis les Constitutions de 1354. Mais les mesures prônées dans le cadre des réformes de l'Ordre vont globalement dans le sens d'un repli tous azimuts sur le cloître afin de mieux marquer la frontière entre religieux et séculiers. On insiste en particulier sur la limitation des séjours des frères hors du couvent, y compris pour les prédicateurs, qui ne doivent pas s'attarder dans les villes et campagnes leur tâche terminée. Il est assez surprenant de constater que la quête, censée incarner la vie mendiante aux yeux des fidèles, n'occupe qu'une place très secondaire dans les textes et en est même parfois absente. Cette discrétion tient probablement à un silence pragmatique et lucide sur une pratique à la fois banale et nécessaire du projet mendiant, mais secondaire au sein de l'économie conventuelle — y compris chez les

---

autem vestrae praesentiae penuriam habebunt, putabunt vos Angelos venientque multi ad vos, et florebit familia ipsa vestra.

Observants — et facilement susceptible de dérives et dérapages. Les autorités de l'Ordre avaient clairement perçu les enjeux et les problèmes de la quête, qui accompagnait la prédication et était difficilement contrôlable, contrairement à ce qui se passait au sein du couvent. La voie de la *reformatio* était donc plus aisée si elle passait davantage par le recadrage, voire l'interdiction, que par la liberté des grands espaces. À cet égard, l'Observance germanique semble, au miroir de ses textes, avoir choisi la voie d'une véritable clôture *extra muros*, en particulier dans la province de Saxe.

La place manque, ici, pour revenir en détails sur cette question.[30] Je me contente de souligner que c'est à la lumière de cette affirmation d'une séparation très stricte entre les religieux et les laïcs qu'il faut interpréter, dans les Statuts saxons, l'abandon des maisons terminaires et la condamnation des *terminarii conventuales*, faisant véritablement apparaître le prédicateur terminaire comme une caractéristique des Conventuels[31]: la maison terminaire est certes vue comme une propriété, or le texte prône l'abandon des biens immobiliers et fonciers ainsi que le refus de l'argent[32]; mais outre cet aspect, c'est tout un système qui est condamné, parce qu'il ne marque pas suffisamment la frontière entre les frères et le monde.

---

30 Je renvoie à L. Viallet, 'La réforme franciscaine au miroir de ses textes. Jalons pour une anthropologie du *vivre franciscain* au XVe siècle', *Quaestiones Medii Aevi Novae* 10 (2005) 331-44; Idem, 'Prière au cloître et refus du monde dans la législation franciscaine du XVe siècle', in: F. Meyer/L. Viallet (dir.), *Le silence du cloître, l'exemple des saints. Identités franciscaines à l'âge des réformes*, Clermont-Ferrand, 2009 à paraître.

31 Chap. III, 5 [AFH 3 (1910) 281] et V, 1 [AFH 3 (1910) 281: *Vitentur discursus inutiles cum summa diligentia. Et occasione predicandi non stent fratres quasi terminarii conventuales per menses vel ebdomadas in civitatibus vel villis, presertim conventui satis propinquis; sed finita predicacione ad sua loca redeant, iterum si opus fuerit illuc reversuri*].

32 Chap. III, 6 [AFH 3 (1910) 281].

En outre, on retrouve cette tonalité particulière de l'Observance germanique, et notamment saxonne, si l'on s'intéresse à la prière contemplative, censée être caractéristique d'une réaction observante face au ritualisme des Conventuels, mais dont la place dans les textes réformateurs varie dans d'importantes proportions. Les Constitutions «martiniennes» de 1430, dont la structure est plaquée sur celle de la Règle, chapitre par chapitre, en disent sur la prière presque aussi peu qu'elle (chapitre III) et reprennent le passage consacré à l'office divin dans les Constitutions de Benoît XII (1336): il n'y est question que de préparer *son cœur* à Dieu en arrivant dans *le chœur* pour célébrer les heures et les messes.[33] Jean de Capistran ajoute en 1443 aux recommandations du chapitre V de la Règle consacré au travail — qui ne doit pas éteindre «l'esprit de sainte oraison» — la notion de *spiritualia exercitia*, dans une optique de complémentarité avec les activités physiques (*corporalibus*).[34] Par la suite, dans les textes réglementaires de la seconde moitié du quinzième siècle et du début du seizième, la place consacrée à la prière individuelle en silence et à la méditation est extrêmement mince, voire inexistante, sauf dans l'espace germanique et en Europe centre-orientale. Presque rien n'en est dit dans les Statuts de l'Observance ultramontaine de 1451, rien du tout dans ceux de l'Observance cismontaine de 1461, ni dans les différents textes toscans ou génois, dans les Constitutions observantes de Bohême (1471) ou chez les Conventuels réformés de Hongrie (1454). En revanche, les Statuts de la province des «Bernardins» de Pologne (1467) imposent la nécessité d'une heure de prière quotidienne[35],

---

33 Michael Angelus, *Chronologia historico-legalis Seraphici Ordinis Fratrum Minorum Sancti Patris Francisci*, I, Neapoli 1650, 93.

34 *Ibid.*, 105.

35 Éd. K. Kantak, *Przeglad Teologiczny* 10 (1929) 342-343 (*De oracione*).

ceux de la province d'Autriche (1516), réformée par Capistran, que les frères demeurent en oraison, pendant l'hiver, une heure avant matines et une heure après vêpres.[36] Les prescriptions des provinces de Strasbourg, de Cologne et surtout de Saxe nous font franchir un degré supérieur, par l'emploi des termes de *privata oratio* et *recollectio mentalis* afin de définir un véritable projet spirituel pour les frères, appelés à revenir le plus possible entre les murs du cloître afin de mieux rentrer en eux-mêmes.[37] Les Statuts saxons de 1467 (révisés en 1494) comportent les mots les plus explicites qu'il m'ait été donné de lire, en une opposition claire entre *l'intérieur* et *l'extérieur*:

> «Item cum principalis et quasi totalis causa multarum exorbitacionum et relaxacionum sit defectus sancte orationis private et recollectionis interne, hortamur et obsecramus in domino, ut fratres in singulis conventibus per eorum superiores ab exterioribus evagationibus et inutilibus occupacionibus cum summo studio retrahantur, et ad interiora quantum erit possibile, ut de deo et spiritualibus ac de sui status sublimissima perfectione in bonitate sentiant, verbis et exemplis diligentissime reducantur; Ut divino offitio devote et cum multa diligentia persoluto, tempus etiam aliquod apte captent, in quo spiritum domini et mentem sanctissimi patris nostri

---

36 Constitutions de la province d'Autriche (qui reprennent les décisions des chapitres antérieurs), chap. I, art. 4, lu dans le texte des Constitutions (amputées de nombreux articles) inséré au sein du cod. 1744 de la Bibliothèque Nationale d'Autriche à Vienne (Bibliotheca Palatina), fo. 25v°.

37 Pour la province de Saxe, voir les Statuts de 1467, chap. II, art. 16 et 29 [*AFH* 3 (1910) 110 et 114]. Pour la province de Cologne, voir les *Ordinationes provinciales* de 1474, art. 13 [*AFH* 7 (1914) 719] et surtout les Statuts de 1524, chap. II, art. 1 et chap. IV, art. 8 et 15 [*AFH* 7 (1914) 721-722 et 725]. Pour la province de Strasbourg, voir les statuts compilés en 1514, chap. II (Munich, Bayerisches Hauptstaatsarchiv, Bayerische Franziskanerprovinz Lit. 54, fo. 99r°) et les prescriptions des chapitres de 1476 et 1481 rassemblées dans la compilation de Trêves, Bistumsarchiv, cod. 122, fos. 157v°, 159r

francisci sibi inbibere valeant, cristi unctione et gratia se eis dulcius infundente.»[38]

On comparera ce texte aux prescriptions des *Ordinationes reformatoriae* de la province conventuelle de France, promulguées en 1452 et on aura une vision assez nette de ce qui pouvait distinguer des projets de vie divergents à l'intérieur même de l'ordre franciscain, puisque le texte réformateur de 1452 insiste sur la messe et sa répétition en continu:

> «Ordino insuper quod Misse ordinate et successive dicantur, ita quod una completa alia incipiatur, sit quoque continuatio Missarum usque ad maioris Misse finem, et maxime diebus dominicis et festis, ut amplior populi devotio crescat et sacrificium laudis ad Dei honorem et populi edificacionem animarumque vestrarum salutem congruo tempore et ordine offeratur.»[39]

° et 162v°.

38 Chap. II, art. 29 [*AFH* 3 (1910) 114], dont on peut proposer la traduction «pragmatique» suivante: «Puisque la principale et presque unique cause des nombreux travers et relâchements est l'insuffisance de la sainte oraison privée et de la récollection interne, nous exhortons et prions dans le Seigneur que les frères soient, dans chaque couvent, écartés avec le plus grand soin par leurs supérieurs des errances extérieures (au-dehors) et des occupations inutiles, et ramenés très scrupuleusement autant que possible, par la parole et l'exemple, vers l'intérieur, afin qu'ils ressentent Dieu, les [réalités] spirituelles et la sublime perfection de son état dans la bonté; afin que, par l'office divin accompli avec dévotion et très scrupuleusement, ils recherchent convenablement le moment où ils pourront se remplir du souffle du Seigneur et de l'esprit de notre très saint père François, l'onction du Christ et sa grâce se répandant plus doucement en eux.»

39 Art. 15 [*AFH* 27 (1934) 87], dont on peut proposer la traduction suivante: « [...] que les messes ordonnées et successives soient dites de façon à ce que l'une terminée, une autre soit commencée et qu'il y ait continuité des messes jusqu'à la fin de la grand-messe, surtout les dimanche et jours de fêtes, afin que la dévotion du peuple croisse toujours davantage et que le Sacrifice de la louange soit offert au moment qui convient et régulièrement pour l'honneur de Dieu,

Les Observants de la province de Strasbourg, qui dès 1481 avaient insisté sur l'obligation de la récollection quotidienne, dénoncèrent d'ailleurs en 1510 l'*abbreviatio* et l'*acceleratio* du culte divin.[40]

Certes, il faut considérer les textes avec précaution, parce qu'ils ne sont pas le strict reflet des pratiques et qu'un silence peut être l'indice moins d'une carence que de dynamiques extérieures liées à des groupes ou mouvements réformateurs de *strictior observantia* — je pense en particulier, pour la Toscane, à la genèse des Capucins à partir de 1525. Il n'empêche, ces textes montrent bien en quoi l'Observance a d'abord été un écart du monde. À cet égard, la tonalité des Statuts saxons constitue un révélateur significatif, qui permet de comprendre un peu mieux non seulement l'impact de la Récollection en tant que branche de l'Ordre, au seizième siècle, sur le monde franciscain germanique, mais peut-être aussi celui de la Réforme protestante. La place supérieure de la prière dans la législation d'Europe centre-orientale résulte, à n'en pas douter, de ce que le monde germanique et rhéno-flamand avait à offrir dans le domaine de la méditation, ainsi que de l'action pastorale de Capistran et de ses relais. Elle témoigne aussi clairement de la volonté de créer, par la législation, l'écart du monde. Un écart qui a pu aussi résulter, ailleurs — dans les péninsules italienne et ibérique surtout — et au moins dans un premier temps, du souffle de

---

l'édification du peuple et le salut de vos âmes». Voir également l'art. 19: «Oneramus etiam guardianum et sacristam quatenus diligenter attendant ut Missas continuare faciant, ut predictum est» [«Nous chargeons le gardien et le sacristain de veiller avec diligence à faire se succéder les messes comme cela a été dit»] (*ibid.*, 88).

40 Voir Trêves, Bistumsarchiv, cod. 122, fo. 173r°. La dénonciation, lors du chapitre de 1510, du raccourcissement du culte divin, concerne celui-ci dans ses trois composantes: l'office, la récollection et les pratiques de piété (la *devotio*). Il s'agit d'un phénomène perceptible dans «certains couvents» et associé à la *sensualitas* — laquelle s'exprime dans le vin, la nourriture et l'habit.

liberté qu'en certains espaces les conditions naturelles, le maillage de l'Ordre, le faible encadrement réglementaire ou même, sans doute, les héritages «culturels» du mouvement franciscain laissèrent passer, nourrissant des initiatives érémitiques peu encadrées.

IV. Perspectives

Je voudrais achever ce tour d'horizon très imparfait en évoquant brièvement trois directions de travail qui retiennent actuellement mon attention, dans une approche destinée à «réinjecter» de l'histoire sociale dans l'analyse des réformes franciscaines[41]. Il s'agit de scruter attentivement les pratiques issues de la nécessité, pour les frères, de concilier le lien avec les élites civiques — lien de dépendance économique, mais aussi idéologique, car l'Observance fut du côté du pouvoir et de l'ordre — et les exigences de la *reformatio*. Or, le lien avec les élites urbaines passait, dans la France du «beau seizième siècle» (c. 1450 – c. 1550) comme dans les villes de l'espace germanique, par une participation à l'exaltation du sentiment communautaire et du patriotisme urbain. Il faut donc ici se tourner vers des phénomènes relevant de ce que les médiévistes français ont appelé «religion civique», les Allemands *politische* ou *bürgerliche Religiosität* — Marek Słoń a récemment proposé *kommunale Religiosität*, expression qui présente l'avantage d'être reprise littéralement dans les langues slaves[42] — voire, avec un

---

41 Ces thématiques font l'objet d'une enquête de ma part, dans le cadre d'un mémoire d'Habilitation à Diriger des Recherches consacré aux mouvements de réforme franciscains du quinzième siècle.

42 Communication lors de l'atelier *Fondations pieuses et religion civique à la fin du Moyen Âge (France et Allemagne)* organisé par Olivier Richard à la Mission Historique Française en Allemagne, Göttingen, 10 juin 2006. Résumé de cette journée d'étude dans

accent spécifique, *Sakralgemeinschaft* («communauté sacrale»), dans ses formes collectives mais aussi plus «individuelles» c'est-à-dire liées à la *memoria*. Or, en Occident, mis à part le culte de saints spécifiquement mendiants, la dévotion aux saints patrons et d'une façon générale les cultes «civiques» étaient avant tout l'apanage des grandes églises séculières: la cathédrale, voire la collégiale comme *ecclesia matrix*. Les pistes proposées ici sont toutes liées, en dernier ressort, à la spécificité revendiquée par la famille franciscaine, celle de l'*alter Christus*, qui a déterminé un *propositum vitae* — malgré les divergences —, une conception que l'Ordre a eue de lui-même et des dévotions développées en son sein particulièrement et essentiellement christocentrés. En ce sens, on pourrait dire qu'il s'agit de scruter certains phénomènes afin de cerner dans quelle mesure ils apparaissent comme autant d'effets d'écho, au quinzième siècle, des idéaux structurants des origines de l'Ordre.

Une première piste de travail concerne le culte de la Passion— y compris dans ses formes mariales — et la façon dont celui-ci a pu être enraciné dans un espace urbain qui faisait ainsi l'objet d'un processus de sacralisation. À la fin du Moyen Âge, en particulier au quinzième siècle et au début du seizième, se multiplièrent les fondations de chapelles de la Passion, de la Sainte-Croix, du Saint-Sépulcre ou de Notre-Dame de Pitié, mais aussi les chapelles dites «de Bethléem». Ces gestes de fondation individuels sont souvent — certes pas exclusivement — à replacer dans l'orbite des communautés franciscaines, qui les encouragèrent avec l'appui de la papauté car elles œuvraient au rayonnement du couvent. Les dossiers que j'ai pu étudier montrent combien ces fondations individuelles sortaient du strict cadre de la sépulture familiale et de l'intercession perpétuelle au profit de la création de pôles de sacralité rayonnant au-delà des sanctuaires qui les abritaient, voire au-delà des murs de leurs cités. Toutes ces chapelles ne devinrent pas lieu de pèlerinage. Mais dans le contexte du quinzième siècle, ces fondations sont à relier à un processus d'enracinement de la piété fondatrice dans l'espace urbain, processus qui trouva son aboutissement, au cours du dernier quart du siècle et des premières années du suivant, dans la création des premiers Calvaires, forme primitive des Chemins de Croix. Constitués d'un Calvaire et de sept piliers, ils résultèrent de l'assimilation du paysage et de la topographie de la ville à ceux de Jérusalem et du Drame de la Passion, et furent souvent étroitement liés à l'Observance. Le souvenir de François avait dès le treizième siècle été rattaché à des lieux, dans la réalité comme dans les différents récits de sa vie, car aux yeux de ses disciples il avait engendré une nouvelle Terre Sainte séraphique en Ombrie: Greccio était ainsi devenu un nouveau Bethléem et l'Alverne, un nouveau Golgotha. À la fin du Moyen Âge, les Mineurs, gardiens officiels du Saint-Sépulcre, ont mêlé étroitement, jusqu'à la fusion, la méditation sur les souffrances du Christ et l'appréhension de l'espace. Ils l'ont fait d'autant plus facilement que ce processus répondait — et renforçait — l'une des aspirations de la ville de la Renaissance, dont l'identité n'était pas sans rapport avec l'image biblique de Jérusalem: faire du cadre quotidien la cité sainte elle-même, la cité du pardon et de la purification.

    Cette dévotion rencontra un succès particulier dans l'espace germanique, où se multiplièrent les écrits de méditation sur la Passion, dans la seconde moitié du quinzième siècle, sous la plume d'auteurs franciscains qui furent aussi des prédicateurs en relation avec les Conseils de ville et des confesseurs de Clarisses. En outre, le lien entre les gouvernements urbains et les communautés religieuses y prit une autre dimension que dans l'espace français comme l'illustre, probablement de façon particulièrement appuyée, le cas de Görlitz. Legs et fondations pieuses effectués à l'église des Mineurs dans la seconde moitié du quinzième siècle et au début du seizième l'ont été à un sanctuaire à forte dimension civique et politique, puisqu'il était un instrument important, voire essentiel de la stratégie d'affirmation et d'influence de la ville dans l'espace régional. La dépendance des religieux franciscains à l'égard des élites municipales fut en outre prolongée par le lien entre la communauté de tertiaires, «sœurs dévotes» issues de la notabilité locale, et le couvent. On touche ici à la deuxième piste de réflexion qui retient particulièrement mon attention, celle des mouvances laïques entourant les couvents, en particulier les communautés du Tiers ordre. La tendance fut forte, en effet, au sein des mouvements réformateurs franciscains, à faire jouer aux différents cercles concentriques entourant les frères un rôle essentiel dans l'économie conventuelle, en stimulant et canalisant le flux des aumônes.

Les Tiers ordres sont liés à un troisième dossier, constitué de la question de l'association spirituelle par l'intermédiaire des lettres de confraternité. L'association spirituelle était un antique usage monastique, mais il est possible que les Franciscains, en particulier l'Observance et en particulier en Europe centre-orientale, l'aient «revivifié», peut-être avec un succès limité dû à la concurrence, notamment, des grandes campagnes d'indulgences. Jean de Capistran semble avoir voulu abondamment utiliser cet «outil» pour récompenser individus, corps constitués et communautés urbaines entières de leur soutien à l'Ordre et donc, au fil de sa grande mission de 1451-1456, à la pénétration de l'Observance. L'association récompensait le soutien matériel apporté aux religieux par une prière perpétuelle qui ne ressortissait pas aux cadres de la fondation pieuse, puisqu'elle n'impliquait pas de transfert de biens ou de rentes; en cela, elle répondait à une exigence fondamentale de l'Observance. Mais elle ne répondait pas qu'à cela, car il faut la replacer dans le cadre de la pastorale franciscaine, qui fut certes une «pastorale de la sainteté», comme l'a bien mis en lumière Jacques Chiffoleau en Avignon, mais qui fut aussi une pastorale de la prière: la prière des frères, surtout, dont découlaient les bienfaits accordés à ceux qui avaient été associés à la famille spirituelle franciscaine et bénéficiaient ainsi du flux de grâce jailli du cœur du *Poverello*. En insistant de façon particulière sur la notion de famille spirituelle et en tissant une vaste toile d'araignée unissant par la prière les vivants et les morts, les frères placèrent au centre de leur action, comme jamais peut-être séculiers et réguliers ne l'avaient fait avant eux, l'idée ecclésiologique du Corps mystique, ainsi que la doctrine théologique de la communion des saints.

Index of Names and Places

A

Abbott, Robert, of Austhorpe, 39
Acastr, Adam de, OFM, 34
Admonitiones, 83, 85
Ainsty, 33
Alan, vicar of Calthorp, 35
Albertus Magnus, see: St Albertus
Aldbrough, church of St Bartholomew, 39
Alexander III (1159-1181), 104
Alexander IV (1254-1261), 62, 180
Alexander, chaplain of Snaith, 24
Alexander the Great, 143
Alexandria, Alexander of 122, 123, 125, 126
Alford, 37
Alnwick, Martin of, OFM, 32
Alva y Astorga, Pedro de, 109
Alverna, mount, 110, 213
Amberg, Frederick of, OFM, 167
Amounderness, 15
Andreae, Johannes (1270-1348), 103, 119, 175
Angleterre, *see*: England
Annals of Dunstable, 60
Annandale, 26
Anonimalle Chronicle, 16
Apologia pauperum, 108
Aquila, 143
Aquinas, Thomas, *see*: St Thomas Aquinas
Aragon, Franciscan province of, 190
Arden, OSM monastery, 33
Aristote, *see*: Aristotle

Aristotle, 99, 100, 132, 139, 174
Ashton, Lord John, 15
Ask, Nicholas de, 32
Assisi, 110
Assisi, General Statutes of (1279), 159, 180
Assisi, General Statutes of (1316), 181
Ast, Astesanus of, OFM, 174
Augsburg, 164
Augsburg, David of, OFM, 14, 38
Austhorpe, 39
Austria, Observant province of, 208
Auxerre, William of, 86, 174
Avicenna, 148
Avignon, 215
Awne, William, OFM, 30
Axholme, Isle of, 31
Aynsham, Geoffrey de, OFM, 20

B

Babwell, Franciscan convent of, 39, 58, 61, 67, 72, 74, 74
Bacon, Roger, OFM, 135, 138, 139, 141, 142, 144, 145, 147, 148, 149, 150
Baghdad, 145
Baldac, *see*: Baghdad
Baldus de Ubaldis (c.1327-1400), 103
Balthasar, Gaspard, OFM, 201, 202, 203
Baltic Sea, 192
Banbury, 20
Banestre, Nicholas, OFM, 30

Barden, 23
Barneby (Barnby), Thomas de, OFM, 18, 31
Bartoli, Marco, 197
Bartolus, 103
Barton, Henry de, OFM, 44
Barton, John de, OFM, 20, 35
Barton, William of, OFM, 19
Batley, 27
Bautzen, 193
Bavaria, custody of, 169
Beauvais, Vincent of, OP, 174, 176
Beckingham, Henry of, OFM, 19
Beckingham, John, OFM, 43
Beckley, 15
Benedict XII (1334-1342), 166, 167, 170, 207
Benjamin the Jew, of Cambridge, 66
Berg, Dieter, 156
Bergamo, Bonagratia of, OFM, 108
Bergson, Henri, 195
Bernardines, 200, 207
Bersted, Stephen, bishop of Chichester (1262-1287), 43
Bertrand, Paul, 75
Bessa, Bernard of, OFM, 173
Beswick, 39
Bethlehem, 212
Beverley, 29, 39
Beverley, Franciscan convent of, 10, 13, 21, 25, 31, 34, 37, 39, 40
Bewchampe, Robert, OFM, 26
Billam, John de, 21
Bilton, 33
Bishopthorpe, 45

Bitton, William, bishop of Bath and Wells (1248-1264, 1267-1274), 26
Black Death, 25, 72
Blackhowe Moor, 42
Blakeney, Carmelite convent, 63, 79
Blyth, 21, 40
Boccaccio, Giovanni, 27, 36
Boethius, 174
Bohemia, 192, 193
Bohemia, observant constitutions of (1471), 207
Bologna, 173
Bologna, general chapter of (1433), 193
Bolton, 39
Bolton Abbey, 43
Boniface VIII (1295-1303), 29
Booth, William, archbishop of York (1452-1464), 31
Boroughbridge, 42
Bosellis, Gregory of, OFM, 15
Boston, 12, 16, 19, 37
Boston, Franciscan convent of, 10, 19, 31, 37
Bourgogne, *see*: Burgundy
Boynton, Thomas, OFM, 30
Bradekirk, Edward, OFM, 31
Bradford, 14
Bradford, Walter, of Houghton, 14
Brantingham, Adam de, OFM, 34
Brescia, Albertano de, 118
Breslau, 199, 200
Breydenbach, Bernard of, 175
Bridlington, 40
Brindisi, 95
Bristol, 15
British Isles, 54

Brittany, John of, earl of Richmond (1306-1334), 42
Brogliano, 190
Bruce, Robert, *see*: Robert Bruce, King of Scotland
Brugman, John, OFM, 203
Bruisyard, Franciscan nunnery, 32
Brunswick, Franciscan convent of, 174
Brusshyn, Geoffrey, OFM, 42
Buckden, 15, 19, 20, 21
Bucknall, William, of Canwick, 22
Bulls:
  Ad statum (1430), 192
  Fratrum ordinis Minorum (1443), 185
  Ite vos (1517), 191
  Quo elongati (1230), 157
  Quorundam exigit (1317), 94
  Super cathedram (1300), 12, 19, 29
  Ut sacra (1446), 185
Burgh, Elizabeth de, 58, 63, 72
Burghersh, Henry, bishop of Lincoln (1320-1340), 20, 20, 20, 31, 46
Burgundy, Franciscan province of, 192
Buridan, John, 99
Burley, Walter, 99, 100
Burnham Norton, Carmelite convent, 63, 79
Burton, Thomas, OFM, 30
Bury St Edmunds, 58, 60, 61, 62, 67, 72, 74, 76, 77, 78, 80
Butrigarius, Jacobus, 103
Byland Abbey, 42

C

Caernarfon, Edward of, *see*: Edward II
Caesarea, Eusebius of, 175
Calthorp, 35
Calvary, mount, 110
Calverley, William de, OFM, 34, 46
Cambridge, 19, 53, 56, 57, 59, 65, 75
Cambridge, custody of, 51, 53, 56, 73, 77, 79
Cambridge, Franciscan convent of, 54, 59, 67, 72, 74, 76, 79, 80, 161
Cambridge, theology faculty, 73
Cambridge, university of, 56, 57, 75
Cantelowe, Elizabeth, 48
Cantelowe, Margaret, 48
Cantelowe, William, alderman of London, 47
Canterbury, Benedictine abbey of St Augustine, 74
Canwick, 22
Capistran, John, *see*: St John Capistran
Cariboni, Guido, 164
Carletti, Angelo, de Clavasio, OFM, 174
Carlisle, 28
Carlisle, diocese of, 28
Carlisle, William de, OFM, 30
Casale, Ubertin de, OFM, 109, 196
Castile, Franciscan province of, 190
Castre, 60
Castre, Simon de, OFM, 46
Cawood, 21
Cazelles, Raymond, 100

Celano, Thomas of, OFM, 86
Celestine V (1294), 109
Certaldo, 27
Cesena, Michael of, OFM, 108, 115
Charmues, Lady de, 32
Chaucer, Geoffrey, 36
Chelmsford, Dominican convent, 79
Chester, 22
Chiffoleau, Jacques, 215
Cicero, 101
Cipolla, Fra, 27, 36
Clare, 58
Clare, Austin Friars, 79
Clare, Richard de, earl of Gloucester (1222-1262), 61
Clarendon, 15
Clareno, Angelo, OFM, 109, 196
Clement IV (1265-1268), 142, 150
Clermont, Franciscan convent of, 203
Cleveland, 27
Colchester, 55, 57, 68, 76, 78
Colchester, Benedictine Abbey of St John, 69
Colchester, East Gate, 67
Colchester, Franciscan convent of, 59, 67, 69, 72, 74, 78
Cologne, Franciscan province of, 208
Commentarii in quatuor libros sententiarum, 174
Compostella, St James, Franciscan province of, 190
Concile, *see*: Council
confessors, 15
Consolatio philosophiae, 174
Constance, Council of (1414-1418), 153, 155, 183, 190
Constitutiones Farineriae (1354), 205
Constitutiones Martinianae (1430), 182, 183, 188, 189, 192, 193, 207
Constitions Générales, *see*: General Constitutions
Conventuals, 188, 189, 202, 203, 206, 207
conventus, 10
Corbridge, Thomas, archbishop of York (1299-1304), 41
Cornwall, 18
Cottis, Thomas, OFM, 38
Couton, John de, OFM, 32
Crokes, John, of South Collingham, 22

D

Dalderby, John, bishop of Lincoln (1300-1320), 12, 18, 19, 20, 30, 42
Dale, John, vicar of All Saints Batley, 27
Darfield-upon-Dearne, church All Saints, 24
Darlay, William, of Leeds, 27
De civitate Dei, 99
Deighton, Roger of, OFM, 19
Delph, 23
De moneta, 95
De officiis, 101
De usuris, 122
De Roover, Raymond, *see*: Roover
Derfield, church All Saints, 13
Desio, Franciscan convent of, 10
Devon, 18

Dewsbury, 37
Diadema monachorum, 174
Dighton, *see*: Deighton
Digne, Hugo de, OFM, 98, 108
Dobson, Barrie, 9
domus formata, 10
Doncaster, 14, 21, 22, 24, 34, 37, 40
Doncaster, Carmelites, 13
Doncaster, Franciscan convent of, 10, 13, 14, 24, 34, 37, 40
Döring, Matthias, OFM, 187, 189, 193
Dorset, 18
Dossat, Yves, 60
Driffield, 40
Dumfries, 26
Dunwich, 58, 72, 78
Dunwich, Franciscan convent of, 60, 71, 76
Durand, Guillaume, 166

E

East Anglia, 63, 75
East Riding, 34
East Riding, archdeaconry of, 31
Ebor', John de, OFM, 12
Eccleston, Thomas of, OFM, 56, 59, 74
Edgecote, battle of (1469), 17
Edmund earl of Cornwall (1272-1300), 15
Edward I, King of England (1272-1307), 43, 78, 80
Edward II, King of England (1307-1327), 43
Egypt, 39
Eleanor of Provence, Queen of England, 15

Elias of Cortone, OFM, 159
Ely, diocese of, 55, 57
Engels, Friedrich (1820-1895), 87, 130
England, 9, 16, 22, 24, 25, 26, 29, 42, 52, 116
epistola approbatoria, 162
Erfurt, 9, 168, 173
Erfurt, John of, OFM, 126, 174
Eschenloer, Peter, 200
Essex, 58
Etymologies, 174
Eugenius IV (1431-1447), 185
Eusebius of Caesaria, *see*: Caesaria
Exchequer, 80
Exeter, 17
Expositio quatuor magistrorum, 92
Extravagantes, 94
Eyre, William, of Saleby, 37

F

Feltham, Thomas, 59
Feuerbach, Ludwig (1804-1872), 130
Fieschi, Sinibaldo, *see*: Innocent IV
Figeac, 60
Fiore, Joachim of, OCist, 87, 135, 143
FitzHugh, Sir Henry, 32
FitzJohn, Alice, 59
FitzJohn, Richard, 59
FitzRalph, Richard, archbishop of Armagh (1346-60), 27
Flavius Josephus, 169, 175
Flore, Joachim de, *see*: Fiore
Florence, 95
Florence, custody of, 167

Florence, Antoninus of, *see*: St Antoninus
France, 95, 103, 108, 190, 204, 209, 211
France, Franciscan province of, 192
Francis of Assisi, *see*: St Francis
Francis, John, OFM, 34
Franciscans, Third Order, 39
Francisgate, Doncaster, 22
Fraticelli, 108, 115
Frederick II, King of Germany and Emperor (1212-1250), 95
Frere breyge, Doncaster, 22
Freris Mynors brigge, Doncaster, 22
Fribourg, Franciscan convent of, 167, 177
Fugeriis, Geoffrey de, OFM, 43

G
Gargrave, 23
Gascony, 15
Gaynesburgh, John de, OFM, 20
General Constitutions (1260), 92
Gênes, *see*: Genoa
Genoa, 95, 103, 125, 126
Gerbrigge, Sir William, 59
Gerson, Jean, 166, 174
Giardina, Andrea, 100
Giffard, Walter, archbishop of York (1266-1279), 29, 33, 40
Glassberger, Nikolaus, OFM, 168, 176, 185
Gloucestre, Anne, wife of Thomas, 47
Gloucestre, Thomas, 47
Goffe, Nicholas, OFM, 17
Golgotha, 213

Görlitz, 193, 213
Gorram, Nicholas of, 173
Göttingen, Franciscan convent of, 164, 166, 168, 171, 172, 174, 175
Grantham, 16
Gray, Walter de, archbishop of York (1215-1255), 40
Greene, Robert, OFM, 21
Greenfield, William, archbishop of York (1304-1315), 33, 33, 41
Gregory IX (1227-1241), 40, 175
Gressebey, Thomas de, OFM, 35
Grimsby, 10, 12, 19
Grimsby, Austin Friars, 14
Grimsby, Franciscan convent of, 10, 12, 14, 19, 37
Grosseteste, Robert, bishop of Lincoln (1235-1253), 15, 20, 31
Grünberg, Franciscan convent of, 174, 175
Guascone, Bernard, OFM, 167, 177
Guillaume d'Auxerre, *see*: Auxerre, William of
Gynwell, John, bishop of Lincoln (1347-1362), 16

H
Haddington, 25
Hagen, Johannes, OFM, 162
Halbwachs, Maurice, 195
Hales, Alexander of, OFM, 91, 174
Halifax, 14
Hampole, 33, 34
Hanlan, Maurice, OFM, 168
Harby, John, OFM, 21
Harling, 39

Hartlepool, 43
Harvy, *see*: Harby
Hastang, Sir Robert de, 32
Hastingford, John de, 59
Haukerword, Richard de, OFM, 20
Haulay, Beatrice, 14
Haute Lusace, *see*: Upper Lusatia
Hawe, Richard, OFM, 22
Heers, Jacques, 126
Henry III, King of England (1216-1272), 15, 40, 58, 61, 62, 62, 70, 78
Henry VIII, King of England (1509-1547), 81
Herice, Richard de, OFM, 20
Hewton, William, of Waltham, 14
Hexham, 32
Hill, Rosalind, 15
Historia ecclesiastica of Eusebius of Caesaria, 175
Hobbes, Thomas (1588-1679), 112
Holbeach, Thomas of, OFM, 19
Holderness, 36, 37, 39
Holy Land, 16, 40, 145, 213
Horrox, Rosemary, 13
Hostiensis, *see*: Segusio
Hotham, John, bishop of Ely (1316-1337), 42
Hothorp, Hugh de, 20
Houghton, 14
Hoveden, John de, OFM, 31
Howden, 40
Hull, 45
Hull, Austin Friars, 45
Hull, Carmelites, 14, 45
Humber, river, 21
Hume, David (1711-1776), 93
Humlocke, George, OFM, 30

Hungary, reformed Conventuals of (1454), 207
Huntingdon, 20
Husthwayt', Thomas de, OFM, 34

I

Imitatio Christi, 86, 184
Ingoldmells, church of St Peter, 31
Innocent IV (1243-1254), 31, 103, 119, 175
Innocent V (1276), 174
Ipswich, 55, 57, 59, 72, 78
Ipswich, Franciscan convent of, 71, 74
Isabella, Queen of England from 1308, 71
Isidor of Seville, *see*: Seville
Italy, 16, 51, 191

J

Jean XXII, *see*: John XXII
Jerusalem, 9, 199, 213
Jesus Christ, 9, 17
Jews, massacres of, 199
John XXII (1316-1334), 93, 94, 108, 115, 186
John, a student of Roger Bacon, 150
Joly, John, OFM, 167

K

Kamenz, 193
Kannemannkodex, 162
Kaye, Joel, 99
Kempe, Margery, 17
Kempis, Thomas de, 86
Kempten, Franciscan provincial chapter at (1498), 168
Kingston, Reginald de, OFM, 41

Kirkstall Chronicle, 16
Kirshner, Julius, 118
Knaresborough, fraternity of St Robert, 40
Knoll, Ralph, OFM, 31
Kyrkham, Thomas, OFM, 30
Kyry, John, OFM, 47

L

Lacy, Henry de, earl of Lincoln (1249-1311), 41
Lakmann, Nikolaus, OFM, 168
Lancashire, 31
Lanercost Chronicle, 16, 26, 42
Lateran Council (1179), 104
Lateran Council (1215), 104
Lator, William, OFM, 25
Lauban, 193
Laxton, church of St Michael, 46
Leclercq, Jacques, 87
Leeds, 27, 39
Lefebvre, Marcel, archbishop (1905-1991), 115
Legbourne, Cistercian nuns of, 35
Legenda et historia de sancto Simperto, 164
Legenda major, 86
Legendre, Pierre, 83, 110
Le Goff, Jacques, 54, 54, 81
Leo X (1513-1521), 191
Lessius, Leonard (1554-1623), 128
Lewes, battle of (1264), 43
Leyc', Richard de, OFM, 20
Leylond, Richard, OFM, 31
Libellus de finibus paupertatis, 98
Liber chronicarum of Hartmann Schedel, 175
Liddington, 20

Liège, 75
limitatio, 9, 11, 12, 14, 18, 27, 29, 30, 35, 44, 48
Lincoln, 12, 15, 16, 18, 19, 20, 21, 22, 35
Lincoln, bishop of, 33, 45
Lincoln, diocese, 31, 45
Lincoln, Franciscan convent of, 10, 19, 20, 21, 35, 37
Lincoln, guardian of, 12, 21
Lincoln, St Katherine's priory, 21
Lincolnshire, 14, 19, 21, 30, 32
Little, Andrew George, 74
Little, Lester, 130
Little Wassant in Holderness, 37
Löbau, 193
Lombard, Peter, 174
London, 25, 43, 44, 47, 52
London, Cornhill, 53
London, diocese of, 55
London, Franciscan convent of, 25, 47
London, Franciscan provincial chapter at (1297), 80
Louis IX, King of France, see: St Louis
Ludeford, Adam de, OFM, 20, 35
Lüneburg, Franciscan convent of, 162
Luther, Martin (1483-1546), 113
Luttrell, Sir Geoffrey (1276-1345), 32
Luttrell Psalter, 33
Lynn, 54, 55, 71, 72, 78
Lynn, Dominican convent, 75
Lynn, Franciscan convent of, 54, 57 70, 72, 74, 80
Lyons, General Statutes of (1325), 181

Lyons, Second Council of (1274), 77, 104
Lyre, Nicholas of, OFM, 173

M

Machiavelli, Niccolò (1469-1527), 112
Magdeburg, Franciscan convent of St Andrew, 173
Malton, 40
Malton, Benedict of, OFM, 34
Marcand, Roger, rector of St Michael's, Laxton, 46
Marchia, Francis de, OFM, 108
Marchia, James, *see*: St James de la Marchia
Margaret of Scotland (d. 1290), 43
Margareta decrecti of Martin of Troppau, 175
Margarita Philosophiae, 175
Marsh, Adam, OFM, 14
Martial, 101, 101
Martin V (1417-1431), 182, 188
Marx, Karl (1818-1883), 87, 87, 98, 130
Masuarii, Robert, OFM, 15
Mediavilla, Ricardus de, *see*: Middleton, Richard of
Mediterranean, 51
Melton, William, archbishop of York (1316-1340), 37, 42, 45
Merlin, 143
Merlo, Grado, 188, 191
Merton, Michael de, OFM, 41, 42
Messina, 95
Meux, Sir John de, of Beswick, 39
Meyronnes, Francis of, OFM, 127, 128
Mézin, 60

Middleton, 22
Middleton, Richard of, OFM, 117, 126
Mirebeau (Poitou), Franciscan convent of, 190
Molina, Juan, SJ, (1535-1600), 120
Mongol Empire, 142
Montfort, Simon de, earl of Leicester (1231-1265), 15
Montier-en-Der, Adso of, 136
Moorman, John, 54, 66
Moreton, John, of Gainsborough, OFM, 19
Morton, Edward, of Little Wassand, 37
Morton, John de, OFM, 35
Mosca, Gaetano, 89
Moxby, OSA nunnery, 34
Multan, Richard de, OFM, 20
Munich, Franciscan convent at, 168, 169
Münster, 162
Myton-on-Swale, 42

N

Nantes, Franciscan convent of, 43
Narbonne, General Chapter of (1260), 158, 159, 179
Nazareth, 110
Nettleham, 20
Newhall, Thomas, of Stoxlay, 27
Newminster Abbey, 22
Newton Reigny, 24
Nichomachean Ethics, 99, 175
Nider, Johannes, 166
Nisse, Grégoire de, *see*: Nyssa, Gregory of
Noort, Juan de, 109
Norfolk, 71

North Riding, 42
Northampton, 21
Norwich, 55, 56, 57, 76, 77, 78
Norwich, Austin Friars of, 39
Norwich, castle, 69
Norwich, cathedral, 69
Norwich, diocese of, 55
Norwich, Franciscan convent of, 59, 69, 72, 74, 75
Norwich, Franciscan *studium* at, 73
Nottingham, 16
Nottingham, Franciscan convent of, 44
Nottingham, William of, OFM, 19
Nottinghamshire, 11, 21, 22, 40, 46
Nozick, Robert, 128
Nuccio, Oscar, 118
Nun Appleton, 33
Nuremberg, Dominican convent of St Katharina, 166
Nuremberg, Franciscan convent of, 176, 204
Nuremberg, Poor Clares, 177
Nyssa, Gregory of, 102

O

Oakham, 21
oblation, 179, 182
Observant Franciscans, 153, 155, 168, 170, 176, 183, 184, 188, 189, 190, 191, 200, 201, 202, 206, 210
Ockham, William of, OFM, 108, 174
Odonis, Giraldus, OFM, 99
Oliger, Livarius, OFM, 182

Olivi, Petrus Johannis, OFM, 99, 108, 117, 118, 119, 120, 121, 122, 124, 127, 196
Ombrie, *see*: Umbria
Opus maius, 142, 148
Ordinationes of Benedict XII (1336), 160, 161, 162, 166, 170, 207
Ordinationes reformatorie of the French conventual province (1452), 209
Oreno, Franciscan convent of, 10
Oresme, Nicholas, 95, 96, 99
Ormesby, 27
Otho, papal legate in England, 60
Oxford, 15, 15, 26, 30, 56, 139, 173
Oxford, custos of, 20
Oxford, Franciscan convent of, 15, 80
Oxford, Franciscan custody of, 21
Oysel, Richard, 32

P

Pareto, Wilfredo, 89
Paris, 137, 173
Paris, General Statutes of (1292), 180
Paris, university of, 140
Paris, Matthew, OSB, 61, 80
Parma, John of, OFM, 135, 136, 137, 151
parva domus, 10
Patrington, Adam de, OFM, 35
Pecham, John, OFM, archbishop of Canterbury (1279-1292), 17, 18, 99, 105
Peke, Richard, of Wakefield, 37
Pellikan, Konrad, OFM, 184

Peñafort, Raymond of, OP, 127, 174
Penrith, Austin Friars of, 24
Peregrinatio in terram sanctam, 175
persona interposita, 189
Pharetra doctorum, 174
Philip, Nicholas, OFM, 25
Philippi, John, OFM, 168
Pickering, 23
Piers the Plowman, 23, 25, 36
Pilate, Nicholas, of Cambridge, 65
Pisa, 95
Platea, Franciscus de, 125
Plath, Christian, 166
Plebe, Armando, 85
Pocklington, 40
Poland, 200
Poland, Statutes of the province of 'Bernardins' of (1467), 207
Poliakov, Léon, 104
Pontefract, 14
Pontefract, Dominicans, 13
Portiuncula, 51, 158
Prague, 169
Preston, 15, 25, 43
Puchelbach, Albert, OFM, 204

Q
Quappelad, Robert de, OFM, 20
Quedlinburg, Jordan of, OSA, 169
Quodlibeta of William of Ockham, 174

R
Rabastens, 60
Radnor, Thomas, OFM, 47
Rationale divinorum, 166
Ravenser, William de, OFM, 20
Reading, 60
Regensburg, Franciscan convent of, 169
Regensburg, Poor Clares of, 165, 169
Registrum Anglie, 10
Reisch, Gregor, OCart, 175
Rennes, William of, OP, 127
Retford, 40
Rhône, river, 201
Richmond, 25, 32, 41
Richmond, archdeaconry of, 16, 31
Richmond, earl of, *see*: John of Brittany
Richmond, Thomas, OFM, 31
Rievaulx Abbey, 22
Robert, OFM, custos of York, 19
Robert Bruce, King of Scots (1306-1329), 41, 42
Robin Hood, 22
Robson, Michael, OFMConv., 9
Roest, Bert, 156, 180
Romans, 204
Romans, Humbert of, OP, 26, 47, 136
Rome, 100, 116, 175
Romeyn, John le, archbishop of York (1285-1296), 29, 40
Roover, Raymond de (1904-1972), 122, 131
Rosedale, Cistercian priory, 33
Rosicz, Sigismond, 200
Rufach, convent of Observant Franciscans of, 184
Ruiz, Damien, 98
Russell, John, OFM, 15
Russell, William, OFM, 25

S

Sabatier, Paul (1858-1928), 83, 186
Sack, Hermann, OFM, 168
Sack, Johannes, OFM, 168, 169
Saints
St Agatha, 48
St Albertus Magnus, OP, 174
St Anthony of Padua, 24, 38
St Antoninus, archbishop of Florence (1446-1459), 120, 174
St Augustine, 99, 111, 143, 174
St Basil the Great, 101
St Bernard of Clairvaux, 174
St Bernardin of Siena, OFM, 119, 120, 191, 199
St Bonaventure, OFM, 86, 91, 92, 93, 99, 108, 137, 138, 141, 166, 169, 173, 174, 176
St Colette of Corbie, 191
St Cuthbert, 17
St Francis of Assisi, 24, 38, 39, 47, 48, 51, 52, 83, 84, 85, 86, 87, 88, 90, 91, 96, 99 107, 109, 111, 114, 115, 116, 138, 175, 188, 201, 213
St Gregory the Great, 173
St James de la Marchia, OFM, 115
St Jerome, 88, 173
St John, 194
St John Capistran, OFM, 186, 188, 189, 189, 191, 199, 200, 203, 204, 205, 207, 208, 210, 214
St Louis, Louis IX, King of France (1226-1270), 95
St Peter, 105, 115
St Thomas Aquinas, OP, 100, 104, 108, 120, 131, 132, 174, 176
Saint Cher, Hugh of, OP, 173
Saint-Michel, Smaragdus of, 174
Saint-Victor, Hugh of, 173
Saleby, 37
Salisbury, custody of, 10
Sandale, John, bishop of Winchester (1316-1319), 46
Sara, servant to the Lady de Charmues, 32
Saxonia, Godfrey de, OFM, 21
Saxonia, John of, *see*: Erfurt, John of
Saxony, Franciscan province of, 189, 192, 206, 208
Saxony, Franciscan provincial of, 168, 189
Saxony, provincial statutes of (1467), 178
Saxony, Jordan of, OP, 140
Scarborough, 40
Scarborough, Franciscan convent of, 10, 34
Schedel, Hartmann, 175
Scheffeld, Robert, de Westbutterwick, 11
Schmitt, Carl (1888-1985), 106
schools, custodial, 160
schools, provincial, 160
Schumpeter, Joseph (1883-1950), 131
Scotland, 41
Scotland, Margaret of, *see*: Margaret of Scotland
Scotus, Bl. John Duns, OFM, 30, 99, 108, 117, 119, 120, 121, 122, 124, 127, 131, 132, 133
Scrope, Anne lady, of Harling, 39
Scrope, John lord, of Bolton, 39
Searle, John, 94
Segusio, Henry, cardinal bishop of Ostia, 103, 120, 127, 175

Selby, 40
Selby Abbey, 13, 24
Selby, William, OFM, 30
Serlle, John, 38
Sessay, church of St Cuthbert's, 38
Seston, 143
Seville, Isidor of, 174
Shelton, Richard de, OFM, 20
Sibyl, 143
Siena, 95
Sigglesthorne, 37
Silesia, 193, 199, 200
Simmel, Georg (1858-1918), 88, 90
Sinningthwaite, Cistercian nuns, 33
Sinnington, 23
Sisted, John de, OFM, 20
Skipton, 13, 23
Sleaford, 21
Słoń, Marek, 211
Smyth, Thomas, of Ormesby, 27
Snaith, 24
Sniterle, see: Blakeney
Sombart, Werner (1863-1941), 104
Somerset, 18
Sothill, John, of Dewsbury, 37
Soto, Domingo de, OP, (1494-1560), 120
South Cave, 40
South Collingham, church St. John the Baptist, 22
Spain, 191
Spalding, 10
Speculum discipline, 173
Speculum humanae salvationis, 169
Speyer, 169

Spirituals, 85, 93, 106, 107, 109, 186, 196
Stabilitas loci, 14
Stafford, Humphrey, earl of Devon (1439-1469), 17
Stainfield, OSB nunnery, 35
Standich, Oliver, OFM, 31
Statutes, cismontane observance (1461), 207
Statutes, of the province of Saxony (1467), 206
Statutes, ultramontane observance (1451), 207
Staunton, Hugh de, OFM, 20
Stayndorp, Robert de, OFM, 43
Stott, John, OFM, 30
Stowe, 16
Stoxlay, church of Sts Peter and Paul, 27
Strasbourg, Franciscan province of, 208, 210
studia solemnia, 161
studium conventuale, 164
studium generale, 160
Suárez, Francisco, SJ, (1548-1617), 120
Sudbury, Dominican convent, 79
Suffolk, 58, 62
Summa angelica, 174
Summa astesana, 123, 124, 125
Summa aurea of William of Auxerre, 86, 120, 174
Summa confessorum of John of Erfurt, 174
Summa fratris Alexandri, 92
Summa Hostiensis, 175
Suse, *see*: Segusio
Swale, river, 42
Swine, Cistercian nunnery, 34

Switzerland, 177
Symys, William, OFM, 30

T
Tabula utriusque juris, 126
Tarantaise, Peter of, *see*: Innocent V
Tartars, 145, 146
Teesdale, 22
terminarii, 206
Terre Sainte, *see*: Holy Land
Testament of St Francis, 86
Thetford, Austin Friars, 79
Thetford, Dominican convent, 79
Thoresby, John, archbishop of York (1352-1373), 21
Thornton-on-Humber, OSA priory, 14
Thurgutthorp, John de, OFM, 20
Thuringia, Franciscan province of, 166
Tibtot, Sir Robert, 59
Tibtot, Una, wife of Sir Robert, 59
Tickhill, Austin Friars, 13
Todde, Richard, OFM, 30
Todeschini, Giacomo, 118, 121
Toulouse, 60
Toumby, Philip de, OFM, 34
Tournon, 201
Toynton, Thomas of, OFM, 19
Tractatus de restitutionibus, 125
Trent, river, 10
Trêves, *see*: Trier
Trier, 208, 210
Trinci, Paul of the, OFM, 190
Troppau, Martin of, 175
Troyes, 123
Tuscany, 210

Tykhill, William de, OFM, 31
Tynton, *see*: Toynton

U
Umbria, 213
Upper Lusatia (Oberlausitz), 193
Urban IV (1261-1264), 61

V
Vallée, Jean de la, OFM, 190
Vatican Council II (1962-1965), 83, 115
Vauchez, André, 54, 81
Venice, 95, 103, 125, 126
Venise, *see*: Venice
Verona, 95
Vienna, 169
Vienne, council of (1311-1312), 103, 104
Visconti, Federico, archbishop of Pisa (1253-1277), 23
visitator regiminis, 193
Vita prima, 86
Voegelin, Eric, 110
Voragine, Jacobus de, OP, archbishop of Genoa (1292-1298), 169

W
Wagner, Leonhard, *alias* 'Wirstlin' OSB, 164
Wakefield, 37
Waldhausen, Konrad of, OSA, 169
Wales, John of, OFM, 17
Walsingham, 17, 58, 60, 62, 69, 77
Walsingham, Franciscan convent of, 55, 56, 63, 64, 72
Waltham, 14

Warter, Nicholas, OFM, bishop of Dromore (1419-1445), suffragan bishop in York (1420-1445), 21
Wattes, master, OFM 17
Weber, Max (1864-1920), 195
Wells, 15
West Yorkshire, 24, 34
Westbutterwick, 11
Weston, Garnius de, 32
Wetewang', Laurence, OFM, 34
Whatton, Robert, OFM, 20
Whelpedale, William, OFM, 25
Whitby, 10, 40
White, William, OFM, 37
Whitkirk, 39
Wilberfoss, OSB nunnery, 34
Willoughby, Sir William, 32
Wiltshire, 18
Witele, John de, OFM, 12
Witton, Oliver, of Skipton, 13
Wodeham, Adam, OFM, 73
Wolf, Kenneth Baxter, 116
Wombwell, Thomas, 13
Woodford, William, OFM, 36
Woodward, John, vicar of All Saints at Darfield-upon-Dearne, 24
Worcester, Franciscan convent of, 80
Wotton, John, 34
Wrocław, *see*: Breslau
Wyclif, John, 16
Wynthorp, Robert de, OP, 35
Wyntringham, Robert de, OFM, 33

Y
Yarmouth, 55, 58, 72, 78

Yarmouth, Franciscan convent of, 59, 70, 76
Yedingham, OSB priory, 34
York, 18, 21, 30, 31, 33, 38, 41, 44
York, archbishop of, 20, 21, 25, 28, 29, 31, 33, 37, 40, 41
York, archdeaconry of, 31, 29
York, archdiocese of, 19, 20, 46
York, custody of, 9, 10, 35, 43, 48, 49
York, custos of, 12, 18, 19, 20, 45, 46, 47
York, dean and chapter of, 15
York, Dominicans, 14, 21
York, Franciscan convent of, 10, 21, 26, 33, 40, 41, 43
Yorkshire, 32, 45, 46
Youghal, Franciscan convent of, 163, 165

Z
Zittau, 193
Zouche, William, archbishop of York (1340-1352), 28